T0308849

Mormon Healer and Folk Poet

Mary Susannah Fowler's Life
of "Unselfish Usefulness"

Mormon Healer and Folk Poet
Mary Susannah Fowler's Life of "Unselfish Usefulness"

Margaret K. Brady

UTAH STATE UNIVERSITY PRESS
LOGAN, UTAH

Copyright © 2000 Utah State University Press
All rights reserved

Utah State University Press
Logan, Utah 84322

Manufactured in the United States of America

Printed on acid-free paper

5 4 3 2 1   00 01 02 03 04

Library of Congress Cataloging-in-Publication Data

Brady, Margaret K., 1947–
    Mormon healer and folk poet : Mary Susannah Fowler's life of "unselfish usefulness" /
Margaret K. Brady.
        p. cm.
Includes bibliographical references and index.
    ISBN 0-87421-299-5 (alk. paper)—ISBN 0-87421-400-9 (pbk. : alk. paper)
    1. Fowler, Mary Susannah, 1862–1920. 2. Traditional medicine—United States—
History. 3. Folk Poetry, American—History and criticism. 4. Mormon women—United
States—Biography. 5. Mormons—United States—Biography. I. Brady, Margaret K., 1947–.
II. Title
    BX8695.F67 B73 2000
    289.3/092 B 21   00-009702

For my daughter Kate Stanley
In hopes that one day she may have even more stories to tell

Contents

Illustrations

Acknowledgments

The same interconnectedness that Mary Susannah Fackrell Fowler experienced throughout her life, the sense of collaboration and reciprocity with family and community, made this book about her a possibility. In 1996 when Barre Toelken and Barbara Walker invited me to speak at the annual Fife Folklore Conference at Utah State University, I was somewhat dubious about the contribution I might make to that year's conference focus on folk medicine. Somehow, in the search for an appropriate topic, I stumbled across the typescript of Mary Susannah Fowler's diary in the Marriott Library at the University of Utah. From that moment on, I have been fortunate enough to have had the support, encouragement, and scholarly advice of a community of friends and colleagues.

Members of the Fowler and Fackrell families have been generous with their time, their precious family scrapbooks, and their memories of a remarkable relative. Eula Fackrell Carlson, Eudora Clements, Eileen Freckleton, Milton Roper, Rae Spellman, Dianne Still, Marice Wilcox, and Lois Worlton shared stories and manuscripts with me. Most importantly, Virginia Fowler Rogers, Mary Susannah's granddaughter, became my friend and guide in this adventure. Always willing to share information—from the recipes for folk cures to genealogy charts—Mrs. Rogers provided a clear and present link to the lively creativity and deep thoughtfulness of her grandmother.

I have benefited from the insights of many colleagues at the University of Utah and around the country. The Fife conference faculty, especially Bonnie O'Connor, David Hufford, Erika Brady and Pat Mullen helped in the early conceptual stages of the project. Later, Erika provided invaluable comments on the entire manuscript, as did Pat who has been a constant support and springboard for ideas throughout. A number of individuals have offered comments and suggestions during the research and writing: I want to thank especially Dean May, Susan Miller, Kim Lau, Janet Kaufman, Karen Brennan, Arthur Traub, and Steve Tatum. My friends

Beverly Stoeltje, Kathy Tatum, Helen Cox, and Dawn Jackson have heard more about nineteenth and early twentieth-century Utah than they probably will ever care to admit—and they have cheerfully been willing to discuss even the most esoteric ideas well into the night.

My research has been generously supported by a Faculty Fellowship and a grant from the University of Utah Research Committee. Pat Hanna, Dean of the College of Humanities and Ron Coleman, Associate Vice-President for Diversity, have also offered wonderful support, both financial and collegial. I am indebted to librarians and museum curators across the United States. In particular, I would like to thank Greg Thompson and Paul Mogren in Special Collections at the Marriott Library, University of Utah; Susan Brady at Yale's Beinecke Library; Janice Esplin at the Orderville DUP museum; Janet Seegmiller in Special Collections at Southern Utah University; and a number of others at these institutions and at the Utah State Historical Society Archives, the Archives of the Church of Jesus Christ of Latter-day Saints, the Daughters of the Utah Pioneers Archives, and the Special Collections of Brigham Young University's Harold B. Lee Library.

Without Brenda Miller, ace editorial assistant and structural engineer, this book would never have appeared in this form—or probably in any other! She is a woman of great patience, infinite creativity, and rare good humor. John Alley at the Utah State University Press has been incredibly helpful in his judicious editorial judgments and in his expeditious shepherding of the manuscript through its various stages—I owe him a deep debt of gratitude. Janet Hough, Kindra Briggs, and Sheila Olsen have handled much of the technical production of the early versions of the manuscript with care and attention to detail. If it had not been for Julie and Bill Reardon at Moon Lake ("Out of This World, but Still in Utah") and Sue Booth-Forbes and Michelle Brown at Anam Cara Retreat on the Beara Peninsula of Ireland, it would have taken me much longer to find just the right spot to write about a woman who so loved the desert.

In Bonnie Deffebach, whose paintings of pioneer women I discovered at the Queen of Arts Gallery in Park City, Utah, shortly after I had completed the first draft of the manuscript, I found a friend, an inspiration, and an incredibly generous artistic spirit. Bonnie's painting of Mary Susannah Fowler that graces the cover reconstructs her life in another vibrant way.

All of these people have provided encouragement, insightfulness, and unflappable good will, allowing me to comprehend on a deeper level the interconnectedness so prized by Mary Fowler. Nowhere is that interconnectedness more fully realized than in the patient and loving support of my children Ned and Kate Stanley, and in the laughter and deep understanding of my friend Jac Campbell. This book is especially for them.

The ground & everything else is covered this morning with a beautiful thin coat of pure white snow come to fill its wonderful mission of beautifying, purifying and gratifying before sinking away into the earth, there to give life and health to vegetation by its magical presence or running in the tiny rivulets to the great rivers & there rushing to perform its part in making the "mighty ocean." I think I would look in vain for a better example of unselfish usefulness.

—Mary Susannah Sumner Fackrell Fowler
December 12, 1899

Introduction

About twenty years ago, just after I had moved to Utah as a young assistant professor of folklore, I received in the mail an invitation to join a postcard chain. The invitation promised that if I put my name and address at the bottom of the enclosed list, and then mailed five postcards to the individuals whose names appeared at the top of the list, I would receive literally hundreds of postcards on the topic(s) of my choice. Delighted at the prospect of receiving so much mail in my new home, I quickly added my name to the list and included my preferred subject matter for the postcards I would receive: photographs of women. In fact, over the next six weeks, or perhaps it was six months, the mailman delivered 187 postcards with photographs of women. There was a picture of a whole line of women sitting under large, beehive-shaped hair dryers, each with a magazine in one hand and a cigarette in the other. In another photograph, a ring of girl scouts, each holding a stick with a marshmallow speared on the end, encircled a fire that illuminated their faces with an almost surreal glow. There was also a sepia-toned photograph of two Victorian women with their skirts hiked up jauntily, long cane fishing poles in hand, enormous, flower-bedecked hats shading their faces, standing in the shallows of a fast-moving stream.

As I examined each postcard, I found myself longing to know more about each of the women whose images fate had placed in my hands. Where *was* that river that offered those two women such a splendid moment of both solitude and relationship—and how did they ever come to be there together? What would happen to those girl scouts as they moved away from the fire, into adolescence, and then young womanhood? Just what was it that fascinated each of those beauty shop customers in the glossy magazines they pored over so assiduously? It was as if the mailman had delivered a whole host of unnarrated lives to me in the guise of these 187 postcards.

Precisely the same feeling of longing to know more came over me almost twenty years later as I gazed at a photograph of thirteen women

Mary Susannah Fowler and the ladies of the Literary Club of Huntington, Utah. Photo taken in the spring of 1900; a photocopy is all that remains of this photograph. Courtesy of Virginia Fowler Rogers

gathered together under the trees in what was quite obviously their finest dress. I had gone to the home of Mrs. Virginia Fowler Rogers, the granddaughter of a Mary Susannah Sumner Fackrell Fowler whose manuscript diary I had found in the archives at the University of Utah's Marriott Library. Wanting to locate more of the fragmentary record of her life, I waited patiently as Mrs. Rogers pulled folder after folder from her own well-kept family history archives. While Mrs. Rogers arranged the yellowed documents for me to examine, I carefully inspected the photograph she'd handed me, trying to identify just which woman in this stately group was Mary Susannah Fowler. A small penciled-in arrow pointed to one of the women, and I gazed into her face, comparing it to the other images Mrs. Rogers had already provided of her grandmother. Together we matched up hair styles, noses, and cheekbones and, in the end, determined that, in fact, the arrow maker had been incorrect. Mary Susannah was actually the woman sitting two places to the left of the one identified by the penciled marking.

But physically identifying Mary Susannah was only the very beginning of finding answers to the questions this photograph raised: Who were the other women in the photograph? What was their relationship? What was the occasion for the picture taking? Whose framed portrait, now almost completely obliterated, hung in the trees above the women? And did the stern looks on the faces of the women convey simple terror at being photographed or did they belie a now-hidden sadness I might never know?

In many ways, that photocopied picture is emblematic of the entire project that has resulted in this book. That longing to know more, that piecing together of an identity, that re-visioning of another's idea about just who this woman actually was, that kind of questioning where answers only lead to more questions—all of these became a part not just of understanding the photograph, but of attempting to truly understand the life of Mary Susannah Sumner Fackrell Fowler. Unlike the pictures on the postcards I had received so many years before, though, this photograph offered me the opportunity to begin to fill in the background almost obliterated by so many attempts to preserve the image. In this case, I might actually be able to find some of the answers to my questions and to hear the stories I had so wanted to listen to as I examined the nameless faces of fisherwomen, girl scouts, and beauty shop customers.

As a folklorist by training, cultural historian by interest, and literary cultural critic by academic affiliation, I brought a theoretically eclectic, interdisciplinary approach to the cultural materials I gradually accumulated in an effort to answer those questions and find those stories in piecing together Mary Fowler's life. Influenced, certainly, by a postmodernist perspective that understands the "self" to be far more complicated than a unified representation of fixed identity, my approach to the "texts" that give access to Mary Fowler's "self" is one that understands that self to be constituted through, and constructed by, language. As Susan Miller has warned scholars engaged in such activities, I realize that "if language is not a transparent pipeline for an always emerging core truth, scholars who work in and across these fields might more pointedly consider how human identity is always layered, within accumulated prior texts and therefore, always politically constructed by disparate but never entirely ephemeral acts of writing."[1] Mary Fowler's identity has been, and will continue to be, constructed by not only her own words, but also by those of friends and relatives whose accumulated texts reveal the stories of her life.

In the very process of reading, listening to stories, and writing about Mary Fowler's life, I, too, become implicated in that construction. Susan Stanford Friedman has proposed a theory of women's writing of the self as a group act by which "women project into history an identity that is not purely individualistic. Nor is it purely collective. Instead, this new identity merges the shared and the unique."[2] I would expand this notion to include an understanding that those actually involved in the process of reading and interpreting that self are part of the collective to which Friedman refers.

The conversation between reader and author necessarily implicates both in the process of identity construction.

I am certainly influenced in taking this position by recent methodological moves in folklore scholarship referred to as "reflexive" or "reciprocal" ethnography. Reflexive ethnography, the postmodern methodology of both the fields of anthropology and folklore, emphasizes the involvement of the researcher with the materials he or she examines. Instead of remaining invisible, behind the screen of scholarly objectivity, the reflexive ethnographer takes into account his or her own role in the meaning-making process.[3] Elaine Lawless has taken this idea of reflexive ethnography one step further in adopting what she terms "reciprocal ethnography," in which both the folklorist and those she interviews work collaboratively by "foregrounding dialogue as a process in understanding and knowledge retrieval."[4] While as a folklorist I have sought to employ such a methodology in the interviews with Mary Susannah Fowler's grandchildren, especially with Mrs. Rogers, who is a vital participant in the process of reconstruction represented in this book, I also need to point out that much of the information on which the book is based is in the form of texts themselves constructed over one hundred years ago. Both contemporary literary scholars and historians have also suggested a similar methodology for readers of historical and/or autobiographical texts; they point to the necessity for the reader of such texts to actively participate in the ongoing conversation of the texts themselves. As early as 1980, for example, James Olney pointed out that autobiographical research "requires a reader . . . to participate fully in the process, so that the created self becomes, at one remove, almost as much the reader's as the author's."[5]

The same reflexivity and reciprocity espoused by folklorists engaged in ethnographic work is at the heart of reading the "self" in autobiography. Reading and reflecting upon autobiographical texts becomes, then, a kind of "mediation between author and reader, between the context of writing and the context of reading."[6] As I read the various constructions of Mary Fowler produced by her family and friends, I, too, become implicated in the production of the Mary Fowler I have come to know through the juxtaposition of the various discursive texts available to me. Barbara Myerhoff and Jay Ruby suggest that in this way "the frame is repeatedly violated and the two stories [the researcher's and the subject's], commenting on each other, travel alongside, simultaneously commanding attention and creating a different world than either represents by itself."[7] In my conversations with Mary Fowler's grandchildren and my reading of her personal writings, I have, of course, been both helped and constrained by my own self-construction. As a folklorist, a woman, a non-Mormon living in Utah, I have come to understand Mary Fowler from a particular perspective, a perspective that has necessarily changed somewhat through learning more about this remarkable woman, becoming closer to Virginia Rogers, and discovering new pieces of Mary's poetry. What this book attempts to do, then, is to present that story of my own coming to understand Mary Fowler along with all the other stories that construct and reconstruct her life.

However, that is simply not enough: you, as reader, are implicated as well. As you read the collaboration involved in these pages, you, too, create a different world, a different story of the Mary Fowler you meet in the juxtaposition of my reading of her life with the primary texts in which that reading is grounded. Along with Francoise Lionnet you may say that as a reader, "I allow my self to be interwoven with the discursive strands of the text, to engage in a form of intercourse wherein I take my interpretive cues from the patterns that emerge as a result of this encounter."[8] As Mary Fowler's own words are contextualized in a variety of ways through the writing of her contemporaries and the stories of her descendants, you as reader enter into a conversation that ultimately produces your own understanding of just who this remarkable woman was—and is. It may be influenced by my construction of her life presented in these pages, but your own reading will, nonetheless, present a distinct and unique conversation with Mary Susannah Sumner Fackrell Fowler.

These understandings necessarily affect the structure of this book itself. Instead of adopting the framework of so many academic books on autobiographical subjects, I do not first present a theoretical chapter that articulates the characteristics of the range of discourses examined throughout the book. Instead, the first chapter introduces Mary Fowler *as I came to know her*. Because my real hope is that you, as reader, will come to understand the reasons behind my own construction of her life and its meaning, as well as develop your own construction, I want to allow you to discover, as I did, what makes getting to know this seemingly ordinary turn-of-the-century Mormon woman such an intriguing adventure. For that reason, chapter 1 includes stories I have shared with my own daughter about Mary Fowler, as well as a brief chronological life history pieced together from the range of discourses I have been able to amass. The following four chapters examine three distinct areas of concern for me as a folklorist. Chapter 2 situates Mary's life within the context of her own folk belief in a particular kind of community—one centered spiritually within a specific Mormon communal system. The intense belief in this conception of community—one shaped by shared beliefs and fostered through selfless service—creates a milieu wherein the values of an often isolated group of individuals bind them together through a reciprocity that is both economic and cultural.

Chapter 3 examines Mary Fowler's role as a folk healer within that community and articulates particular metaphors of self that emerge from her role as community healer: healing as maternal nurturance and women healers as mediators. A detailed reading of these metaphoric representations suggests that the idea of interconnectedness underlies and weaves together these themes in the construction of Mary Fowler's life.

Chapter 4 provides the cultural and literary context for an understanding of Mary Fowler's poetry. The literacy practices of her own family as well as those of the larger Mormon community help illuminate the kinds of discursive options available to Mary as she fashioned her own poetic self-construction. Chapter 5, then, draws on the work of Roger deV. Renwick and Pauline Greenhill and explores Mary Fowler's folk poetry as a culturally constructed form that allows her to examine, critique, and celebrate the values of her community at the same time she is constructing that self.

The final chapter allows us to reflect on the entire matrix of discourses that have created an intertext for understanding Mary's own life writing. In this chapter, both the generic differences among these discursive forms, their particular strengths and limitations, and the part each plays in the construction of Mary Fowler's identity are foregrounded. In this way, you as reader may evaluate the relative weight each of these discourses will have in your own reading of this life story. If, as an academic reader, you are more comfortable with beginning your own experience of identity construction with a more familiar theoretical positioning, I suggest you read the first chapter for some essential background and then flip quickly to the last where you will find such a theoretical perspective, one that otherwise emerges out of the understandings developed in the middle chapters.

The belief in the importance of the reader's own separate experience of, and conversation with, these multiple discourses also has an effect on the way in which the texts themselves are presented. In attempting to "preserve the immediacy of a handwritten page and to simultaneously provide the accessibility of a printed volume,"[9] I have attempted to present these texts with as little editorial intervention possible. Instead of bracketing spelling corrections or including numerous [*sic*]s throughout these texts, I have chosen to trust the reader to make sense of the words of these authors *as they wrote them*. The very act of poring over a text in an effort to figure out exactly what a particular word might be affords the reader a direct engagement with the text that a more intrusive editing might sabotage.

Similarly, there are occasions when the conventions of capitalization and punctuation familiar to us today simply are not present in these texts. It is often difficult, for example, to distinguish capitals from lowercase letters, and in those instances I have made a judgment based on Mary Fowler's usual practice. Frequently, periods are omitted from the ends of sentences, or the end of a line is used as the only signal of the completion of the sentence. In these cases, I have allowed Mary's own sense of punctuation to prevail. As you grow familiar with Mary's own stylistic choices, you will be quicker to interpret commonly used abbreviations and cryptic references; in the process, you will enter into a more intimate conversation with Mary than reading an expurgated diary text or poem might allow. In the transcription of the oral interviews, I have followed a similar principle, allowing pauses to be indicated by ellipses, and refraining from correcting the occasional grammatical irregularity.

Likewise, I have chosen to use several different configurations of Mary Susannah Sumner Fackrell Fowler's name throughout the book. Since I want readers to become constantly aware that Mary Fowler was not, and is not, a static representation of a cohesive, fixed identity, but rather a constantly constructed "self," these various appellations—Mary S. Fowler, Mary Susannah Fackrell, Mary Fowler—will serve as reminders of the very constructedness and changeability of that identity. Certainly, all of these names were used by Mary Fowler's family and friends on different occasions; here they serve also to remind us of the ways each of those members of Mary's close community was actively engaged in constructing his or her own versions of her identity.

Laurel Thatcher Ulrich, author of the Pulitzer Prize–winning biography of midwife Martha Ballard, has commented, "Opening a diary for the first time is like walking into a room full of strangers; the reader is advised to enjoy the company without trying to remember every name."[10] I would add that if you stay at the party long enough and have truly engaged conversations with the other guests, you will come away knowing more about your fellow partiers, and more about your hostess and yourself as well. Please consider this introductory preface your own invitation to a gathering in honor of Mary Susannah Sumner Fackrell Fowler.

I

"Another Leaf in Time's Old Book"
A Life Story of Mary Susannah Fowler

Old time is flying very fast!
Another year will soon be past!
Another leaf in time's old Book
Will turn to us, that we may look
Upon the clean unblemished side
With purity our thoughts to guide.

One wintry afternoon a few months ago, my daughter Kate asked me to tell her about "that woman you're writing about in the book." We had just returned from a snowshoeing adventure in Neffs Canyon east of Salt Lake City, and as we sipped hot chocolate and snuggled under quilts and fleece blankets in front of the fire, I began to tell Kate about the time that Mary Susannah Sumner Fackrell Fowler, her young husband Henry Ammon, and their two tiny children had gotten trapped in a sawmill far away from their home town of Orderville, Utah. As the snowflakes whirled outside our living room window, I started the story that would become the first of many the two of us shared about Mary Fowler:

Mary and Henry Ammon had been sent up a canyon near Orderville in southern Utah to take care of the sawmill. In those days—it was probably 1883 or 1884—they belonged to a kind of Mormon commune started by Brigham Young, and everyone shared the work needed to keep the town of Orderville going. So Mary Susannah and Henry Ammon took their two little children and traveled the fifteen miles up the canyon to the sawmill some time that fall. The winter that followed was a particularly bad one and the snow got terribly deep. They really weren't very well prepared, and when another major snowstorm swept down on the area, they were cut off from any way to get supplies or to send a message that they needed help. Mary had to comfort her two little ones and try to help Henry Ammon keep the fire going and figure out what they were going to do.

Orderville sawmill where Mary Susannah Fackrell Fowler and Henry Ammon Fowler and their two small children were trapped in a snowstorm. Photo used by permission, Special Collections, Gerald R. Sherrat Library, Southern Utah University.

Back in Orderville, though, Mary's own mother, Susannah Fackrell, was also worried. She hadn't heard from her daughter in a long time, and she knew the problems a storm that large could cause. So she decided to send two of Mary's brothers through the snow with supplies and words of encouragement to the young family. The brothers couldn't make it by themselves and so enlisted two other men to help them dig through the snow, and even then it was several days before they could reach the mill. You can imagine how thrilled Mary Susannah and Henry Ammon were to see the frosty faces of their rescuers!

Henry, or Ammon as he was most frequently called, had already fashioned some kind of cross between skis and snowshoes from boards at the mill, so he and Mary strapped these on. One of the men, Mr. Cox, tied the older child, Arno, to his back, and Mary carried the tiny baby. They could scarcely go far at all before one of them would fall into a snowbank. Mary fell over and over again, each time carefully thrusting her tiny infant up through the drifts. Once when Mr. Cox fell, little Arno, who had been dumped in the snow, just laughed and said, "Wo, Jane!" Even though they were exhausted and numb with the cold, everyone else had to laugh: the Fowlers' horse was named Jane, and Arno must have heard that phrase whenever the animal got out of control; as far as Arno was concerned, Mr. Cox apparently had the same balking disposition as the horse.

By the time the Fowlers finally reached Orderville, the night's darkness was so deep that only the still-falling snow disturbed its completeness; it was difficult to even make out their village's fort-like enclosure on the desert landscape. During the journey Mary and Ammon's clothes had become so wet from the snow that they were now frozen to their backs. The exhaustion that overtook them was so complete that it was difficult for Mary even to find the strength to put her babies to bed. But in spite of the cold and the damp and the tiredness, at least they knew that they were safe at home at last.

As I think back on the snowy evening when Kate and I shared hot chocolate and this story, I realize that it was more than just the context of the snowstorm that caused me to select this particular narrative out of the hundreds of other stories I have come to know about Mary Susannah Fowler, the Mormon woman who had lived in southern Utah as a polygamist wife, healer, and folk poet a hundred years ago. I suppose what I really wanted thirteen-year-old Kate to understand from this particular story was that no matter how old or how mature she might become, a mother's love would always be there if she needed me. I also hoped that, as she approaches womanhood, Kate might see the courage of this remarkable woman, might find in it a kind of inspiration in times when being courageous herself might not prove such an easy thing to do. I wanted to let the actions of Mary Fowler's brothers convey to her the importance of family and the lengths to which one might go to protect a relative. And to the sometimes-too-serious Kate, I also hoped to reaffirm that humor is always a lifesaver in tense situations. All of these things, no doubt, influenced my choice of this individual narrative. And over the next several months, time after time I found myself choosing other stories to tell Kate about Mary Susannah Fackrell Fowler for a multitude of other reasons. I now realize that in selecting these stories to tell my daughter, I was also choosing those narratives that most clearly revealed the qualities I most valued in Mary Fowler's own discourses.

Once, when Kate was confined to bed with a broken ankle, I told her about the time that Mary Susannah cooked mud over a wood-burning stove in her kitchen until it was just warm enough to apply thickly to Eliza Norwood Fowler's arms and legs when she suffered miserably with a particularly painful kind of rheumatism. My intention, of course, was to demonstrate that things really could be worse for my daughter, but the part of the story that most amazed and even amused the grumpy Kate was when I revealed that Eliza was Henry Ammon's second wife. Kate was certain that Mary took a kind of delight in slapping the heated mud onto her sister-wife's sore limbs. No amount of detailed examples taken from Mary's own writings could convince her that Mary really liked Eliza and was only interested in providing the best care she knew for her. And since that day, if either teenaged angst or stiff muscles threaten to cloud Kate's usually upbeat outlook, the mere mention of "mud in a frying pan" is a fail-safe way for me to lighten things up without being overbearing.

Sometimes, too, when Kate has asked for stories about Mary Fowler, I've chosen narratives that simply seem to me to capture the woman I've come to know over the last three years. I want her to come to know the Mary I have learned to cherish as I have discovered more and more about her. Once, for example, I told Kate how the women and girls of Orderville would keep silkworm eggs in their bosoms to help the cocoons stay warm until they hatched. As she walked along on her way to school one day, Mary was amazed to find little worms crawling out from under the collar of her homespun dress.

On another occasion, I told Kate how Mary Susannah Fowler would take care of sick children all over the town of Huntington where she had moved with her family. One time Mary spent days and days trying to ease the suffering of a friend's baby. Finally, she stayed with the mother and child through the night until baby Arvilla died. Then Mary prepared the baby for burial. Only three months later Mary went to the same house to help her friend with the birth of a new baby girl, whom Mary washed and dressed and handed to the tired but happy mother.

Once when we were talking about women we knew and cared about, Kate wanted to know more about the women Mary Fowler chose as friends. So I described the reading group that Mary had started in Huntington long before Oprah Winfrey's book club was a common household phenomenon. Then there was the story about how Mary and her friends set out to close down the two saloons in Huntington while fighting for the temperance movement. Years later, some of the same women met to sew bandages and other items for the Red Cross during World War I.

Each time Kate either asks for a story or I seize the opportunity to use a Mary Fowler example to clarify a point I want to make to my daughter, we together construct a version of this woman who was born more than a hundred years ago. At the same time we create a relationship with Mary, though, we are also strengthening and re-creating our own relationship to each other. This is something I think would especially please my friend Mary Susannah Fowler; the interconnections she so prized are now mirrored in the storytelling sessions Kate and I share.

BEGINNINGS

The very fact that I have such an extensive repertoire of stories about this woman from which to draw is quite frankly astonishing to me now. Less than three years ago, I had no idea where Orderville, Utah, was, how silkworms metamorphosed, or even who Mary Susannah Sumner Fackrell Fowler might be. What I *did* know was that I was in desperate need of a topic for a talk I was to give at the Fife Folklore Conference just four short months away. Searching through the card catalogue at the University of Utah Marriott Library with an eye toward any entry vaguely related to folk or traditional medicine, the focus of the conference that year, I came across an entry for the manuscript diary of Mary Susannah Sumner Fackrell Fowler. Her very name was so impressive I determined to at least take a look at the diary in Special Collections. The fragment of Mary Susannah Fowler's diary, written from November 1899 to July 1900, revealed a woman whose own values and sense of connection with her community were voiced so strongly that I was immediately swept up in what life must have been like for her a century ago. Even after my conference presentation was finished, I found that I had only just begun the odyssey started when I first peeked inside that thin volume. I spent the next three years trying to understand the pages of that foolscap notebook by searching for every bit of evidence I might find to explain the often cryptic entries in the diary that had so enthralled me on first reading.

At first, I had no idea of the identity of any of the people named in the diary. "Who is 'Pa'?" I wondered, for example. "Was he Mary's father or

David Bancroft Fackrell and Susannah Sumner Fackrell, Mary
Susannah Sumner Fackrell Fowler's parents. Photos courtesy of
Virginia Fowler Rogers and the Orderville Daughters of the Utah
Pioneers Museum.

her husband?" By the time the Fife Conference took place, I had been able
to locate only one other work that illuminated in any way the confusion
the diary had presented. Mary Fowler's youngest son, Fred, had written a
forty-eight-page biography of his mother in 1945, twenty-five years after
her death. That volume, housed in the Utah State Historical Society's
archives, allowed me to take the first steps toward understanding just who
Mary Susannah Sumner Fackrell Fowler was and is; it provided me an outline of her life, and even more, it hinted at many of the thematic resonances
I had already begun to see emerging in the words of her own diary.

The Emergence of a Life History

Through her son's biography I was able to begin to piece together a
thumbnail sketch of Mary Fowler's life, one that would allow erasures and
redrawing as other renderings of that life were added to the picture. Mary
Susannah Sumner Fackrell was born in Woods Cross, Utah, on October 23,
1862, the seventh child of David Bancroft Fackrell and Susannah Sumner
Fackrell. Her parents, both of English ancestry, had met in Bountiful after
each had journeyed across the plains. David Fackrell had left Vermont as a
fifteen-year-old with wanderlust; after traveling around the Midwest and
South for almost fifteen years, David joined the gold rush and set off for

California. When the company with which he was traveling stopped in Salt Lake City, he happened to hear about a family named Fackrell who had settled just north of the city in Bountiful. Surprised to find someone with the same last name, David sought them out and discovered that they were his own parents, James and Amy Crumb Fackrell, who had converted to the Mormon Church after he had left on his journey, and who had then come west with the Mormon pioneers.[1]

Mary Susannah's mother, Susannah Sumner, had an equally astonishing trip to Bountiful. Born in England, Susannah had emigrated to the United States as a young child with her mother and stepfather, John Parker. When Susannah was twelve years old, both her mother and stepfather died of cholera; after spending a year with a family who lived nearby, Susannah eventually joined a group of Mormon pioneers on their journey to the Salt Lake Valley. There she met James and Amy Crumb Fackrell, who invited her to live with their family. Only a few months later the wandering David appeared to reclaim his long-lost family and marry the orphan girl they so generously had taken in.

Their early years in Bountiful were somewhat rudimentary, as Mary Susannah's sister Olive explains:

> After their marriage in Bountiful, father and mother took up 160 acres of land there. He built a log house with a dirt floor and roof. He built a bunk in one corner and their chairs were made of sawed-off logs. Their cooking utensils were a bake oven and skillet, and they had two tin cups, two tin plates, and grandmother gave them two knives, forks, and spoons. They did not have a stove but cooked over a fire place. (Well, I'm sure they were very proud of this very first furniture, etc., for it was their very own.)[2]

From these meager beginnings the young couple soon expanded their "holdings." They purchased sheep and cows that Susannah helped to care for. She carded the wool and wove it into cloth for the family's clothes; she also wove for other people in the community. The Fackrells added more than livestock to their family. David and Susannah had fifteen children, eight of whom survived to adulthood. Living the Mormon principle of polygamy, David also married a second wife, Hannah Proctor, on October 15, 1862, only eight days before Mary Susannah was born. During her earliest years, then, Mary Susannah was cared for by both her mother and her "Aunt" Hannah.

When Mary Susannah was only six years old, President Brigham Young called a group of the faithful to go to a section of what was believed to be southwestern Utah, but that ultimately turned out to be a part of southeastern Nevada called the "Muddy." David B. Fackrell was one of those called. Taking his second wife, Hannah, and their two young sons as well as

Susannah's oldest son, Joseph, to settle this new section several hundred miles southwest of Salt Lake City, David left Susannah and her six children at home in Bountiful. Two years later he returned to take Susannah and her children to the Muddy, but before the family could reach their destination, the mission was abandoned. After spending the winter in St. George in southern Utah, the Fackrell family moved first to Mt. Carmel where other members of the Muddy mission had decided to settle. There they built a log cabin, cleared the land, and planted their first crops. Mary Susannah and her family lived in Mt. Carmel for four years; it was there that she was baptized on September 17, 1871, a month before her ninth birthday. In the Spring of 1875 the family moved two miles north in Long Valley, eventually settling in what became Orderville, a communal endeavor set up under the direction of Brigham Young.[3] There Mary Susannah Fackrell lived from the time she was almost eleven until she was twenty-six. It was in the United Order that she met her husband Henry Ammon Fowler.

Henry A. Fowler had come to Orderville in the fall of 1875 to visit his sisters, and at their urging decided to stay. Henry Ammon's early life had been filled with as much tragedy as the early years of Mary's own parents. Like Mary, he was the descendant of English converts, William and Ellen Bradshaw Fowler, who emigrated with their young children, Henry, Harriet, and Florence, in 1863 when Henry Ammon was almost six years old.[4]

Although his early childhood was spent in a loving home with devout parents, Ammon (as he was commonly called) was to know tragedy all too soon. Before emigrating, Ammon's father, William, had been an LDS missionary in his native England and during that time wrote the well-known hymn "We Thank Thee, O God, for a Prophet." Shortly after the family's arrival in Salt Lake, Brigham Young, recognizing William's scholarly gifts, sent the Fowlers to Manti, Utah, where William was to become a school teacher. Unfortunately, according to Fred Fowler,

> the exposure of the long journey from England by boat, rail, and wagon train greatly weakened his lungs, which were already weakened from his apprenticeship and work as a skilled craftsman in the cutlery trade. He contracted consumption and had to turn the work of teaching over to his wife, who also courageously cared for him and the three children.[5]

When Ammon was only eight years old, his father died. After returning to Salt Lake City for a brief time, his mother Ellen went back to teaching in Manti. It was there she married her second husband, a blacksmith and farmer, about two years later. When he was fourteen years old, Ammon took a job working for a neighboring farmer and was able to save enough in his first six months of work to buy his mother her first stove.[6] She was only to enjoy it for a short time, however; when Ammon was fifteen, his mother died.

After working at various odd jobs, farming, sheepshearing, driving oxen and mules, Ammon followed his two sisters to Orderville. As he related to his granddaughter, Elizabeth Fowler:

> In the spring of 1875, my two sisters, Harriet and Florence, moved from Manti to Orderville, having been persuaded to go by Harriet's father-in-law, Mr. Charles Allen, who had joined the order. I remained in Manti but as both our parents had died, my sisters prevailed on me to join them. I traveled as far as Kanab with John Porter and Walter Windsor, driving two yoke of oxen. While at Kanab I made arrangements to go to school and work for my board at the home of W. D. Johnson. I decided to pay a visit to my sisters in Orderville, and they would not concent for me, then a boy of fifteen, to go to Kanab to live. So the thought of school ended and I joined the order. The first winter I hauled wood from the canyon, some days making two trips. The snow was deep but as wood was our only fuel, we could not complain. When the wood was brought in, it was taken to the public wood pile which was near the kitchen. Then members of each family chopped enough for their home and some for the public dining hall and kitchen.
>
> During the summer I worked on the farm which was located a short distance above the Washington Dam. This tract had been purchased by the order as they intended to raise cotton. Three families and some single men had been sent down there to work. I worked one year and returned to Orderville. I was put into the shoe shop to learn the shoemaker's trade. Other boys were put at other trades. Here I learned to make shoes as all the shoes the people wore were made in this shop. Sometimes six pairs were made in a day. Most of the leather was made in the tannery owned by the order. I worked in the shoe shop nine years, the last three of which I was foreman and had charge of the men.[7]

It's unclear whether Henry Ammon met Mary Fowler in that shoe shop or through one of the many activities engaged in by the young people of Orderville. They both were members of their respective Mutual Associations, groups designed for spiritual, intellectual, and recreational purposes; in fact, they both wrote for the same Mutual newspaper and both were involved in dramatic presentations sponsored by these groups. Henry Ammon Fowler's own brief autobiography is almost cryptic in its account of the events leading to his marriage to Mary Fowler: "I knew and courted Mary S. Fackrell for some seven or eight months and on the 29th of September, 1880, I took her to the St. George Temple, and we were married."[8] He describes the events with slightly greater elaboration when telling his granddaughter:

> I was married while living in the order. No preparation was made for the event, but I was given $2.50 (about the only cash I saw during the time I spent in the order.) We bought a small glass lamp, a mirror, a pair

of scissors, a comb, and two window shades, also some spools of thread. Of course, I had credits in the order that went to secure my house and we lived from the general fund.[9]

By the time of their marriage Mary Susannah had been teaching school in Orderville for two years. Henry was still working at the shoe shop (being appointed foreman January 31, 1881), and he was also helping shear sheep in the summer months. They moved into a "shanty" of their own after the marriage and continued to work together with the other members of the community. Their first child, David Arno, was born July 14, 1881, and his brother William Rey soon followed on December 14, 1882.

The communal system of Orderville began to break up about this time, due to both political and economic pressures.[10] In the fall of 1883, in concert with the gradual dissolution of the United Order, Henry Ammon Fowler built his young family a house in the orchard owned by the order and constructed his own shoe shop in the back. It was here that Mary Susannah gave birth to Joseph Eben on July 10, 1884. Within the next four years, Henry Ammon would marry another wife, Eliza Norwood, whom he had employed as a nurse when Mary gave birth to her daughter Laura in 1886; he would flee from federal agents searching for polygamists; and, following yet again in his sisters' footsteps, he would move his entire family to the town of Huntington in south-central Utah:

> In the fall of 1888, my sister Harriet's husband Albert Allen, and his brother Isaac, came down to Orderville with their teams and I sold my house and bought a team and wagon and several cows, and a riding pony and saddle for the boys to ride to drive the livestock up to Castle Valley. I had decided to move to Huntington because I thought I had a better chance of getting a farm and home there. Isaac and Albert Allen both lived in Huntington and they told me about the country there.[11]

When the family finally reached Huntington after an arduous journey, Henry Ammon bought a lot with a log house on it where Mary and her children lived, and he rented a house for Eliza and her children across the street. Fanny Fowler, the first of Mary's surviving children to be born in Huntington, describes their first house as

> built of logs with one large room and a lean-to kitchen. The logs were chinked up and whitewashed inside with factory for the ceiling. Dirt or sod took the place of shingles which was partially washed off occasionally when there were severe storms and then it was necessary to shift furniture around and catch the little streams of water in buckets and pans to keep from having things spoiled. When the storm was over it was a simple matter to replenish the "shingles." The floor in the front room was

Mary Susannah Sumner Fackrell Fowler and her children; photo taken in 1900 to send to her husband, Henry Ammon Fowler, while he was on his mission to Oklahoma Indian Territory. Photo courtesy of Virginia Fowler Rogers.

covered with a hand-made rag carpet stretched over a generous amount of straw which gave a crunchy sound when we walked over it.[12]

It was into this two-room, dirt-roofed, dirt-floored house that Mary Fowler moved with her husband and five young children. By the time they moved in, there were already families well settled with whom they had worked in Orderville. No doubt, this made the tremendous task of resettlement somewhat easier for the Fowlers. Their daughter Laura Ellen Fowler Roper suggests that "it was a trial to Mother to leave her folks and a comfortable home, and it was many years before things grew anywhere near as luxurious as they had been in Orderville. However, Mother was patient and cheerful and faithful, prayer being her mainstay. The people were all poor together and had to be resourceful."[13]

Still, it is somewhat of a surprise to learn that just a few short weeks after her arrival, Mary Fowler had become the editor of the Young Ladies' Mutual Improvement Association journal, the *Gem*. Such an accomplishment suggests the relative ease with which a young woman might move from one Mormon community to another and even assume an important position within a religious organization. This also indicates the importance of church service to Mary Fowler, who certainly had plenty to do with a new home and five young children under eight years of age, yet undertook the time-consuming task of editing a frequently published journal.

Life as a young wife and mother in Huntington was itself incredibly demanding. One of the Fowler children, Fanny Fowler Harper, writes:

> Our living was very meager, having little money to spend for food. We ate what we could raise or the fruits, vegetables, honey, etc. that could be stored for winter. The fruit was mostly dried and we also had dried squash, corn, and beans.
>
> Our clothes were all home-made, from our wraps to our factory outing-flannel underwear. Mother corded, spun, and dyed the wool to make our stockings, mittens and facinators. Father made our shoes and we didn't even know about overshoes and rubbers. One pair a year was the rule and they were made on the same last so they could be worn on either foot to make them last longer.
>
> There were eight of us youngsters growing up in those two rooms. In the winter we each had our various amusements and occupations and I wonder how Mother put up with so much confusion.[14]

As these comments suggest, during her first decade in Huntington Mary bore six more children, three of whom died in infancy: Susannah Mary was born November 8, 1889, and died a few months later on March 8, 1890; Fanny Harriet was born on December 19, 1890; Bertha Elizabeth arrived on March 24, 1893, but died on June 19, 1893; Harry Cyrenus was born May 29, 1894; Karl Fernando was born on August 17, 1897, living only one day; Fred Milton was born November 29, 1898. Mary's twelfth and final pregnancy resulted in stillborn twins.

The unending tasks of caring for so large a family with so little money in so small a house are summed up by her son Fred:

> From the present vantage point of modern conveniences it is hard to appreciate the sheer physical demands upon strength and energy in bearing and rearing a large family where cooking was done on a wood or coal stove; washing was done by hand; ironing was done with flatirons heated on top of the stove; water was dipped and carried from the irrigation ditch running in the street in the summertime (in highwater time or after each storm the roily water had to be settled before use), or hauled in barrels from more distant streams in the wintertime when the water no longer ran in the irrigation streams; bathing was done in tin washtubs set on the kitchen floor; pants, shirts, dresses for husband, sons and daughters were sewed; socks and stockings and mittens, and other articles were knit from yarn spun from wool carded in the home; vegetables were grown and stored and fruit dried and preserved for winter food.
>
> Both from necessity and by design labor was shared by the children. Through wise management each member did his appointed tasks as

a matter of course. All learned to take responsibility willingly. Family living was a cooperative enterprise. But even so the strain was great upon
the mother, and it is all the more wonder that so much time was found
for doing the many things which she did.[15]

The range of Mary Fowler's activities, in fact, was quite astounding.
Apart from caring for her large family in all the ways her son Fred has enu-
merated above, Mary was actively engaged in church organizations, not
only editing the YLMIA journal, but also becoming secretary of the Relief
Society in 1900. Her literary and scholarly efforts extended beyond such
church associations; Mary Susannah Fowler was a leader in establishing a
women's literary club in Huntington, and she pursued her own literary
interests unceasingly, writing verse for her personal edification, for friends'
birthdays and funerals, and for ceremonial occasions in the larger community. In addition, Mary was a nurse, healer, and midwife, unceasingly serving especially women and children, often leaving her own family to tend
to the medical needs of others.

Henry Ammon Fowler found work in Huntington as a shoemaker
and also became even more accomplished in stone masonry and carpentry.
Although he worked extremely hard, later writing, "I will say that I worked
at everything that I could get a chance to work at to support my two big
families. There was no work about building houses that I didn't do,"[16]
Fowler also found time to continue his lively interest in and love of music.
In Huntington, as in Orderville, dances were held on numerous occasions
and Henry A. Fowler played violin and snare drum at these events. He also
played piccolo or fife or snare drum in a martial band that he later was chosen to conduct.[17] Ammon joined the choir as soon as he reached
Huntington, as he says: "The people who lived there and had known me
in Orderville, knew that I led the choir at Orderville and they wanted me
to take charge of the choir. I wanted to get better acquainted so I told them
to wait until spring. In the spring I accepted the position of chorister. . . .
Besides being chorister I acted as janitor."[18]

Both Henry Ammon and Mary Susannah found that their previous
experiences in Orderville prepared them for the work they were to engage
in in Huntington. In fact, their early experiences in Mormon communal
living dramatically shaped the rest of their lives. For Mary, the nurturing of
her family, caring for the sick, service to her church, and personal expression through her own writing continued to develop as central themes.

Yet, in identifying specific significant events, her son's biography of
Mary Fowler, the reminiscences of her family, and the autobiography of her
husband all reveal only a handful of occasions that stand out from the everyday tasks of her life in Huntington. Apart from the births and deaths of her

children, the notable events all have to do with travel, with either leaving or returning to Huntington. In the spring of 1890, for example, Mary returned to Orderville to nurse her mother who had become seriously ill. Henry Ammon's "diary" relates that "in the spring of 1890 Mary's mother was very sick and I took Mary and her children down to Orderville with my team and wagon to see her mother. . . . Mary stayed in Orderville all summer. In the fall, she came to Gunnison with her brother, and I went to meet her."[19]

Another family trip, one that is not mentioned by either Henry Ammon or Mary in any of their writings now available, was especially significant to their daughter Laura Ellen, who writes in her personal history, "When I was twelve years of age [1898] we went to Salina to meet mother's parents and several of her brothers and sisters who were going to make their home in Idaho. That was quite an event in my life as a child. We traveled in a covered wagon."[20] Laura, who was only a toddler when the family had moved from Orderville and still only four when they went back for the visit mentioned above, chooses this trip to Salina in a covered wagon as one of the most significant events in her childhood.

Just two years later, Henry Ammon received a call to go on a mission for the LDS Church to the "south-western states." On October 5, 1900, Henry Ammon, accompanied by Mary, Rey, Laura, Fanny, Harry, and Eliza's son Ralph, traveled to Price, Utah, where Henry boarded a train for Salt Lake to begin his mission. Mary's diary for October 6 reveals her own commitment to her husband's journey:

> We went to the station to see Pa off. I now begin to realize what it will be to be a missionary's wife. It is an experience I have always desired yet always dreaded. My outlook is not very encouraging. But though I feel sad I am thankful for the privelege of parting with my husband for a little while to spread the glorious gospel which is dearer than anything on earth to me. And I believe our Heavenly Father will take care of him & us.[21]

Mary's concern about the twenty-five months that Henry would spend in Oklahoma and Texas was certainly not unfounded. Without even the meager income that Henry was able to supply from his many jobs, Mary herself became the school janitor, adding this backbreaking work to all her other duties. In order to make ends meet, she found herself relying on the generosity of friends and taking on even more odd jobs when the possibility arose. As early as October 12, just one day after her husband had left Salt Lake to begin his mission, Mary Susannah writes in her diary: "Picked up potatoes for W. Avery. Laurie Asa Leo and myself earned 5 1/2 bu. Answered Pa's letter."

During her husband's absence, Mary also took care of her sister-wife, Eliza, who became seriously ill shortly after Henry Ammon left on his mission. Because of her illness, Mary found herself supporting not only her own children, but Eliza and her children as well. In addition, Mary worked to make enough to send Henry money for his room and board in Oklahoma and for the purchase of necessary clothing and supplies.

The added work and worry did not dim Mary's enthusiasm either for her husband's missionary life or for her own other activities. On her birthday that same October she writes: "My birthday. This is as bright a birthday as I have seen for many years. Our prospects seem just as good as they ever do & it is a great comfort to have my husband laboring in the missionary field. My children are a great comfort & help to me. I attended Young Ladies meeting with Laurie, was asked to speak in meeting" (October 23, 1900). Besides her church work, Mary also continued ministering to the sick, meeting with her friends, and attending political rallies: "Sat [October] 27 Attended Primary conference also Republican Raly in evening. Nelson of Manti and Smith of SLC speakers. They are good men but I don't like their politics"; and on Tuesday, November 6: "Voted Democratic ticket."

By the time Henry Ammon Fowler returned to Huntington in early November of 1902, Eliza had recovered completely, the children were all well, but Mary had exhausted herself. She became so ill that Henry took her to Salt Lake City to be seen by doctors there and then they went to the Salt Lake Temple to be blessed.

A few months later in the fall of 1903, Henry Ammon moved Mary and her children to Provo at Mary's urging so that Arno and Rey could attend Brigham Young Academy (the forerunner of Brigham Young University). Mary took this opportunity to receive finally some official training in nursing, taking classes at Brigham Young to supplement her already considerable knowledge of the field.

During their time in Provo, Henry was frequently away, working in other locations in Idaho and Utah. For example, during the late spring and summer of their first year in Provo, Henry took Arno, Rey, and Eben with him to Idaho to work:

> I stopped at Blackfoot to work in the sugar factory. The boys went west to Lost River to shear sheep. In July I sent Mary $20 to come up and see me and her folks, who lived at Riverside. They lost the money in the mail so she had to wait until the next payday, when she came and stayed a month and brought Fanny, Harry and Fred. We all returned together in the wagon.[22]

By the time the Fowlers left Provo to return to Huntington in the fall of 1907, Eben, Arno, Rey, and Laura had all married. Henry had gone back to Huntington to work on plastering the schoolhouse, and afterwards he "took the dirt roof off our own house and raised it higher and put shingles on and built a kitchen, pantry and clothes closet at the back. When it was finished I took the team and wagon and went to Provo for Mary and the children. We moved all our things back to Huntington again."[23] While Mary Fowler's family had grown considerably smaller, her house had become somewhat larger. Then in 1910 Mary's extended family became smaller still; Eliza, who had stayed in Huntington while the others were in Provo, decided to move to Price to be close to two of her children, so Henry sold her house in Huntington, bought a lot in Price, and built her a new home.

Reduction in family responsibilities provided the time for Mary to visit some of her siblings whom she had not seen in many years. Besides visiting her Idaho relatives during the time they lived in Provo, in the winter of 1911 Henry Ammon took Mary to visit her brother Cyrenus, whom she had not seen in twenty-five years. Henry had gotten a plastering job in Enterprise, Utah, where Cyrenus lived, and as Henry put it, "that paid our way there and back."[24]

The next journey for the husband and wife was not such a pleasant one. "In the spring of 1915," Henry Ammon writes,

> I took down with a severe pain in my stomach and bloated real bad, but by hard work Mary reduced the bloat. The doctor said it was peritonitis and said it was gallstones that were troubling me. I did not think so as I had not had a spell for a long time. . . . Dr. Graham from Castle Dale said that I must go to the hospital, but I was not financially able to do so, and so made no move to go. This was a Sunday evening when he told us this. On Tuesday he came again and said if I wanted to live I must go, so we sent for Bp. Antone Nelson. He came to see me and said to go to the hospital and the church would pay the bill. So the next morning we got Reuben Brasher to take us to Price. The Dr. wanted to go with me but I thought Mary was good enough. She had morphine to give me in case the pain during my ride to Price was too hard on me. We had only a short time to wait at Price for the train. When we reached Salt Lake City, there was a hospital ambulance there to meet us. The next morning I was put on a wheeled stretcher and taken to the operating room. They did not notify Mary when they would operate so she did not get there until they had begun to work. They cut out the gall sack and there was over 100 stones from the size of grains of wheat to a good size marble.
>
> Through the neglect of one of the nurses, I got pneumonia about two weeks after the operation and nearly passed away. If my wife, Mary, had not been there I surely would have done so. She first went to one and then another until she convinced them I had pneumonia and they got busy right away doctoring me for it. I was in the hospital from the 1st of April until the 1st of May.[25]

Throughout Henry Ammon's married life, it was Mary who attended him during every illness and injury, of which there were many. He relied on her both for physical and spiritual support as this one example clearly indicates.

No doubt Henry also relied on Mary's supportive nature when two of their sons, Harry and Fred, enlisted in the service in 1917, traveling to Ireland, England, France, and Italy during World War I. Mary became actively involved in working with the Red Cross during the war, no doubt feeling she was contributing not only to her country, but to her boys as well.

As if sending her two youngest sons off to war were not hard enough, during the fall of 1917, the Fowlers' house burned down while they were out working in the fields. As her daughter-in-law Jessie Manwaring Fowler describes it, "Eben's mother and I were doing some canning and had a good fire going in the kitchen stove. Suddenly, the house was on fire. We fought the flames but it was useless. Almost everything in the house was destroyed."[26] Although the neighbors were able to carry out many of the belongings on the ground floor, everything upstairs was lost in the fire. Henry Ammon and his son Eben, were able to construct a 28-by-32-foot bungalow and ready two of the rooms for habitation by the following New Year's Day. By the summer of 1920, the downstairs was completed and the plastering was done upstairs.

Mary's delight in her new house was to be short-lived, however, as Ammon describes:

> After fixing our home up with closets and bedrooms downstairs, etc. Mary did enjoy it so much. She did like to go upstairs to bed. She was not to enjoy her home very long though. The injury which she received years before from being kicked by a horse had grown worse until in october of 1920 she had a real bad spell. I called in Dr. Hill and he told us she must go to a specialist where an x-ray picture could be taken so I sent her to Salt Lake City. She attended Conference and felt so well she thought of not having the operation but before she came home she had another bad spell and went to the hospital. The x-ray picture showed a growth in her colon on her left side. She was operated on October 27, 1920 and lived just forty-eight hours after the operation. I got a phone message that she was dead. It was an awful shock. I went right up to the city.[27]

Mary's last earthly journey home to Huntington mirrored her first trip from Orderville some thirty years before; several of her children, Eben, Laura, Fanny, and Harry, accompanied her casket through a steady fall rain to Huntington, where the community welcomed her home at a "very large funeral . . . in spite of the rain and muddy weather, and many nice things were said of Mary's various works in public ways and her nursing the sick."[28]

PIECING TOGETHER A LIFE

This brief history was pieced together from many sources; these various discourses began to open up the life of Mary Fowler in new and often unexpected ways. Once I had begun to get a sense of the contours of Mary

Fowler's life through her own diary and her son's biography, I realized that I simply *had* to know more. As even the brief preceding life sketch indicates, there were so many aspects of Mary's life history that were too intriguing to go unquestioned, unpursued, and so I went in search of anything I could find that might illuminate Mary Fowler's life. In what seems now like a very short time, the few pages of "data" I had originally encountered at the library grew to include hundreds upon hundreds of pages: additional portions of Mary's own diaries, her poetry, essays, travel narrative, and genealogy notes; her biography written by Fred Fowler; her husband Henry Ammon Fowler's missionary diaries, short personal history, lengthier autobiography, and autograph book; the personal histories of many members of her family; her sister-in-law's autograph book; minutes of the Relief Society and the Young Ladies' Mutual Improvement Association which reported on her activities and often her speeches; tributes written by friends at her death; and memoirs of her contemporaries in Orderville and Huntington. Finding these documents took me from the University of Utah to Brigham Young University, from the Historical Department of the Church of Jesus Christ of Latter-day Saints to a tiny one-room museum run by the Daughters of the Utah Pioneers in Orderville.

The search to understand this woman became for me an adventure, a mystery; like all readers of good mystery novels, I became obsessed with the desire to discover more clues, clues that might explain those fascinating experiences only hinted at in the material I first encountered. I wanted to know more than a mere chronological life history sketch could offer; I wanted to understand the "whys" behind the events, reasons that could not simply be arranged in any convenient temporal sequence, reasons that would explain the life patterns that emerge without respect to temporality. And like any of my favorite female sleuths (and like most folklorists), I soon discovered that the most important part of any search is getting to know the right people, the people with the "real story."

In this case, those people were Mary Susannah Fowler's grandchildren, whose names I first located in the LDS Church's Family History Library. Through the oral narratives and the collected memories of her granddaughters and grandson whom I first contacted by letter, I came to know Mary Fowler in a way no printed text alone could ever reveal. To my delight, I discovered that Virginia Fowler Rogers, the granddaughter most involved with family history and a former employee of the genealogy library, lives only ten blocks away from me. Mrs. Rogers became my partner in the search. Through her I was able not only to locate many written sources, but she also put me in contact with several other relatives who shared family stories about Mary Susannah Fowler. And in the process Mrs. Rogers and I became good friends.

The discovery process involved a whole range of experiences from digging in archives to photographing American Indian jewelry. One day, while I was grading final exams for an introductory folklore class, Mrs. Rogers called and asked if I could come over to her house. Glad for the distraction and eager to talk some more with her, I rushed over to find Mrs. Rogers waiting for me in the kitchen. She gave me a big smile and announced, "We're going to make grandmother's stomach powder!" Together we carefully measured and poured the ingredients necessary for concocting Mary Susannah Fowler's home remedy for both constipation and flatulence. As Mrs. Rogers warned with a laugh, "Take just a *little* pinch for gas, more for the other problem." As we worked together, measuring and pouring, she would comment on the usefulness or availability of each ingredient. When I questioned whether we had to actually grind up the "gizzard peel," for example, she told me that you can get a substitute at the pharmacy these days and she pulled an unmarked jar from her kitchen cabinet. Adding a little extra sugar, Mrs. Rogers shook her head and said, "I used to give this to my own kids, but after each one had tasted it once, there was just no getting them to take it again! You better have a little more sugar." Today the little bottle of "stomach powder" sits in my university office, a constant reminder of the day I first felt I'd begun to be unofficially adopted into the Fowler family. In this case, the "adoption papers" consist of a torn scrap of notepaper listing the ingredients Mary Susannah Fowler had first put together, copied carefully for me by the hand of her granddaughter, Virginia Rogers:

Stomach Powder
2 tsp. Golden seal
2 tsp. Bayberry
1 tsp. gizzard peel
1 tsp. egg shell
7 tsp. powdered sugar
Blend thoroughly—Keep in air-tight container. Use for gas.
More as laxative.

In small ways, then, the connections between Mary Fowler and myself had become even stronger. She was no longer the shadow of someone who lived a century ago, but the provider of advice and even remedies for common problems. The sense of the reality of Mary Susannah grew even stronger when I visited her grandson Milton Roper in Huntington one summer afternoon. While we talked about his grandmother, Milton Roper's own granddaughter came in from the garden, the same garden Mary Fowler had planted so long ago, and offered me freshly picked carrots—the biggest carrots I'd ever seen. As I tasted the sweetness of those carrots, I could visualize much more clearly how Mary's own life in Huntington revolved around both the garden and the two-room house which used to stand next to it. Through both Mary's great-great-granddaughter and her grandson, an understanding of the ways family connections can be represented in land tilled over generations was dramatically enacted.

Occasionally, the discoveries of the range of growing connections came in unexpected ways. At the end of an especially long day of reading microfilms of newspapers and minutes of church meetings from Huntington, Utah, in the LDS Church Historical Department, I decided to finish up that particular portion of my research by taking a quick look at the journal Henry Ammon Fowler kept while he was on his church mission. Although I doubted that there would be anything particularly useful to my interest in Mary Fowler's life, I assumed that I would be able to quickly eliminate this citation from my growing list of "sources to consult." Instead of the microfilms I expected to see emerge from the bowels of the archives, I was pleased to find that the archivists had retrieved Ammon's original journals for me to peruse. Carefully opening the first worn leather volume, I read in almost utter disbelief:

> Journal of the Travels
> of Henry A. Fowler
> of the
> Church of Jesus Christ
> of Latterday Saints
> While
> in the South Western States
> Mission
> Oklahoma and Indian
> Teritory
> Chickasaw Nation

My own Chickasaw grandfather, Stilwell Russell Polk, had been born in 1903 in the very area where Mary Fowler's husband had done his missionary work two years before. As I read the eleven small volumes composed by Henry A. Fowler on his travels through southern Oklahoma and northern Texas, I could map out the times he might have encountered my great-grandparents, although they were never referred to by name in his journals. Perhaps, the nonscholarly side of me began to think, finding Mary Susannah's journal was not just coincidence after all. This was not, however, the end of the "Indian connection."

A few months later when I was once again visiting Mrs. Rogers, she brought out a long list of relatives she'd been working on for me. Almost every time I would talk with her, my friend would manage to remember another cousin or aunt or nephew that perhaps I hadn't yet spoken with. On this occasion, she had noted that I might want to meet Eileen Freckleton, another of Mary Susannah's granddaughters, who lived in Bountiful near the place where Mary Susannah had been born. When I called Mrs. Freckleton, she was really quite gracious in asking me to come for a visit, but she warned me, "I was born long after grandmother Mary had already died. And I really don't know much about her at all. In fact, I don't even have copies of any of her diaries or poems."

Disappointment almost distracted me from Mrs. Freckleton's next words: "Really, all I have is a few of her things." I actually felt my heart rate begin to quicken. For months I had been searching for some clue to the location of Mary Susannah Fowler's "curio collection," which had been mentioned in one line of her son Fred's biography. No one, not even the assiduous Mrs. Rogers, knew where it might be. Knowing that it was probably highly unlikely that a granddaughter who hadn't even met Mary Susannah would have acquired such a collection, yet hoping beyond hope that she had, I asked tentatively, "What *kind* of things?"

"Oh, just some old Indian pots and things that belonged to her" was the answer that was my reward for even risking hope. I quickly set up a time to meet that afternoon, and a few hours later, camera in hand, I was standing at Mrs. Freckleton's door in Bountiful.

The "things" turned out to be more than "just old Indian pots": the collection was comprised of Navajo jewelry, braided horsehair ornaments, and a series of incredibly beautiful examples of Navajo pottery. Even more startling was the fact that Mary Susannah Fackrell Fowler had carefully attached to each piece a small, white tag on which she had written the date, the artist she had acquired the piece from, and, when necessary, a brief description of the object. Mary Susannah Fowler was a folklorist! In fact, she may have been the very first "folklorist" to be interested in the culture of the tribes of southern Utah: the Utes, Paiutes, and Navajo.

As I photographed the collection and reflected on the notations left in Mary Fowler's handwriting, now blurred and in some cases obliterated with age, again I marveled at the connections between this Mormon woman and myself—a non-Mormon, part Chickasaw academic who had written her first book on Navajo narratives almost a hundred years after Mary had begun collecting Navajo material culture. Now as I think back on the day I took those photographs, or on the afternoon I helped make stomach powder, or the time I tasted carrots from Mary Fowler's own garden, or the first time I opened the pages of Henry Fowler's missionary journals from Oklahoma, I realize that the interconnections between us go far deeper than I could ever have imagined when I first glanced at the opening lines of Mary's diary three years ago.

It is precisely this idea of interconnectedness I have learned from both my own experiences and from those of the Mary Fowler whose life emerges in a pastiche of images that each of the representations of her life (the diaries, poems, Relief Society minutes, biographies, life histories, et cetera) evokes. Because both Mary Fowler and I are folklorists in our own ways, the issues and concerns that shape my construction of her life are not surprisingly those of someone with a folklorist's sensibilities. In the chapters that follow, then, instead of simply adding a greater number of specific events to "fill out" or "fill in" the chronological sequence presented earlier, I want to examine Mary's grounding in a particular folk belief about the idea of community, her use of traditional medicinal practices, and her delight in writing folk poetry as the organizing principles for my own reconstruction of the many stories of Mary Susannah Fowler's life.

2

"Home with Our Families,
Near Home with Our Friends"
Folk Belief and the Mormon Community

Our Mission dear sisters is not far extended
Tis at home with our families, near home with our friends.
Tis not mongst the nations this is not intended
But yet to vast labors our mission extends.

The particular concept of community that shapes the thematic resonances of Mary Fowler's self-construction is quite obviously influenced,
some might say determined, by the ideas of interrelationship with which she
grew up. As Dean May has suggested in his landmark article, "The Making
of Saints: The Mormon Town as a Setting for the Study of Cultural Change,"
in many nineteenth-century Mormon towns in Utah "community harmony and solidarity was a supreme value."[1] Certainly that was no more fully the
case than in Orderville, the longest lasting and most successful of over two
hundred Mormon communal endeavors. For Mary Fowler and other young
people who grew up in Orderville, the particular folk beliefs surrounding
this concept of community indeed profoundly influenced the development
of their ideas about the relationship of self to "other."

Orderville as it existed between 1874 and 1885 was in many ways pro-
totypical of the village community that Dorothy Noyes refers to in
describing a slide of the Irish village of Braunton, Devon:

> The village community gives us the idea made visible, the performance
> made permanent in architecture. Here group is territory and perfor-
> mance, social ideal and lived reality. Here is the community as "bounded
> individual," like a body writ large. Here is the emblem. Here are the city
> walls as the limits of interaction.[2]

In fact, her description could be adapted almost in toto for a picture
of Orderville, with its fort-like enclosure, its Mormon ideals enacted most
fully, and its continual performance of what it means to be both Mormons

and members of this United Order. While Noyes makes the point that as folklorists we should not be susceptible to always thinking of local community as "primary and natural," in this case the conscious construction of an idealized community in Orderville provides an excellent example of the ways in which such a marriage of the ideal and the real has occasionally been effected. In this case, the "imaginary" community consists both of Brigham Young's conception of the United Order and the individual Ordervillian's recontextualization of that ideal as it is transplanted to southern Utah; the real community is the working out of those imaginings in the day-to-day performances of the men, women, and children of Orderville.[3]

Such embracing of the communitarian ideal was not always the case among Utah Mormons. In contrast to Orderville, for example, in Kanab, Utah—only about twenty miles south of Orderville—"when the communitarian United Order was introduced in the late spring 1874 the town began to break into two factions, divided primarily over whether a full communal organization or a loosely structured producers' cooperative was most desirable. Bitter controversy continued for four years and feelings remained high for decades thereafter."[4] In fact, several of those Kanab settlers, still desiring to participate in a communitarian society, eventually joined the Mormons of Orderville. The enacting of the social imaginary in a historical reality demands the participation of all members of the community (to a certain extent) and the continual performance of those community ideals.

The identification with the Orderville community, effected through such ongoing performances, was an intensification of the kinds of social constructions found in Mormon towns all over Utah in the late nineteenth century. Whether fully communitarian in practice or not, the people of Mormon Utah considered themselves first and foremost the "people of Zion." Brigham Young used the words applied to ancient Israel in 1 Peter 2:9, that "ye are a chosen generation, a royal priesthood, an holy nation, a peculiar people" in calling for Mormon people to "flee the world—'Babylon,' as they called it—and gather with the Saints."[5] Joseph Smith had designated Jackson County, Missouri, as the new Zion in 1831, but two years later the Mormons were driven from Jackson County and from Missouri entirely in 1839. After a period of time in exile in Illinois, Brigham Young led an advance party of Mormons to the Great Salt Lake Valley in 1847. Shortly thereafter he sent out a famous apostolic letter announcing that a new gathering place had been found in Utah: "Flee to Zion—there the Servants of God will be ready to wait upon them and teach them all things that pertain to Salvation. . . . Should any ask, where is Zion? tell them in America; and if any ask what is Zion? tell them the pure in heart."[6]

As Dean May notes, "Under a new Joshua, the Saints were moving into a promised land. They now were entrusted, as a spiritual obligation, with the task of erecting bricks and mortar of Zion in a remote region hitherto unsettled by whites."[7] As the new people of Zion, then, Mormon men and women considered their communities as integral parts of the Kingdom of God on earth. That conception of community, based as it was in a religious ideology that conceived of "building the City of God" as an effort not of individuals but of this "peculiar people," circumscribed the attitudes of the faithful in both their worship services and their daily interactions with each other. In describing Alpine, Utah, in the 1870s by envisioning a walk through the village, May imagines:

> We would see that people were interacting with others outside their household almost everywhere we looked and that most were engaged in or planning voluntary activities. And each time people met and talked . . . each time these encounters took place, strands of vaguely defined outward obligation and connection were being teased out, twisted, and in time securely tied. The obligations were never made contractual or explicit, and in their very indeterminate quality lay their power. For who can say when debts owed to one who took time from life-sustaining activities to teach embroidery, literature, or that the meadow lark sings "Alpine is a pretty little place!" are repaid? The Alpine people, without quite willing or realizing it, were constructing a web of obligation and attachment that held most emotionally and physically to the town.[8]

Certainly, a walk through Orderville at the same time would reveal similar, if not even more intense, webs of obligation and signification. In a communitarian village where each member freely gave up individual ownership in favor of the communal good, the children of Orderville came to prize values of reciprocity and mutual interdependence.

THE UNITED ORDER IN ORDERVILLE

The members of the LDS Church who moved to Kane County in southern Utah in the early 1870s had already developed a sense of unity and a spirit of camaraderie, since most of them had toiled together in southeastern Nevada along the Muddy River. That particular effort at colonization had been an extremely difficult one: "The valley was hot and dry and subject to insect infestation, flash floods and disease. The settlers eked out a living in a condition approaching outright destitution."[9] By the time these travelers reached Long Valley, they were even more firmly united in the desire to create a community that would flourish. Earlier exploring parties had found over thirteen hundred acres of tillable land and vast grazing ranges in this area. Timber was plentiful and water for irrigation and power would be provided by the Virgin River.[10]

After building a transitional community at Mt. Carmel where there was already a small group of Mormon settlers, the refugees from the Muddy eagerly accepted the urgings of John R. Young, who met with the Mt. Carmelites in March of 1874, to establish a United Order.

> This United Order was a later manifestation of what LDS church mem-
> bers in Missouri had previously referred to as the "United Firm," "Order
> of Enoch," or "United Order." Efforts to establish an ideal, communal
> society were initiated by Mormon founder Joseph Smith as the result of
> a series of revelations. The "Order" was an attempt to redefine the rela-
> tion of individual to property, and was socialistic in nature. The earth was
> considered the Lord's; the people were stewards only over their posses-
> sions, which were to be known as stewardships or inheritances. Those
> who had surplus property, more than required to provide a frugal living
> for the family were to consecrate it by deed to the Church, to benefit the
> poor. Surplus production beyond family needs was to be turned over to
> the bishop's storehouse.[11]

When the Mormons were expelled from Missouri, the Order of Enoch ceased to formally exist, although cooperative ideals were certainly operative in Mormon social interactions. In 1874, then, Brigham Young called for a restoration of the order. In part, Young's reinstitution of the order was a response to the growing presence of "Gentiles" in Utah, the economic uncertainty resulting from friction with the United States government, and a belief that self-sufficiency and a favorable balance of trade were critical for the survival of Mormonism in Utah. "If the Saints lived frugally, bought nothing from without, and produced an exportable surplus, they might . . . become rich people. Moreover, by uniting their individual means, the Saints might evade mortgaging themselves to outside capital."[12] In addition, the national Panic of 1873 had a serious effect on the Utah economy.

Although Young's plan for the United Order extended to all of Mormondom, it achieved its greatest success in southern Utah. There, the members of the United Order took to heart the connection between these economic and religious principles, renewing their covenants by baptism and joining together to create truly communal settlements, which would "provide the material and social conditions essential to individual and collective happiness and progress."[13] Ninety-four of 112 Mt. Carmel Saints over the age of fourteen agreed to join the order. Community historian Francis L. Porter recorded that "the Order was the possessor of everything appraisable, from real estate to chickens, featherbeds and ladies' wardrobes."[14] Though the land was more hospitable than Nevada had been in some ways, numerous trials faced the new order members: "Grasshoppers ate the first wheat crop and frost killed the corn. Many were in rags. An epidemic of measles swept the valley and carried off numbers of children."[15] In the face of such trials, by the first summer some friction arose between several families who were dissatisfied with the order and those who accepted the call wholeheartedly. As a result, after consulting with Howard Orson Spencer who had been sent by Brigham Young to settle the differences, the order members moved their community two and a half miles up the Virgin River and established a settlement in March 1875. Located at the mouth of a canyon on the north side of the valley, the community was first named Order City and then, later, Orderville. David B. Fackrell, his wives Susannah and Hannah, and their children were instrumental in both the physical and spiritual organization of the Orderville community.

Originally settled in 1864, Orderville (or the settlement that preceded it) was abandoned in 1866 because of trouble with neighboring Indians that resulted in what has been called the Black Hawk War. By about 1871 settlers had begun to return to the area, and in 1875 when the members of the order arrived, they found a suitable location to plot out a townsite:

> While some of the settlers cut a canal and planted 300 homesteaded acres to wheat, corn, oats, barley, potatoes, sugar cane, alfalfa, garden and orchard, others surveyed the land and layed out a townsite, 30 rods square. All of their economic property, both real and personal, valued at approximately $21,500 in 1875 prices, was deeded to the community corporation. This property included 335 acres of land, 18 houses, 30 hogs, 400 chickens, a threshing machine, reaper, mower, cane mill, 30,000 feet of lumber, and a variety of farming equipment, provisions and supplies.[16]

Orderville was particularly well-located for this kind of communal venture; because it was distant from densely populated centers of economic wealth, the isolation contributed to a successful climate for the abandonment of capitalistic ideals.

The organization of the townsite proceeded within a fairly detailed plan. Each family occupied a separate home, consisting of one- and two-room apartments or "shanties" that were connected together in a kind of fort-like arrangement.

> The typical family occupied quarters consisting of a living room 12 by 12 feet and a bedroom 8 by 12 feet. Such a "shanty" as it was called was constructed of rough boards standing vertical with battens over the cracks, and roof boards running from square to ridge similarly battened.[17]

Public buildings such as the community dining hall were located between the rows of shanties. A large apartment house, known as the "Big

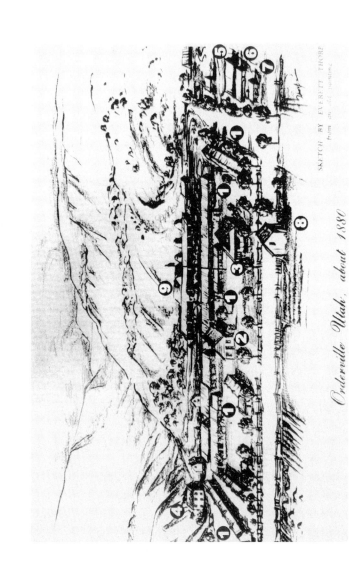

Orderville, Utah, about 1880

SKETCH BY EVERETT THORP
from an old painting

A sketch of the town of Orderville, Utah, taken from an early painting based on another drawing by Issac V. Carling about 1880. Photo used by permission, Utah State Historical Society. 1. Shanties (living quarters). 2. Dining Hall. 3. Big house. 4. Relief Society hall. 5. Carpentry shop. 6. Commissary. 7. Order office and shoe shop. 8. Blacksmith shop. 9. Stables.

House" was constructed to house the leaders of the order and their families; it also contained the United Order office with a storeroom and shoe shop attached. It was a two-story building consisting of twelve rooms and an attic. Later a blacksmith shop, carpentershop, cooper shop, tannery, and telegraph office were added. Barns, sheds, a garden house, and eventually a woolen factory were later additions as well.

Phil Robinson, an early English visitor to Orderville, described the community in this way:

> The settlement itself is grievously disappointing in appearance. For as you approach it, past the charming little hamlet of Glendale, past such a sunny wealth of orchard and meadow and corn-land, past such beautiful glimpses of landscape, you cannot help expecting a scene of rural prettiness in sympathy with such surroundings. But Orderville at first sight looks like a factory. The wooden shed-like buildings built in continuous rows, the adjacent mills, the bare, ugly patch of hillside behind it, gave the actual settlement an uninviting aspect. But once within the settlement, the scene changes wonderfully for the better. The houses are found, most of them built facing inwards, upon an open square with a broad sidewalk, edged with tamarisk and mulberry, boxelder and maple trees, in front of them. Outside the dwelling-house square are scattered about the schoolhouse, meetinghouse, blacksmith and carpenters' shops, tannery, woolen-mill and so forth, while a broad roadway separates the whole from the orchards, gardens, and farm-lands generally. Specially noteworthy here are the mulberry orchard—laid out for the support of the silk-worms, which the community are now rearing with much success—and the forcing ground and experimental garden, in which wild flowers as well as "tame" are being cultivated. Among the buildings the more interesting to me were the school-house, well fitted up, and very fairly provided with educational apparatus; and the rudimentary museum where the commencement of a collection of the natural curiosities of the neighborhood is displayed.[18]

Of course, the community that Robinson describes was the result of almost eight years of hard work, dedication, and commitment. The people of Orderville were well prepared for such an undertaking, having suffered together on the Muddy; most had little to give up to communal coffers, yet they strove diligently to make the experiment a success. In the beginning, twenty-four families (approximately 150 people), including David B. Fackrell, his two wives, and their children, founded Orderville; within five years there were more than 700 members of the community.

One of the first structures erected by the settlers was the dining hall: approximately twenty-two feet by forty feet, it was built of rough hewn lumber, pegged together and lined with adobe. Erected in the middle of the square, it served not only as a community dining hall, but also for prayers, religious meetings, and social gatherings, since it was large enough to seat the entire community. Later, a kitchen and bakery were attached to the dining hall. At the first dinner in the completed community dining hall, held on July 24, 1875, food was prepared by a male supervisor and six women for more than eighty families.[19]

Just ten days earlier, on July 14, the community was incorporated under the name of the "Orderville United Order." All the activities of the order were carried on under the direction of a president, who was the ward bishop, and an annually elected board of directors. The nine members of this board assigned the labor and planned the operations of the community. Each family earned credits for their labor in the various departments and drew upon those credits to provide for their needs. Initially, all the men were credited the same wage, regardless of the job: $1.50 per day; women were credited 75 cents per day; children from eleven to seventeen were credited 75 cents, and those under ten, 12 1/2 cents per day. Board for adults was generally about $50 a year. Clothing for a man was $17.50 a year; for a woman, $16.50. Children were charged approximately 1/2 to 3/4 of these rates.[20] On October 22, 1877, wages were cut 50 percent to bolster the struggling economy. At the end of each year, if a man's credits exceeded his debts, the surplus was turned back to the common fund; if the debts exceeded the credits due to illness or accident, the debts were forgiven and everyone began anew with a blank record.[21] For almost eleven years, the order grew under this system with several modifications along the way.

THE FACKRELLS OF ORDERVILLE

Mary Susannah Fackrell's father, David Bancroft Fackrell, was one of the first members of the board of directors of the Orderville United Order, elected July 26, 1874; as secretary of the order, he was one of five men who traveled to Toquerville, Utah, the Kane County seat, to file the articles of incorporation a year later. He had recently written an article that appeared in the *Deseret News* on July 7, 1875:

> Order City is the name of a town we are building some two and a half miles above Mt. Carmel. The brethren who are doing so organized in the United Order some 16 months since; all except four families were on the Muddy mission. Some four or five withdrew from us last season. We have been greatly blessed in our labors. Our faith has been increased in the faith of the Lord and we feel determined to persevere in the Order. We had no very great display on the 4th, it being Sunday, still it will be long remembered by the saints here. Our dining hall is far enough completed to hold our meetings in. Our families were nearly all gathered in it to dinner. All those who have moved up from the old place eat together all

of their meals. . . . As each family move up they fall into line and help to
swell the family circle. We have all lived from the general fund for some
time and all fare alike. We have no individual property. Our Bishop
Howard O. Spencer is, indeed, a father to the people and much beloved
by all. The Spirit of the Lord is with us. Our aged brethren, some that
were in Zion's Camp, say these are the best days they ever saw. . . . We
wish to see the United Order increase and spread forth until the saints
become one in very deed.[22]

From records of the order it is clear that Fackrell and his wives served
many important roles in Orderville's early days. One of the most significant jobs was the supervision of the order's dairy farm at Castle Ranch
twenty miles up the canyon, a task that involved the entire family. Along
with supervision of the order's store, David Fackrell frequently traveled to
Salt Lake with wagons to trade Orderville's surplus wool for necessary supplies. On one of these trips, his daughter Laura Fackrell Chamberlain
remembers that "Susannah went with him to Salt Lake and returned with
new false teeth, the first false teeth we ever knew of."[23]

As storekeeper, David Fackrell kept track of the debits and credits of
individual members of the order, and in 1877 he was appointed as one of
three members who were selected to straighten out the order's accounts.
In addition, Fackrell and his children were the principal soapmakers of the
community. A poem composed on the anniversary of the order says:

Brother Fackrell made soap out of old grease and scraps.
It would take the skin off the face; cover hands with rough chaps.[24]

Susannah Fackrell served the order in many different capacities: she
helped with the store and was an assistant to Persis A. Spencer in running
the boardinghouse.[25] Perhaps most importantly, she was one of the first
nurses, midwives, and schoolteachers in Orderville, setting an example for
her daughter Mary Susannah who would soon follow in her mother's footsteps. Mary Susannah was only nine years old when she reached Long
Valley with her parents. She left seventeen years later, a wife and mother of
three children, an accomplished poet, a valued member of church organizations, and a recognized healer and midwife. The years in the United
Order had fostered a sense of community and service that would shape the
rest of Mary Susannah Fackrell Fowler's life.

Growing Up in Orderville

As a child growing up in Orderville, Mary Susannah Fackrell learned such
values in a number of ways. In order to foster the communitarian ideal, the
Orderville community structured its activities carefully, so that Mary found
her days governed in part by a regimen not unlike that of the fort her

community physically resembled. Brother Thomas Robertson called everyone to prayer, to work, and to the dining hall for meals by playing his coronet. At seven, twelve, and six o'clock he played different tunes for each meal and certain special songs on Sundays.[26]

The regimen of these calls of reveille was also echoed in the educational experience of Orderville youth. The first school Mary Susannah attended was in a bowery, or as Martha Jane Carling Webb Porter describes it, "a school-room made from green, leafy branches leaned against a framework of poles built around the porch of the 'Big House.'"[27] The informality of the "school-room" disguised the rigor of the first Orderville teacher, Robert Marshall, who had several means of disciplining students who were distracted in this idyllic setting. He would sometimes have problem students stand on one leg for long periods of time and once a young child "was put in a barrel one day, which was another form of punishment."[28] As soon as the weather turned cold the following winter, school was moved into the attic of the Big House, which was more comfortable, but not nearly as exciting. A schoolhouse was one of the first buildings to be constructed in Orderville; "it was a room fourteen by sixteen, not adequately equipped, but some good teaching and learning went on within the four walls."[29] Discipline ordered by regimen was as central to the education delivered in this new schoolhouse as it was in the bowery. Charlotte Cox Heaton recalls, for example, that in order to have the children line up in an organized fashion, "they drove round-headed tacks into the floor, making numbers which the children had to toe by. My number was 18. These numbers never wore out."[30] Nor did the disciplinary conditioning the numbers afforded.

Along with their school obligations, the young girls of the United Order were also obliged to serve the community's meals in the dining hall. By the time the order had been established in Long Valley, Mary was old enough to join the other girls in this work. Three senior girls and three junior girls of eleven or twelve years of age served each week, and the assignments thus rotated through the community. This chance to become partners with a senior girl often "aroused emotions almost bewildering. It was a supreme moment; a real affection grew up between the senior and junior girls."[31] This early experience of a female community likely played an important role in Mary Fowler's later participation in a wide range of female-centered associations.

Guided by the sure hands of the older girls, the younger girls' duties were to set and wait on the tables. Since there were no tablecloths, the tables were thoroughly washed after each meal; the benches were washed as often as needed. White sand was used to scrub the floors twice a week because soap was so scarce. And on the Saturday she was acting as junior server, Mary would help the other servers scour the silverware with sand and water to keep the utensils perfectly clean. Although cleaning silverware for that many people often seemed an impossible task, Emma Seegmiller suggests that at times it wasn't really so bad: "Usually some of the boys would saunter along, if not to help, to tease and amuse us as we sat outside in the shade of the building, busy with scouring sand, towels and great pans of water."[32]

Instead of finding such tasks mere drudgery, the girls delighted in adding special touches to the meals. In the springtime they would often get up early in the morning to gather the wild roses that grew profusely along the creek banks. Placing a rose under each overturned plate, the girls waited for the adults to arrive, turn their plates over, and fill the room with the heady scent of fresh flowers.

Mary also learned about her place in the female community as she observed her mother and the other women who cooked for the entire population of Orderville. Although a man, William Black, was the overseer of the kitchen, six Orderville women cooked for a week each before another six rotated into the positions. This allowed women to attend to cooking chores only periodically, so that they had more time for their other duties in the intervening weeks. Each day over three hundred pounds of flour was mixed into bread in large troughs; many loaves at a time could be baked in the large brick ovens attached to the kitchen. Potatoes, squash, and meat were cooked in large quantities, and "occasionally pies, cakes, cookies, and puddings" to please the children.[33]

The weeks when she wasn't serving at table, Mary Fowler joined her peers in the dining room. Marie Sorensen Jensen recalls:

> All the children ate at one long table. There were some women who stood behind us. One woman we all remembered, Auntie Harmon. She saw to it that we all cleaned up our tin plates of all the food, and when we were through eating, I learned to say to her, "Auntie Harmon, please, I'm done." She would nod her head and away we would go as full and satisfied as if we had sat at a Queen's table.[34]

A COMMUNITY OF WOMEN

For Mary Fowler, close-knit female associations in Orderville became the basis for a life lived in the company of other women. The concept of interconnectedness that was to tie together the other central metaphors of Mary's self-construction in many ways was grounded primarily in an understanding of female relationships developed and sustained in Orderville.[35] Her own mother, Susannah Fackrell, played the most instrumental role in such a development by exemplifying in every way the ideal of Mormon womanhood for

Mary. Through Susannah Fackrell's dedication to communal work, service to her church, and love for her family, Mary Fackrell Fowler observed firsthand what it meant to be a member of the United Order and a Mormon woman; under Susannah's tutelage she began rehearsing and participating in a life constructed in many ways around the female networks of association that bound the community's beliefs and values together.

As Mary observed her mother serve the community in a number of varied roles, she gained the knowledge and skills necessary for her to even-tually take on similar positions herself both in Orderville and in Huntington. From their first days in Orderville Susannah Fackrell under-took many of the most influential and significant tasks in order to ensure the success of the communal undertaking. First of all, Susannah Fackrell contributed to the daily functioning of the community as well as to its basic physical needs. Along with cooking in the community kitchen when it was her turn, Susannah taught in the school, worked in the silkworm industry, sewed clothes for the community, worked with the weavers to produce cloth, helped in the making of straw hats, ran the Castle Dairy, and was one of three women who decided how to dole out supplies from the community store to each Orderville family. Her daughter Olive adds that "Mother was one of the ladies chosen to oversee a lot of the work. She and Lil Brown directed pickle making, butter churning, and other tasks. Of course, I was too small yet to help, but kept quite busy following my moth-er around."[36] These various jobs were accomplished almost always in the company of other women, and most frequently Susannah's daughters par-ticipated along with her in feeding, clothing, and providing for the physi-cal and intellectual needs of their community.

When Mary Susannah Fackrell began teaching school in Orderville in February of 1880, she was following closely in the footsteps of her mother; Susannah Fackrell was one of the community's first teachers, serv-ing several years while her children were young and then returning to teaching after they were grown. Charlotte Cox Heaton recalls that "I start-ed school when six years old and Susannah Fackrell was my first teacher. She was a big fat woman and I was first in the chart class. We had no books but learned the alphabet from a large chart hung on the wall. We didn't learn to read as quickly as children do now. I learned by spelling. What a slow process!"[37] With few supplies and children of various ages needing attention, no doubt the task was not easy, but it was one Susannah embraced eagerly.

Although teaching and caring for her own children took much of her time for several years, Susannah Fowler joined the other women of the community in clothing the men and children of Orderville, as well as themselves. As Olive Fackrell Norwood notes, "The girls all learned to

Utah women engaged in silk production. Photo used by permission, Special Collections, Marriot Library, University of Utah.

knit. Mother helped weave the cloth on the looms. I twisted some yarn for knitting. The girls all did, and just as soon as we were old enough we all learned to knit. We'd take our knitting to school and knit while we learned our lessons."[38] As she taught reading, spelling, and mathematics, Susannah Fackrell no doubt also corrected dropped stitches and unknotted troublesome yarn.

For the women of Orderville the process of clothing an entire community began much earlier, though, with growing the cotton and collecting the wool their husbands sheared from the communally owned sheep. "The women, with girls to help, took over the tasks of washing and carding wool, dyeing and spinning of yarn. They made cloth on several hand looms at first. To dye the yarn and cloth, they used herbs and bark of trees."[39] That process is vividly described by Charlotte Cox Heaton:

> Before Diamond dyes were on the market if you wanted to color your dress a different color you wouldn't go buy Ritz or Diamond Dye— they didn't have it to sell. In a dry spot north of the ditch bank grew a patch of madder, the roots of which were used to color red. People would come there in the spring and get starts to set out a row of madder so they'd have something to color red with in the fall. This madder mixed with indigo blue made a rich brown. We could always buy indi-

Orderville Woolen Factory where the women of the United Order produced fabric and clothing. Photo used by permission, Utah State Historical Society.

go, which was blue in color, but we could never buy green. In order to get the right shade of bright green we wanted, the article was first soaked in this indigo water; then when it came time to make the color green Mother would set the big white chamber pot out on the floor and tell us all to use it through the night. The pot was about full by morning, when she would take it outside to the vessel in which the goods were soaking in indigo water. The article to be colored was put in the urine. It would soon turn green—and what a pretty green it was! And it didn't fade.[40]

After this dyeing process was completed, Emma Carroll Seegmiller remembers that

from the spun yarn, dyed in different colors for women and girls, men and women's hose were knitted as well as gloves, mittens, caps, hoods, and comforters. Spinning time was a happy time, especially to the younger set. Spinning wheels were often taken out under the side-walk trees in the dense shade and in a spirit of good-natured rivalry the day's work was carried forward, each girl trying to outdo the other. Many of the women and older girls became expert in spinning the fine and better grade yarn.[41]

Mary E. Chamberlain adds that "after the cloth was made the next step was to make it into clothing. They made all the underwear, dresses and men's suits as well as knit the socks and stockings. A few sewing machines were owned by individuals [who did all the sewing]. Susan Heaton, Mary E. Cox, Mary Ellen Clayton and Susannah Fackrell each had one."[42]

Labor intensive though this process was for Susannah Fackrell and the other Orderville women, it was absolutely necessary to transform the somewhat drab homespun into articles of clothing that would be aesthetically acceptable. What made it possible, even pleasurable, was that as time-consuming as these tasks were, they were accomplished within a strong female community. Whenever a young woman in the community was to be married, the other women gave her flannel and helped her to make a new dress, "and they called this their wedding dress."[43]

Even when individual women were dyeing cloth or sewing up suits at home, they were relying on the support and mutual interdependence of other women. When a factory mill was established just outside Orderville at Factory Lake, the young women continued to rely on each other as they produced cloth on the newly imported machinery: "All hands were at work, some at spinning, some at the carding machine, others at the looms."[44] As Mary and her friends good-naturedly vied for the chance to be the most prolific spinner or to weave the tightest piece of cloth, they also learned the kind of cooperation that would last throughout their lifetimes.

Perhaps the most communitarian of endeavors regarding cloth and clothing wasn't the weaving of cotton or wool cloth, but the investment of the entire community in the silk industry. As part of his plan for economic self-sufficiency Brigham Young encouraged the United Order in several communities to undertake the task of establishing a source of silk for both their own use and for export. In Orderville, Mary's father David Fackrell drove to Salt Lake to obtain the first silkworm eggs that had been sent from Japan; these eggs traveled to southern Utah in Fackrell's wagon, wrapped and rolled carefully in paper. Mulberry trees had been planted to provide leaves to feed these first worms, who matured to produce the first silk in Orderville. Charlotte Cox Heaton remembers that when the

> mulberry trees began to leaf out in the spring the eggs were hatched and the worms fed the leaves till time to spin their cocoons. The women folks helped with this hatching process by placing the papers covered with eggs in their bosoms to keep them warm till time for hatching. Then they were placed on a table in front of a sunny window where the little worms would start hunting for food as soon as they could crawl. They grew fast and soon needed a whole room full of space.
>
> Every day the big girls would climb the trees and pick the leaves and drop them to the ground where the children would gather them up into home made willow baskets. When the worms would grow to the size of a big tomato worm it was time to bring into the room large branches which were hung on the walls from ceiling to floor, over the

windows, and all over the floor. On these branches the big worms would attach themselves, stop eating, and begin to spin.[45]

The elaborate process is described further in Arlen Clement's anthology about the Fackrells in Orderville:

> When the worm is ready to spin, he fastens himself to the tray and starts to spin a silk thread. . . . The silk spins out from his mouth and winds around his body. When he is all through he is about the size and shape of a large peanut, and is called a cocoon. They are then placed out in the sun for about three days and turned over and moved around in the sun occasionally. This kills the silk worm. However, a few are kept for breeding. The silk from the breeding cocoon would not do for weaving cloth, but is utilized for silk batting for baby quilts.
>
> The dead cocoons were then placed in a dishpan of hot water on the stove. This dissolved the glue substance and enabled the workers to unwind the silk and wind on reels. It took quite a number of cocoons full of thread to make one thread for weaving.[46]

A more personal perspective on this work describes how much expertise was required to accomplish these tasks successfully:

> Reeling these silk threads together took a lot of experience to do a good job. I've watched my mother put a dozen or so cocoons in a pan of soapy water, let them soak for a few minutes, then from each cocoon she would pick up the end of the fine thread and putting several together would fasten them on a reel and turn it till the cocoon was gone. When sufficient reels were filled the threads were doubled and twisted till strong enough for weaving.[47]

The expertise necessary for this work could only come from shared experiences of trial and error. The women of Orderville together experimented with strategies for producing silk until they were successful, and in the process they wove together their own friendships on the warp of common goals and the woof of shared belief in this ideal community. As the silk threads were twisted together to form a stronger weave, so, too, the fabric of the community grew ever stronger through the shared work of Orderville's women and girls. Perhaps the greatest artifact and testament to their accomplishment in this endeavor is an American flag, woven from Orderville silk that had been dyed with locally produced dyes.[48]

Even without the focus on the specific task of creating a silk industry for the United Order, women came together to share work and each other's company.

> We womenfolk had lots of working bees and we would go to help each other sewing carpet rags, also quilting and other sewing. We also had fruit cutting bees in fruit times. Another thing we girls did was to take our

knitting and spend the evening with each other. We got a lot of knitting done that way.[49]

When Susannah Fackrell was "assigned the responsibility for supervising the Castle Dairy which was located many miles from Orderville the children went along and did their share of the many tasks to be done."[50] Emma Seegmiller describes these tasks as she observed them on a visit to Castle Dairy:

> Allowed to spend a few days at the dairy, we were initiated into a new experience; to watch the toilsome milking of many cows and the proper handling of the calves; strict care of milk buckets, pans, and churns, which must be well washed and scalded and set to air in the bright sunlight, were stepping stones in our practical education. A woman presided over the work indoors with girls working under her. The girls also helped with the milking. Credit was given on the books for each day's work.[51]

In her account of those days at Castle Ranch, Henrietta P. Fackrell suggests, though, that the experience was far from "all work":

> There was a raised place in the mountain between the ranch and the Sevier River, sort of a high round [k]noll, a white large rock that looked like a large building or castle (which suggested the name). This was surrounded with lots of pine trees. It must of been a very lovely place. Castle Rock was on top of the high "make believe building" or mound. Mary used to love to fish, and often passed by this Castle Rock to fish in the Sevier River. They had sort of a spear or prong they often used to catch fish with. . . . They had a lot of fun mixed with the work they seemed to enjoy. At this time a very dear friend Lucy Spencer before her marriage spent several days visiting her friend Mary Fackrell at the Castle Ranch. They dressed as boys in white pants. They rambled thro' the country, through the trees, having a lot of fun.[52]

Under the guidance of her mother and in the company of several young women friends, Mary Fackrell found time for both a "practical education" and the freedom of wandering the countryside, fishing in rivers, and "having a lot of fun." In providing for their larger community's need for milk and other dairy products, Susannah Fackrell, her daughters, and their friends also found the female camaraderie that working intensely and playing joyously together can bring.

A Female Community of Caring and the Polygamous Life

Grounded so firmly in this female community of caring, Mary Fowler began her young adult years already fully immersed in the interconnectedness she would find so central to her conception of self. In fact, Mary

Fowler's days as a young wife and mother in Orderville, and later in Huntington, were often comprised of joining with other women in work activities (braiding rugs, sewing, or taking care of the sick, for example). These informal associations with other women, begun first as a young girl in the United Order, continued to be Mary's support and sustenance throughout her adult life. And like her mother, Mary's network of friendship and work also included a sister-wife—for Susannah Fackrell it was Hannah Elizabeth Proctor, and for Mary Fackrell Fowler it was Eliza Norwood Fowler.

The ideal of a particular kind of polygamous community was lived most fully in Orderville, where many of the influential leaders of the order were polygamists. David Bancroft Fackrell had actually married both his wives before moving to Orderville.[53] Susannah, who was fifteen years old when she married the thirty-year-old David Bancroft on July 6, 1851, according to her granddaughter Laura Fowler Roper, had given "permission for David to marry a Danish immigrant girl, named Hannah."[54] In a collection of oral narratives put together by a daughter-in-law, Hettie Fackrell, the story of this second marriage is elaborated upon:

> At this time polygamy was recognized by the Church, and many men had more than one wife. Many of the people there [in the Salt Lake Valley] met the Emigrants as they came into the valley. They met them at the Public Square where they stayed until they got places to go. Issabella Blackburn Proctor, and her daughter, Hannah Elizabeth Proctor were converts of Elder Heber C. Kimball. They lived in Preston, England. Hannah's father died there. They crossed the Plains with others, arriving in Salt Lake City in the Fall of 1862. David and Hannah were married in the Endowment House, in Salt Lake City, 15 Oct. '62. Susannah, David's first wife went with them. They all lived together, there in Bountiful.[55]

What is particularly significant about the timing of this marriage is that at the time, Susannah Fackrell was more than eight months pregnant with Mary Susannah Sumner Fackrell, whom she delivered only three weeks later. In a strikingly parallel turn of events Mary Susannah's own husband, Henry Ammon Fowler, would meet his second wife, Eliza Norwood, a divorced mother of two, when she came to help with the birth of Mary's own daughter Laura. What might seem an incredibly stressful and awkward bit of timing surely was less dramatic for Mary Susannah, who no doubt had heard the story of her own father's taking a second wife immediately before her own birth.

For both Susannah Fackrell and Mary Susannah Fowler the idea of polygamous union, or "living the principle," was simply a tenet of faith that they accepted and lived fully. As Lois Worlton, a descendant of Susannah

Fackrell's brother says, "Well, this family was very adamant, they were very religious and they really believed in the principle. They did. The older ones took second wives, but of course the younger ones did not."[56] Later Lois Worlton told me a family story that reveals the depth of that belief in the principle:

> Now one of the interesting things about this is that when David Bancroft, before he came west was in Des Moines and he fell in love with a young woman named Ellen Carroll. And she died and I'm not sure what she died of. I tried to see if there were any records, but it was too early for records and anyway when he came to Utah one of his children by Susannah he named Ellen Carroll . . . and that child died. And I read in these other little notes here that he . . . "My wife Susannah Sumner Fackrell acting as proxy was sealed to me for Ellen Carroll, her mother Hannah Wilcox Carroll and her sister . . . to be my wife"! So, can you imagine? Susannah not only had to live with a second wife but she had to live with the dead wife too![57]

It was in this atmosphere, with this fervent attitude of belief in the principle of polygamy, that Mary Susannah Fowler grew up. The idea of interconnectedness promoted in Orderville through close association with other women was also characterized by a particular understanding of what it meant to have a "sister-wife." In fact, because Mary's husband was shared with Eliza, who lived across the street in her own house, the opportunities for further developing strong ties with other women friends during days and nights when he was frequently absent were even greater.

While there has been much written on the topic of polygamy in Utah,[58] there is really very little in Mary Susannah's later diary to provide any real understanding of her personal feelings about her sister-wife, Eliza. Little by little I have been able to piece together a shadowy picture of the nature of what must have been an intensely intimate relationship. Virginia Rogers, Mary Fowler's granddaughter, told me this about the nature of what must have been one of their first encounters:

> And I was told . . . well, Aunt Eliza came to nurse grandmother while she was in bed with the baby and grandfather fell in love with her. They were married, and grandmother divided everything with her. Eliza had two children that she brought. I have seen the sealing record in the St. George Temple where grandfather adopted those two children. And grandmother Mary, she divided everything—she even divided her underwear![59]

Mrs. Rogers has told me that same story on at least three other occasions, emphasizing the fact that even though Mary Susannah's husband chose to marry as a second wife the woman who had come to nurse her in childbirth, Mary still welcomed her completely.

From this narrative of Virginia Rogers describing Mary dividing even her own underwear with her husband's new wife, to the single reference in Mary's travel narration about the trip from Orderville to Huntington in which she notes, "With the help of the children Harriet [her husband's sister] Eliza and my self did some washing patching and drying the bed clothes that had been wet several days,"[60] to the numerous notations of the participation of both Mary and Eliza in Relief Society meetings in Huntington, it is possible to form a rough outline of these two women's lives lived in such close connection for decades.

Throughout their lives in Huntington, Mary and Eliza attended Relief Society meetings together. The Relief Society minutes themselves indicate a kind of mutual interdependence.[61] On April 6, 1899, for example, the minutes note that first Mary and then Eliza Fowler bore their testimonies; on December 2, 1897, Mary Fowler gave the opening prayer in Relief Society and then bore her "testimony to the truth of the gospel," after which the minutes note that, "Eliza N Fowler felt like performing her duty . . . the minutes read and accepted on motion of Eliza N Fowler."

One of the most telling dates recorded in the minutes of the society is September 7, 1899, when "Sister Mary S Fowler bore testimony to the Blessings that the Lord had granted unto her" and "Sister Eliza N Fowler bore her testimony to the gift of healing." In the autobiography of their husband Henry Ammon Fowler, in the biography of Mary by her son Fred, and in the entries of Mary's own diary we find several instances where the healing required by Eliza was performed by her sister-wife Mary Susannah Fowler. In this brief entry in the Relief Society minutes we find Eliza's public recognition of the power of that healing before all their women friends. It is a "testamony" not only to the power of the Lord, but also to the healing abilities of Mary Susannah Fowler. Those same healing abilities were used to cure Eliza's children, occasionally necessitating Mary leaving her own little ones at home while she went across the street to nurse Eliza's ill offspring.[62]

Although the bond between these two women is not often acknowledged formally in the extant diary writings, there are subtle indications that the two women shared a closeness that went beyond the fact that they were married to the same husband. For example, on several occasions Mary's diary indicates that the two women spent time either together alone or with their children, as on January 7, 1900, when she concluded a fairly lengthy entry about her Sunday activities with simply "Spent the evening at Eliza's," or on February 1, 1900, when her "children took dinner to school on account of cold," and Mary notes that she "Ate dinner with Eliza and Ellen," Eliza's daughter.

No doubt there were tensions between the two women as well, but these do not appear in either Mary's brief diary entries or in her grandchildren's narratives about the relationship between Mary and Eliza. It might appear from this discussion that I have idealized the nature of that relationship, since as my daughter Kate points out, it is hard to believe that one could so easily accept the idea of polygamy, not to mention the trials of its practice in everyday life. While other accounts of polygamous relationships between sister-wives reveal real difficulties, even overt hostility between the women, Mary's own writing virtually never indicates such animosity towards Eliza.

In fact, Mary Fowler's poetry reveals further, often more dramatic, glimpses of the closeness she and her sister-wife Eliza shared. Since much of the poetry was written during the period of time when Mormon polygamy was targeted for prosecution by the federal government, it is even more likely to suggest the climate of those tense times. The poem Mary wrote in August of 1890 when she visited Orderville after moving to Huntington, "I went back to the old home Liza," is addressed to her sister-wife and recalls the times they shared before "much trouble":

> I went to the dear old place Liza
> To your old home and mine!
> I saw the dear old house and
> The shrub the tree the vine.
> Twas long ere I could go there
> For at the sight of the place
> Such mem'ries would crowd to my bosom
> And 'spite of my self I'd retrace.
> I scarcely can tell how it is Liza
> But when I pass by the old home
> I feel like I'd like us to be there
> And have the past back to us come.
> I think of the time that we spent there
> Before we had known so much pain
> And it seems that those true heart felt pleasures
> Can never come to us again!
> As I view those past scenes how my heart aches
> If I'm wrong oh may I be forgiven.
> You know 'twas before you'd much trouble
> Or my sweet little girl went to Heaven.
>
> The trees and the vines have grown larger
> But the weeds and the grass have grown too
> And only the old rusty buildings, have not
> changed in sise or hue.
> Like this it may be that our changes
> And trials have not been in vain
> For experience has grown though in weakness
> And our shield let me hope is the same.
> And through tribulation if faithful

We'll gain what we can't otherwise
A reward with the meek and the humble
When we've finished these course endless lives.

Yes I went to the old home Eliza
And good is the lesson it taught
For 'tis marked may the wisdom of Heaven
That the haughty of earth have found not
And oh that our lives might be nurtured
Like those trees in the way that is best
Not waiting to murmur at others
But preparing our heart for each test.

In these lines, Mary uses the visit to her Orderville home as providing guiding metaphors for interpreting the hardships life in Huntington
had brought. In addressing these remarks to Eliza, Mary acknowledges the
fact that only Eliza can truly understand what she has been through during this period. In what we shall later discover to be characteristic "Mary
Fowler style," she draws on the natural world ("trees," "vines," "weeds," and
"grass") to evaluate both the trials and the blessings of the changes that
have taken place in their lives since they left Orderville. This poem, then,
also demonstrates the kinds of internal journeying that always accompanied physical travel for Mary Fowler. In this particular case, the reference
to the "trials" undoubtedly suggests the constant stress of the pursuit of
polygamists by federal agents. Henry Ammon himself had run from these
agents immediately before the family's move to Huntington in 1888, and
Mary's own father David Bancroft Fackrell was arrested for polygamy and
bound over for trial with his second wife, Hannah, in Beaver, Utah, in
1891, less than a year after this poem was written. As Lois Worlton tells the
story, "On the way, and this was in the dead of winter and they had to go
from Orderville to Beaver by wagon, and on the way there or back
Hannah caught pneumonia or something and she had a stroke and died
within two weeks after their return from the polygamy trials. . . . So he was
no longer a polygamist."[63] Mary Susannah Fowler's own mother, the first
wife who had stayed home to take care of the children (both her own and
Hannah's), became mother to Hannah's little ones when Hannah died.

For Mary Fackrell Fowler and Eliza Norwood Fowler, the constant
worry about their ability to continue living the principle undoubtedly fostered the development of both shared concern and mutual support. Other
polygamous families in Huntington at this time were experiencing incredibly tense situations. Chastie V. Stolworthy Esplin, in telling the story of her
early life to her daughter Ila Jean Esplin, details her own terror and confusion growing up as the daughter of a "second wife":

About this time the persecution of those living polygamy became very severe. Typical of the heartaches of those troubled times was the "shawl incident." Mother and Aunt Lydia had plaid shawls just alike. All of the women wore shawls, but there were no other shawls of the same color and design as these. My half-sister Lucy could not understand why we were being persecuted, and she felt hurt when we had to go away without even telling her where. One day she was going to the store in Huntington when she saw a woman wearing a shawl like our mothers had. The woman had her back turned, but knowing her own mother was home, Lucy thought this must be her Aunt Johanna.

She ran to her calling, "Aunt Hannah! Aunt Hannah!" But the woman turned a corner and disappeared. Poor bewildered Lucy! She went home crying and told her mother she had seen Johanna in town and she wouldn't even speak to her.

"But, Lucy," her mother said, "that could not have been Aunt Johanna. You know she would not be in Huntington." "Oh, yes it was," Lucy cried. "I would know that shawl anyplace." Lucy was brokenhearted because she loved her aunt and missed her.

What Lucy did not know, was that the woman she thought was her Aunt Johanna was really Sister Walker, with whom we were staying. Sister Walker had borrowed Mother's shawl and was wearing it to town.

Mother and I often had to move secretly from one place to another—anyplace where she felt we would be safe for a time. We even went as far as Mancos, Colorado. . . . Once during the winter at Walker's, Mother and I had to spend a whole day huddled in a cellar, hiding from the Marshalls. Mrs. Walker brought us food and blankets, but the cold and dampness affected Mother's lungs. She always had a bad cough after that.

We had been living under the assumed name of Brown. When we went to stay with the Day family at Lawrence, I heard Mother talking to Mr. Day about changing the name to White, so I thought the change had been made. One day Mr. Day said, "Well, my girl, what's your name today?" I blurted, "Chastie White—no, Chastie Brown—no, White." Mr. Day laughed, but I cried. I thought I had given away our secret. Sometimes I wasn't sure *who* I was.[64]

Perhaps this intense fear of discovery evidenced in Chastie Esplin's recollections, and the personal and familial havoc that discovery would cause, kept Mary Fowler from reflecting on the issue of polygamy directly in her own diary. Or perhaps, because she was the first wife, the intensity of the fear of persecution was somewhat less. Or it may have been simply that by the time she was writing the only pieces of her diary that still exist today, the intense threat of prosecution by the federal government for polygamous practice was past. Whatever the case, it is obvious that the support and encouragement of their women friends was incredibly important for these sister-wives as they dealt with the exigencies of life lived according to the principle. It was also these informal networks that formed the real underpinnings of Mary Fowler's sense of interconnectedness through community.

WITHIN THE CIRCLE OF MORMON SISTERS

Mary Fowler's own conception of community, born in the Mormon ideal of communitarian living in Orderville, matured most fully within the circle of female friends whose lives constantly intersected in a number of different ways in Huntington, Utah. Mary's diary is filled with notations regarding these informal associations. Within a nine-month period of time, Mary mentions working and visiting with her women friends over 175 times. Several of the accounts focus on food shared, for example:

> [December 13, 1899] Cold, cold. Sister Grange gave us a "mess" of beets and carrots this morning. Arno not quite so well. Sr. Brace sent mess of fresh pork. Pa got pig from Mort Jensen. Sr. Lenard sent some pickles, and chilli sauce, also butter.
>
> [December 19, 1899] I left Fred and went to see Sister Brace's little new sweet red baby girl. Sr B was delighted and so was I. Took her a chicken and fruit.
>
> [January 25, 1900] Baked bread for Sr Gardner. Sweat Sr. Robins.

Even more frequently, Mary mentions visiting with other women in the context of work mutually shared. When Mary's son was quite ill, her friend Ellie Norton "stayed until after midnight to help with Arno" (December 3, 1899). And a few days later, Sister Norton who had stayed several more nights during Arno's illness, "came and helped me with some patching and other little chores for which I am grateful" (December 14, 1899). The very next day, Mary wrote, "Wash day. Mary Brace helped us." This is the same Sister Brace who Mary visited just five days later to see her "new sweet red baby girl"!

While these women friends are mentioned frequently throughout the diary, other women also receive individual mention for their help and concern. For example, on December 22, 1899: "Sr Westover knit stockings for Fanny"; on December 27, 1899: "Sr Norton came to see us. Sr Gardner sewed for me in the afternoon"; and on February 7, 1900: "Sister Robins came after some yarn to knit Laurie a pair of stockings of and staid the afternoon. Had some mush and milk with us." Mary also reciprocated by lending her services, not only applying mud sweats and delivering healing herbs, but helping with housework as well: (Wednesday [January] 10) "Fine day. Cleaned house for Sr Norton."

Sometimes the women got together to share their chores, as on January 23, 1900, "Washed. Sr Norton brought her washing and did it with me. Sister Robins very poorly. Gave her a mud sweat." Or on May 31, 1900, "Hot weather. Helped Sr Gardner white wash a little while. Hot weather." On July 17, 1900, "Sr Norton came and helped us put up some fruit and prepare to leave home for a few days to see my boy Rey, who has been herding sheep for a long while." Whatever the chore, from washing to knitting to getting ready for a trip, Mary Fowler and her women friends found time to assist each other and spend time talking together in the process. There are also several times when Mary simply mentions going to visit various friends, often in the evenings, simply for the chance to share time together.

What is overwhelmingly evident in reading her diaries is that for Mary Fowler, life really was lived primarily in the company of other women. While she does mention interactions with her husband, referred to throughout the diary as "Pa," Mary was frequently left alone to create her own social networks, networks composed almost entirely of other women. Sometimes "Pa" was away working in the mines, sheepherding, or doing construction work in other towns; sometimes he was staying with Mary's sister-wife Eliza. Toward the end of the period in which the journal was written he was away on his mission to Oklahoma. Whatever the case might be, Mary's own self-construction is grounded most frequently in affiliations with her women friends.

Significantly, however, these informal relationships were always framed by and connected with the more formal voluntary organizations that, in many ways, structured Mary Fowler's days, and weeks, and years— as such associations did the lives of women all over America in the last half of the nineteenth century.

Reading the pages of Mary Fowler's diary, the minutes of Relief Society and Young Ladies' Mutual Improvement Association meetings, and the memoirs of her women friends, I was amazed at the extent and range of organizations and activities in which she enthusiastically participated. It seems almost unbelievable that a woman with so many children, so little financial security, and so great a commitment to maintaining the health of her family and larger community would have the time to belong to even one "club" or "church group," much less the large and varied number in which she actively participated. And yet, somewhat surprisingly, recent research indicates that Mary Fowler is not the exception, but rather the norm for women in late-nineteenth-century America. Scholars' examination of both institutional and personal records document the fact that "by 1860 most American communities of any size, particularly in the north

Huntington Saloon closed down due to the efforts of Mary Susannah Fowler and several other women. Glass plate photo reproduction used by permission, Utah State Historical Society.

and middle west, had developed a dense web of women's associations for a wide variety of formal purposes."[65] And the last thirty years of the nineteenth century continued to witness an exponential growth in such women's organizations.[66] Like Mary Fowler, many of the women who belonged to these associations across the country found themselves maintaining overlapping memberships in organizations with often related goals. Yet in every case, their memberships provided what Anne Firor Scott has called "a safe setting in which women could begin to question the dominant ideology with its emphasis on competition and profit as the highest values."[67]

An examination of the range of these associations reveals certain organizational patterns: church-related organizations (directly descended from missionary and benevolent societies of earlier nineteenth-century origins); women's clubs of various kinds; the Women's Christian Temperance Union; and national suffrage associations and their local branches.[68] Mary Fowler belonged to a number of organizations that might be included in each of these categories. Certainly most important, however, were the church-related associations, especially the Young Ladies' Mutual Improvement Association and the Relief Society, that formed the nexus from which each of the others sprung.

CHURCH-RELATED ASSOCIATIONS:
THE YOUNG LADIES' MUTUAL IMPROVEMENT ASSOCIATION
AND THE RELIEF SOCIETY

As she had in work-based female friendship networks, Susannah Sumner Fackrell provided a significant model for her daughter Mary in participating in church-sponsored associations. In fact, their roles within church-related organizations are often mirror images of each other. For example, when the first Orderville Relief Society was organized in 1874, Susannah Fackrell was appointed one of two counselors; two years later in 1876 when the Young Ladies' Mutual Improvement Association was organized, Mary Fackrell was named one of its two counselors. Still later, Mary Fackrell Fowler herself became an important leader in the Huntington Relief Society. In fact, as her son Fred writes in his biography of Mary Fowler,

> It was during the years of the United Order that Mary began accepting responsibility for service to her church. From her youth to her final passing there were only short periods when she did not have at least one regular church responsibility—teaching classes in Sunday School, Children's Primary Association, Mutual Improvement Association, and president of the latter organization, secretary of the Relief Society, and Stake President of the Primary Association.[69]

As one of two founding counselors when the Young Ladies' Mutual Improvement Association was first organized in Orderville, Mary Fackrell played a significant part in the organization of the group. The YLMIA, an outgrowth of the "Junior Retrenchment" associations first suggested by Brigham Young in the late 1860s in an effort to provide for the spiritual needs of his young daughters and their contemporaries throughout Mormondom, was intended to provide older teenaged girls and young married women with an understanding of the gospel and a place to develop their religious life.[70] In Orderville, meetings were held in the afternoon, usually on Fridays. While one of the main agendas of the association was to provide a place for young women to bear testimony,[71] there were other, more social and intellectual activities that were tremendously important as well. Frequently programs consisting of readings of poetry and dramatic monologues, singing, and oral recitation were the focus of the Friday meetings. Every alternate Saturday, the women in this group met jointly with the men of the Young Men's Mutual Improvement Association to present similar programs, to stage theater productions, and to read aloud from the jointly produced journal of the organizations. While each group sometimes produced their own newspaper, they often cooperated in writing and

Orderville barns and fences after the break-up of the United Order. Photo
used by permission, Special Collections, Marriot Library, University of Utah.

editing a joint edition. Called variously the *Pearl*, the *Honey Bee*, the
Clipper, or the *Mutual Star*, this newspaper was handwritten on foolscap
and sewn together by the editors and included original essays, poems, and
articles concerning current events.

It was as writers and editors of these journals and participants in their
respective Mutual organizations that Henry Ammon Fowler and Mary
Susannah Fackrell became better acquainted, as the minutes of these joint
meetings attest:

> [December 28, 1878] Henry A. Fowler among those to write pieces for
> the next paper.
> [January 29, 1879] Prose reading by Mary Fackrell.
> [June 14, 1879] Mary Fackrell to write pieces for the paper.
> [September 20, 1879] Prose reading by Mary Fackrell. [Also notes
> that she will write pieces for the paper.]
> [November 8, 1879] Henry A. Fowler appointed editor of the
> *Honey Bee.*

The minutes also subtly reflect the change in marital status of the couple when just a month after their wedding, the following appears: "A program of the joint meeting that was held November 27 1880. An opening

address by Sister Mary Fowler." Although there were certainly other opportunities in Orderville for Mary and Henry Ammon to meet and get to
know each other,[72] it is within the context of their memberships in these
Mutual Improvement Associations that they were able to share their interests in literature and writing, interests so central to both their lives. It is especially noteworthy that Mary met her husband within the formal activities
of a close group of women friends, where she could find the support and
understanding that embarking on a marriage requires.

It is not surprising, then, that when Mary moved with her husband,
her sister-wife, and their children from Orderville to Huntington in the
autumn of 1888, she immediately became involved with the Young Ladies'
Mutual Improvement Association in her new town. Within three months
she had become editor of Huntington's Mutual newspaper, the *Gem*, as the
YLMIA minutes note on January 16, 1989, "Sister Mary Fowler encouraged the girls to write to the Gem"; and a week later, "The Gem was then
read by the editor Mary Fowler" (January 23, 1889). In Huntington, however, the connection between the young men's and young women's associations seems to have been less formally structured and less significant.
Here the young women focused even more explicitly on the development
of their own spirituality in concert with their literary productions.
Throughout the winter and spring of 1889, for example, the minutes relate
Mary Fowler's attention to the spiritual life of her women friends in the
Mutual association. On February 13, Mary offered the opening prayer and
then read from the *Woman's Exponent*, a newspaper produced by the Relief
Society in Salt Lake City and distributed worldwide. On February 27,
Mary made a few remarks after her husband's polygamous wife, Eliza
Norwood Fowler, had spoken "a short time and gave some good instruc-
tions." Besides offering the opening prayer on April 9 and April 30, Mary
also gave "a lecture on the Father, Son and Holy Ghost" on April 16 and a
Bible exercise on May 14. As an older (twenty-seven-year-old) woman,
Mary Fowler assumed a leadership role in the young women's organization
in Huntington, leading her young "sisters" in prayer and lecturing to them
about spiritual matters. At the same time, she provided a connection
between spirituality and literary production that we shall see in even more
detail in the following chapter.

THE HUNTINGTON RELIEF SOCIETY

Mary Fowler's reading of the *Woman's Exponent* in YLMIA meetings cues
us to both the significance and influence of women's writing in such associations, but also to the strong connection between the YLMIA and the
Relief Society. As an outgrowth of the Relief Society and existing under

its larger umbrella, the YLMIA sought to make the concerns of the Relief Society relevant to younger Mormon women. It is no surprise, then, that Mary Fowler as a young wife and mother in Huntington belonged to both associations. Created in 1842, the Relief Society was a body of Mormon women who sought to enrich their own spiritual life and to provide for the needs, both spiritual and physical, of the larger Mormon community. Eliza R. Snow, wife, first, of Joseph Smith and, later, of Brigham Young and founder of the Relief Society, pointed out the close connection between spirituality and philanthropy in describing a typical Relief Society meeting in a 1903 article in the *Woman's Exponent*:

> The meetings were opened and closed with a prayer, and systematic order was observed throughout. In each meeting reports were given by those whose duty it was to visit from house to house and inquire into the circumstances of the sick and the destitute—donations were received and those subjects discussed which appertain to women's duties, influence and responsibilities.[73]

In this way, then, often the informal associations discussed above, where women looked in on each other, provided food and nursing care, and collaborated on household work, were directly related to the more formal structures of Relief Society activities. It is often difficult to determine where one left off and the other began. Mary Fowler's journal for the period of time her husband was on his mission includes a list entitled "Ministering Angels" where she records the names of a number of friends and family, mostly women, and their contributions to her family's welfare. An excerpt from this list demonstrates the way in which these "angels" provided the Fowlers with everything from money to overalls to postage stamps:

Jan.	Sister Leonard	apples
	Sister Brasher	one lb butter Loaf bread
Feb.	Sr. Ettie Norten	4 lb. Sap Greece
	Esther Grange	One qut coal oil two quts preserves 4 pounds meat
	Brother Wall	six oranges
	Sister W	cotton batting
	Ethel and Violet Grange	cloth for dress with two yds of lining one spool of thread & velvet & gimp trimming.
	Sister Robins	2 yds skirt lining
	John Brasher	two bu. potatoes & carrots
Apr.	Sr Riley	hat for Fanny
	Sr Woolman	calico for dress
	Sr Rowberry	lime for whitewashing

May	Sister Brace	large bar castile soap
	Sister Eunice Harmon	hat
	Stanly Andersen	photographs of club & band for Pa.

And so the listings continue, mentioning vinegar, apples, string beans, stamps, and many other necessities of life with a few surprises (like candy) thrown in. The list of the family's needs might have been compiled by Relief Society home visitors, or Mary's friends might simply have ascertained where her needs lay and what they were each able to contribute. But certainly, for the women themselves, such distinctions between formal philanthropy and friendship were insignificant. What was important was that there was a community of caring in which women moved both formally and informally to sustain each other, their husbands, and children, a community that is given voice in Mary Fowler's poetic epigram to this chapter, where she notes that:

> Our Mission dear sisters is not far extended
> Tis at home with our families, near home with our friends.
> Tis not mongst the nations this is not intended
> But yet to vast labors our mission extends.

The Relief Society was certainly a central organizing force in Mary Fowler's life. It was through local Relief Society meetings and activities, as well as through her informal friendship networks, that Mary discovered the needs of her neighbors and revealed her own. It was also through affiliation with the larger, churchwide Relief Society that Mary was able to come into contact with ideas and issues from which she might otherwise have been isolated.

These ideas came to Mary and her sisters in Orderville and Huntington primarily in two different ways: visits from the officers of the Relief Society and publications of the Relief Society, such as the *Woman's Exponent*.[74] As a young girl in Orderville, Mary Fackrell was present when Eliza Snow and Zina D. Young first came to the community to endorse their early efforts at establishing women's organizations like the Relief Society and Young Ladies' Mutual Improvement Association and the children's Primary in which Mary soon became a teacher. Her own sister, Olive Fackrell Norwood, describes one of these events that occurred on February 16, 1881:

> When Sister Eliza R. Snow and Zina D. Young came to Orderville to organize the Primary, they called a meeting of the chosen officers to meet in the "big house" where lived our Bishop along with Hoyts, Spencers and Chamberlains. I went with mother to the meeting. In this meeting, Sister Eliza R. Snow, Joseph Smith's wife, showed us the Prophet

Joseph's gold watch. She let me hold it so I could say "I held the President's watch." Both women talked at the meeting before they organized the Primary. We had three Primaries. Mother, Sister Louise Spencer, and Lydia Young were the Presidents.[75]

In her history of Kane County, Adonis Robinson comments further on this auspicious occasion:

> Eliza R. Snow spoke in tongues and Zina D. Young gave the interpretation. Sister Eliza showed the children the watch which the Prophet Joseph Smith had on when he was martyred in the Carthage jail. It had been given to Eliza when she was made president of the Relief Society organization.[76]

As Mary and her sisters listened to these erudite women speak in tongues and then describe the place of women's roles within the LDS Church, they also broadened their understanding of what those very roles might encompass. Both spiritual and philanthropic goals were integrated in the articulation of the Relief Society's mission. And many of the charitable works were focused within their own community, as well as in others (such as American Indians they might hope to convert).[77] The Relief Society also planned social events, especially for the women in the community; they raised funds for and constructed a Relief Society Hall to be used for those social events; and they carried out a variety of welfare programs.

The minutes of the Huntington Relief Society amply demonstrate Mary Fowler's own understanding of the dual mission of spiritual improvement and philanthropy. In fact, these minutes offer a fascinating perspective on the way in which Mary Fowler's own contributions to the Relief Society mature between 1889 and 1920 and, at the same time, reflect the changing needs of the developing organization itself. When the minutes first make note of Mary's presence in late 1889 and early 1890, they reveal a young woman intent on the development of her own spiritual life in the presence of and through the encouragement of her women friends. Frequently, Mary Fowler spoke in these early years about her relationship with God and the importance of her Mormon faith:

> [April 3, 1890] Sister Fowler spoke a short time on our troubles we are called to pass through but felt that God was all to cheer us up if we would only put our trust in him thought we ought to pray often to our Heavenly Father.
> [August 6, 1891] Sister Mary Fowler bore her testimony to the truth of the LDS work also to the instructions we had received.
> [September 3, 1891] a Lecture was delivered by Sister Mary Fowler from the Book of Mormon Sisters Mary J Woods and Mary S Fowler were then sustained as Teachers in the Relief Society of Huntington

As a Relief Society teacher, Mary visited other women and encouraged them in their efforts to deepen their faith; later, she reported on those visits in the Relief Society meetings.[78] Mary's own faith is constantly displayed through her participation in Relief Society meetings; she is one of those listed most frequently as giving the opening prayer, as bearing her testimony, and as providing lectures on a variety of religious topics:

> [September 5, 1895] Opening prayer by Sister Mary S Fowler. . . . Sister Mary S Fowler lectured from the Doctrine and Covenents.
> [September 15, 1898] . . . a lecture was then given by Sister Mary S Fowler from the life of Nephi Second Chapter

Also, on November 15, 1900: ". . . an incident of Church History related by Sister Mary S Fowler." Clearly Mary's voice was a strong one within this group of Mormon women; she was entrusted with explicating the gospel and explaining church history. This role would remain hers throughout her life, as we can continue to find frequent references to her participation as spiritual advisor right up until her death in 1920.

This role of spiritual advisor was reciprocal. Rather than a hierarchical arrangement whereby only certain women were marked as worthy to teach and comment on spirituality in such meetings, any woman could— and did—speak concerning spiritual matters. In fact, Mary's support and commendation of other speakers is another constant that runs throughout the records of the Relief Society:

> [January 9, 1893] Mary S Fowler expressed herself as being well paid for coming to meeting and in listening to the remarks made by the sisters.
> [November 6, 1913] Sister Mary S Fowler had had her testimony strengthened in listening to the lesson

Often, too, Mary seconded the points made by another woman:

> [September 7, 1893] Mary Fowler felt to endorse what had been said concerning the rearing of our children
> [May 14, 1899] Sister Mary S Fowler bore testimony to what Sister Pearson said in regard to the Word of Wisdom

Through mutual respect and the belief that each woman was capable of enlightening the others as they together sought spiritual understanding and the ability to live the gospel more fully, Mary Fowler and the other women of the Huntington Relief Society worked collaboratively toward the spiritual well-being of both individuals and the community as a whole.[79]

This is not to say, however, that there were not leaders within the organization, and certainly Mary Fowler was such a Relief Society leader. First elected secretary of the society on February 2, 1901, Mary continued to serve in a variety of leadership roles for the rest of her life. Her genuine delight in her election is reflected in this diary entry:

> I was chosen as one of the board of directors of the Relief Society in Jan & sustained at the regular business meeting Feb 2nd receiving every vote in the room both times. Was set apart by Bishop Johnson to the office of Sec'y. he blessed me with health & strength with wisdom to perform my dutys acceptably to my Heavenly Father to myself & to my sisters.

Interestingly, stylistic shifts in the minutes occur as soon as she takes over the society's secretarial duties: her minutes are more detailed, fuller, and apparently more inclusive. As in her healing practices, Mary brought to the job of secretary a disciplined and thoroughly professional perspective.

As she became more involved in the leadership of the society, Mary Fowler also attended larger stake meetings, general church conferences, taking notes and reporting on these experiences when she returned to Huntington. For example, the minutes for April 17, 1902, note: "Sister Mary Fowler reported on the conference at Price." As secretary of the society, she was also directly involved with fund-raising efforts to secure the necessary financial assets for the Relief Society Hall. This undertaking taxed her physically as her husband's journal history indicates: "[Mary] was secretary of the Relief Society, which was building a large hall so that when I came home from my mission she was nearly worn out. She broke down about a month after, and was very bad for weeks."[80]

Still, Mary continued her Relief Society work. Her remarkable ability to lead, both through her speeches and through listening and responding to her sisters, was recognized not only within the close community of Huntington, but also became a well-known and much appreciated fact even in the much larger cities of Provo and Salt Lake City, where she visited with such women as Emmeline B. Wells, the Mormon suffrage worker and Relief Society secretary and president.

All of these "ways of speaking"—offering opening prayers, giving lectures on biblical topics, serving as a visiting teacher, commending others for their homiletic expertise, bearing her own testimony, contributing precise and detailed minutes of the Relief Society meetings—continued to develop throughout Mary Fowler's life, and her own competence and confidence in speaking quite clearly grew as she matured.

Huntington's Ladies Literary Club

Besides the opportunities for speaking and organizing within the context of the Relief Society, Mary Fowler found additional possibilities for the development of her growing skills in other contexts as well. While the

Relief Society focused primarily on spirituality and related concerns, other groups of Mormon women organized around issues that could not at this time be fit neatly under the Relief Society's discursive purposes and goals. As in the larger cities and towns of Utah, Huntington women heard the call of the women's club movement, which had been gaining momentum all across the United States since the late 1860s.[81] Just as their Mormon sisters in Salt Lake organized the Reaper's Club, the Authors' Club, the Press Club, and the Daughters of the Utah Pioneers, among others, the women of Huntington joined together to educate themselves and expand their literary horizons under the leadership of none other than Mary Susannah Fackrell Fowler.

The first mention of such a club occurs in the minutes of Huntington's Relief Society itself on February 9, 1898: "The following Ladies spoke very interesting on different subjects also spoke on the feasability of organizing a Ladies Club in Huntington The following Ladies was chosen as a committy to visit the Ladies of Huntington on behalf of the club"; Mary Fowler's name, along with that of her sister-wife Eliza Norwood Fowler, were included in this list. However, in early May of that year a special meeting of the Relief Society was called wherein "Elder Le John Nuttle addressed the sisters and gave some reasons why we were organized as we are at the present. . . . Brother Nuttle refered to the danger there was to the Latter Day Saints joining the clubs that are gotton up on the out side."[82] There is never another mention of this club in the minutes of the Relief Society.

Mary Fowler's own diary, however, suggests that this was not entirely the end of such an organization; in fact, the diary charts almost the entire course of this club's life. On Tuesday, January 9, 1900, she writes, "Went with Sister Wall to see about beginning the meetings of the Ladies Improvement Class which were postponed in the fall," then two days later says, "I also attended a meeting of Ladies Improvement class. Would like to resign my position as president but they will not listen to it." Mary was a leader in the organization not only in title, but also as a motivating force behind the meetings themselves. It appears that in the two years since Brother Nuttle's pronouncement in the special Relief Society meeting, the organization of this club had become separated from the society and found its own niche within the network of Huntington women. This is not to say, however, that male church leaders did not exert an influence over the new organization, for on Tuesday, January 30, Mary's diary notes, "Also went to see the Bp in regard to getting the house to have a theatre for the benefit of the improvement class. Asking for his approval for the same. Both granted." Two days later she went to visit Sister Wall to make arrangements for the "theatre." Having secured the bishop's approval for both the theater and the women's club, Mary immediately began to work to accomplish what she had set in motion.

Mary Fowler was involved in every aspect of the creation of this women's club. On February 13, 1900, she writes that she "Met with the ladies of the Improvement class in a special meeting called for the purpose of considering the problem, how can we procure funds to carry on our meetings profitably and join the womans federation of clubs. Also attended committee meeting in behalf of our theatre." Desperately poor herself, without even enough money to buy material to make clothes to wear to Sunday School, Mary Fowler nonetheless tried to find a way to make the club fiscally sound, and able to join the American Federation of Women's Clubs. Understanding the benefit of seeking connection with the larger network of women's associations, Mary again displayed the profound belief in the collaborative interconnection of women she has been committed to throughout her life. On February 22, Mary notes that they had decided to join the "State Federation of Womans clubs," and adds, "Our beloved Bishop Johnson was at meeting. Extended his approval support and blessing to us."

Over the next months, Mary's diary reveals her active participation in helping to host activities to increase the solvency of the club. She directs the theater project and attends many rehearsals; the final production on March 10, 1900, is proclaimed a "grand" success:

> Made $25.00. I never had my prayers answered more directly than at this time. The play [was difficult] on account of lack of interest in some of the performers and lack of time with others. Nearly all were beginners and there were only 6 rehearsals. I asked the aid of my Heavenly Father for the "players" & asked Him to make the people pleased with it. Every one is talking about what a grand affair it was.

At the same time that Mary is assuring the financial well-being of the club, she is achieving success in her own right. As both the director of the play and the president of the women's organization, she can take a great deal of credit for the production. In fact, only two days before the play she had been reelected as president of the club, and she notes in her diary that, "They gave me the distinguished title of peace maker."

Along with raising funds, Mary took responsibility for disbursing them. In the midst of several entries noting participation in Improvement club meetings, Mary writes that she "attended a special meeting of the L. I. class. Disposition of funds on hand made. $10 donated to help build the R.S. House. Name of association changed to Ladies Literary Club of Huntington" (March 15, 1900). It is important to recognize that the relationship between the literary club and the Relief Society is still a strong one, but at the same time that it is contributing to the construction of a meeting hall for the Relief Society, the club has taken a major step in clearly defining its own separate educational purposes and goals by renaming itself under Mary Fowler's leadership. The professional quality of Mary's leadership is evident again when she notes that on Wednesday, April 7, 1900, she "spent afternoon and evening in helping Revise by-Laws of Ladies Club." In fact, the business of the club takes much of Mary's time during early 1900; she frequently remarks on her activities on behalf of this organization. And Mary Fowler's leadership of the club went far beyond her organizational prowess; for example, she often selected the reading for club meetings. On April 3, 1900, her diary says, "Selected sentiments from Byrons poems for Ladies Club." Through the club and her influential role in its conception and development, Mary Fowler constructed herself as literate, professional, organizationally gifted, and personally persuasive. For a woman raising eight children in a two-room house with a husband who was absent much of the time, this is indeed a remarkable achievement.

One can only imagine, then, the strength of sentiment lying just beneath the surface of these lines penciled in her diary for April 18, 1900:

> Attended a special meeting and had the privelege of shaking hands with Apostle Teasdale. He doesn't heartily approve of the ladies club. But says we may go on if our actions are approved of by the Bishop, which they have been all the time. But unless we get a warmer consent than that I am not in favor of continuing.

In an entry written four days later, we find the following:

> A letter was read in meeting stating that those who belong to any but Church societies would not be considered in good standing, aluding to our Ladies club. I don't know why he should give his private consent and then send a letter to be read in public. Those who are against us are rejoicing. I am glad for once that I was not at meeting.

Mary's emotions are closer to the surface here, and her questioning of the entire process seems clearer. However, it is also clear that she will obey whatever the patriarchal authorities demand, when on April 26 she writes simply: "Met with Ladies club. Disorganized club. Presented $10 to meeting house. Ladies manual to myself. Two chinese lanterns to Sr Wall. the records to the Sec'y. Song book to Sr Ipson, 3 yds calico to the R.S. 8 yds Moskito bar and treasurers book to Primary, and new record book to Y.L.M.I.A."

There are only two other entries in the diary related to the club. The first, on May 2, 1900, details a dispute regarding the final dispensing of funds suggested above:

Had the satisfaction of having my prayers answered today. The Ladies of the Club that was, had a disagreement as to how the money should be given to the meeting house. A few wanted it put in a certain thing, so we would know what we had donated. While the majority wanted to give the money and merely receive credit on the book. The feelings resulted in harsh words and one sister was so wounded she declared she wouldn't have a thing to do with it, only to make all the trouble she could. I felt deeply grieved by the trouble and began to fast before supper last evening and my heart went up to my Heavenly Father that He would unite us together and overrule the transaction for good. I felt troubled all day, but when the time for us to meet and attend to it came, I went down. I asked those who came to pray for a spirit of peace, but they said they had done and said all they could, and wouldn't "put up" with any more, and contrary to their wishes I went to see the party who felt the worst, and after lots of persuasion she consented to go, just, she said, for my peace of mind. I assured her it would, and when she got to the meeting, very much to the surprise of all she went with us to see the bishop and every thing went off as well as if there had been no trouble. At the Bishop's suggestion it was decided to try to present to the meeting house a bible.

This entry, certainly one of the longest in the entire diary, reveals precisely how significant her role as president and peacemaker of the "Ladies club" was to Mary Fowler. In assuming the duties of her office, Mary had developed her own rhetorical and discursive talents to the extent that she was able to do the one thing that was so central to her own self-construction, bring others together in collaborative, mutual exchange and interconnection. Mary Fowler's final comment concerning the club is one line in the middle of an entry discussing knitting, a surprise party attended by her children, and the receipt of a dress pattern in thanks for her work with a sick child. It reads simply, "Was photographed with Ladies of the Club" (May 9, 1900; see page 2 herein). The sentiment held within that one short statement cannot be adequately conveyed, I imagine. For a woman who had devoted much of her time in an otherwise extraordinarily busy life to bring together a group of women for the purpose of mutual education and the extension of their connections in a variety of ways, certainly this last photograph must have contained both the lost hopes and the renewed commitment to discover other ways to reach those goals.

Mary Fowler's granddaughter Rae Spellman provides a view of these events as they are recalled within family stories:

> She [Mary Fowler] held high standards for her husband and her children and for the sisters. There was a time in Huntington when the sisters got together and they had a club and they read classical literature. That's where she got the name of her first son, David Arno. She had been reading about

Italy in the Middle Ages and she read about the River Arno and she liked the name, so that's what she called him. That was my father.

Now this group of women caused a considerable amount of talk. People didn't know what to think about this. When it was conference time and one of the apostles came, they asked him about this book club and he thought about it and he thought that maybe the sisters were getting a little ahead of themselves and that maybe they would get off on the wrong foot and get some wrong ideas. So he said that they should quit having the book club.[83]

When I asked Mrs. Spellman what Mary Susannah thought about that, she replied,

Well, she was very unhappy about it, but there was no confusion about it for her. Now today there might be more discussion, but then every one of the sisters felt that they should obey the priesthood. So they just stopped having the club.[84]

For the Mary Fowler constructed by the narrative of her granddaughter almost a century later, there is no doubt that patriarchal obedience was the most significant determinant in the abandonment of the Ladies Literary Club of Huntington. It was simply a question of "high standards," standards that are often looked to as models of Mormon faithfulness by her family today.

During this entire period, Mary Fowler had continued to attend Relief Society meetings and to speak powerfully on a range of topics, most of them related to the spiritual life of her family and her community. Diary entries reflect her own understanding of the importance of her voice in the meetings. For example, on November 1, 1900, she writes, "Attended RS meeting. Opened meeting by prayer. All felt the divine influence of the Holy Spirit." How important the continuation of her active discursive participation must have been for this woman who had been forced to abandon the literary discussions she had worked so diligently to create. So significant a part of her life was this Relief Society participation that even when she moved to Provo in 1903 for only four years, Mary became an integral part of that particular Relief Society. Her daughter Laura Fowler Roper remembers, "While in Provo she so worked her way into the hearts of the Relief Society members and others, that when they learned she was to remove to Huntington in 1907, they tried in every possible way to persuade her to remain in Provo."[85]

THE "NEW" RELIEF SOCIETY AND LECTURES ON MOTHERHOOD

By the time Mary and her family returned to Huntington from Provo in 1907, a major shift had occurred in the structure of Relief Society meetings throughout Utah, at least partly in response to the fact that society membership had dwindled in the wake of the many new women's organizations, especially those in Salt Lake City where the General Board of the Relief Society met and determined policy. Somewhat ironically, Mary Fowler, whose own women's club had been deconstructed by patriarchal order, found herself with an almost entirely new role to play in the Relief Society, and a role not dissimilar from the one she had undertaken as president of the Huntington Ladies Literary Club.

Most interestingly, the changes in Mary Fowler's own life as a result of her sojourn in Provo actually coincide with and exemplify in many ways the changes in the Relief Society itself. As Jill Mulvey Derr and her colleagues who chronicled the history of the Relief Society suggest, not only was Relief Society membership decreasing after the turn of the century, but also "increasing church membership demanded the more formal operation [of the Relief Society], yet loss of the old intimacy, the personal concern, the long-established sisterhood was costing the society dearly, both in membership and activity. Change was imperative."[86] The first step in bringing about that change was to draw in new society members by offering mother education courses in Relief Society meetings. In an editorial in the *Woman's Exponent* in 1903, Eliza Roxcy Snow noted that while "the dear old ladies who study the Bible, the Book of Mormon and the standard Church works" might still be "able to tell our young mothers many things for their edification and benefit in rearing their families, . . . the tendency for the age is for new ideas and new methods."[87]

In their own Mary Fowler, the Huntington Relief Society found both the comfort and intimacy of "the dear old ladies" *and* the "new ideas and new methods" of the twentieth century. Steeped in the communally nurtured healing traditions of southern Utah, experienced with the development of Huntington's own women's literary society, and fresh from an education in nursing at Brigham Young Academy, Mary Fowler was able to provide both continuity and growth for the Relief Society members she so loved. The change in Mary's topics of discourse within Relief Society meetings reveal this new role that she apparently assumed with enthusiasm. As we have seen, Mary Fowler's earlier turns at talk within the Relief Society meetings focused on bearing her testimony, giving opening and closing prayers, reporting on church conferences, and giving talks about biblical topics, as well as discussions of the Book of Mormon and church history.

Yet, as we have also seen earlier, Mary's participation in the Relief Society before she moved to Provo in 1903 occasionally *did* reflect a dual focus on spirituality and philanthropy. For example, once, as an acknowledged healer within the community, she was called upon to speak in a Relief Society meeting concerning her particular knowledge about the care of the sick. On September 20, 1900, several years before her move to Provo,

Mary's diary reveals that she "came from Sister Leonards [where she was nursing her sick friend]. Looked over the notes for my lecture. Subject— care of the sick or use of herbs. Went to RS meeting & delivered lecture."

The Relief Society minutes after her return from Provo suggest a far greater amplification of this role and quite a different discursive pattern from that of spiritual advisor she had so regularly assumed before her move:

[October 17, 1907] Sister Mary Fowler was very glad to get home again, and hoped to be able to help in doing her duties as a member of the Relief Society.

[November 7, 1907] Sister Mary Fowler spoke of the priviledges that we have in gaining knowledge for ourselves, and that we should not let them slip by without doing our parts.

[December 5, 1907] Sister Mary S Fowler bore her testimony, and spoke very interesting.

[January 16, 1908] Sister Mary S. Fowler said that we should all repent each day and study things that will go with us when we leave this earth.

[April 16, 1908] Mary Fowler spoke on associating with our children.

[September 3, 1908] Sisters . . . Eliza Fowler . . . and Mary Fowler each bore their testimonies and spoke on prohabition.

[September 14, 1908] Mary S. Fowler spoke—had been greatly impressed with the instructions we had received regarding our children. We should find out what our little ones know by talking with them— the uses of their bodies—spoke of the duties we had to perform—we should see to it that we understand our duties and then perform them.

[November 5, 1908] Sister M. S. Fowler spoke—honoring aged on Thanksgiving day. Announced lesson for next meeting.

[December 17, 1908] Parent and Child—lesson 3—"Resp of Motherhood" given by Ruth McKee and Mary Fowler.

[January 21, 1909] Parent and Child—lesson 4—"Beauties of Motherhood" by Mary Fowler. Benediction by Mary Fowler.

[May 20, 1909] Pres Lemmon was pleased to see so many out, then turned the meeting over to Sister Mary S. Fowler who gave the lesson in Parent & Child on clothing.

These minutes clearly indicate that Mary Fowler's devotion to "duty" embraced the Relief Society's new mandate to educate the young mothers in a "modern" way. While Mary continued to offer opening prayers and benedictions and to occasionally bear her testimony, her most frequent contribution to the discursive practices of the Relief Society after her return from Provo was to provide lessons on "Mother and Child."

The Huntington Relief Society had taken up the charge to develop a course of study that would focus on the moral, physical, and spiritual needs of children and their mothers; according to the General Board of the Relief Society in Salt Lake such courses were to be taught either by Relief

Society members or by guest instructors who had studied in these fields.[88] Mary Fowler was perfect for this role, and, as is obvious from the preceding minutes, her lectures were interesting enough to bolster the flagging attendance at Relief Society meetings (one of the chief objectives underlying the new mandate).

Not only was Mary a skilled nurse and an accomplished public speaker, but more importantly she was an experienced mother. When she returned to Huntington in 1907, Mary Fowler's oldest children were already married and beginning families of their own and her youngest child, Fred, was a preadolescent. She had endured the days of worry over her sometimes wayward sons and had rejoiced in their return to righteousness. As Fred writes in her biography:

> It is significant, too, that without exception her children responded to the quality of her motherhood with an adoring devotion that was almost worship. Consciousness of having fallen short of her expectations was accompanied by a sense of having wronged her almost more than of having fallen short of the moral precepts which were violated. This oneness or identification of her and all of the highest ideals in the attitudes of her children was not the result of studied and intended effort on her part. She was far too humble in spirit for that. It was rather the by-product of her never failing goodness and of her passionate desire that her children should emulate in their lives the ideals dear to her.[89]

Certainly, her children did not always unfailingly emulate those ideals, as indicated by some of the diary entries Fred quotes:

> A few extracts from a diary kept intermittently for a period of two or three years afford glimpses into her attitudes and feelings toward her children. Under the date of October 1, 1900 she wrote, "Rey boy came home after an absence of five and a half months. All of our trouble was forgotten in the joy of his coming." Another entry made the next day said, "Rey brought $31 home after buying a suit of clothes. He sent $25 home in August. The boys are all good to work and have their wages used for the benefit of the family."
>
> On a Sunday sometime after her husband had left on his mission a note in her diary tells much. "I went to Sunday School and Meeting. Arno won't go out on Sunday because his clothes are too shabby. Eben won't go today because his shirt doesn't suit. He won't wear a white one. Laurie and Rey will go when they are at all decent. This is a blessing to me."
>
> On her birthday nearly a year later she wrote, ". . . it is a great comfort to me that my husband is laboring in the missionary field. My children are a great comfort and help to me." A short time later she entered the following revealing note in her record, "A beautiful Sabbath day . . . Arno is getting to be so steady and good. In fact they all are good. I thank my Heavenly Father every day for my children."

The following fragments recorded at later intervals add to the picture. ". . . I think Eben is quitting tobacco. He is such a nice big boy and it will make me so happy if he will be good."[90]

As Fred's quotations from Mary Fowler's diary suggest, her children were not always perfectly in tune with her own religious ideals, but she gave them the room to correct their own mistakes. Often this was accomplished without any direct advice or preaching as the following family story demonstrates:

> She instinctively understood that decisions and choices underlying the attitudes and behavior of her children had to be their own. She had the patience to bear seeing mistakes made and missteps taken rather than make and enforce her own decisions in the lives of her children.
>
> That she had great tact is shown by the following incident which the writer vividly recalls from his childhood. Along the way travelled to school a most enticing "candy emporium" was conveniently located. "Uncle Ame", the operator of this establishment encouraged children to buy his wares using eggs for the pay inasmuch as money, especially in the hands of children was rather scarce. The writer had a habit of occasionally surreptitiously slipping two or three eggs from our Minorca hens in his pocket to be used for this purpose, and supposed that his practice was unknown.
>
> At the dinner table one Sunday afternoon all the married sons and daughters and their families were gathered according to usual custom. The conversation turned to the merits of various breeds of chickens. Opinion differed as to the size of their eggs. The opportunity, if not deliberately made, was at least taken advantage of to let the errant son know that his sly delinquencies were known. She carefully made the conversational remark without any apparent weighting of words or voice, "Uncle Ame says that our eggs are as large as any that come into his store." It may be that others did not attach any special significance to the remark, but it was a bombshell to the miscreant and no more eggs were taken without permission.[91]

No doubt, the advice concerning child rearing that Mary Fowler delivered to the women of the Huntington Relief Society was based as much on her personal experience with situations such as this (which apparently occurred at precisely the time she was undertaking these lessons) as it was on any formal written materials available through the general offices of the society. It was Mary's incredible ability to discipline her own children with enduring love that made her such an ideal speaker on topics of motherhood and child rearing.

However, after months of delivering such lectures, by July of 1909, Mary had apparently decided that she had fulfilled her duty and the minutes state simply that "Sisters Esther Grange and Mary S. Fowler the committee on Parent & Child wished to be released as it was impossible for them to attend to it right and on motion and second they were released with a vote of thanks for their services." By January of the following year, however, Mary was involved in teaching a class on parenting in the Huntington Sunday School and urged her Relief Society sisters to attend.[92] And two years later she had resumed her position of Relief Society lecturer as the minutes state that "4th lesson from motherhood—sub infancy—discussed by Sister Mary Fowler. There was many good things to be learned in regard to rearing infants and proper care they should have" (May 16, 1912).

What is particularly interesting about Mary's return to teaching about child care is that once again her personal discursive practices are precisely in line with changes in the patterns of organization and discourse in the Relief Society itself. In this case, one month before the preceding minutes, a standing committee of the General Board of the Relief Society, after a lengthy debate about whether there should be a standard list of subjects for meetings, had published an optional outline for Relief Society lectures, listing ten possible topics for talks that were to be based on local expertise; these topics ranged from "faith and integrity in families" to "tree planting" to the "use of the franchise."[93] Following this pronouncement, Mary Fowler frequently spoke in society meetings on subjects related to the these suggestions:

> [November 21, 1912] The following sisters spoke interesting on the subject of "keeping the girl a girl" . . . Mary S. Fowler . . .
> [January 16, 1913] Julia Wakefield spoke on the subject Mother also Mary Fowler.
> [May 15, 1913] Then Mary S. Fowler took charge of the lesson and gave us all a chance to express our thot's on the lesson,—Fish, Poultry and Game.

Within the entire Relief Society and its related organizations, the words that Relief Society president Bathsheba Smith had proclaimed in a society conference in 1907 seemed to be taking more and more effect on the actions of individual stake societies and members: "There is nothing good, which is suitable for woman's work, that cannot be properly brought in the Relief Society. The study of the best literature, science, nature, cooking, in fact the whole field of domestic science, child study, nursing, home making, house furnishing, ethics, civics, Patriotism, Moral, Manners, the Gospel, the Virtues—all, and kindred subjects are within scope of the Relief Society."[94] As Jill Derr notes, "The mother's work had catapulted the Relief Society into a program that would seem for women of later generations its chief purpose: education."[95] Mary Fowler was at the forefront of that educational agenda in Huntington.

As in other communities across Utah, in Huntington women's educational prerogatives also burst out of the confines of the Relief Society meetings themselves and began occupying discursive spaces of their own: "Mary S. Fowler stated that on thursday next would be held the Home Economic class in this building and invited all to attend."[96] Within the Relief Society itself, though, the growing sentiment for a more varied discourse was finally institutionalized through the January 1914 publication of the new *Relief Society Guide*. This guide, edited by Susa Young Gates, provided lesson outlines for four meetings a month: one on charity work and business, another on the study of genealogy and the bearing of testimony, a third on home ethics and gardening, and a fourth on literature, art and architecture. Immediately, Mary Fowler took up the charge to lead the discussions on these topics, lecturing widely on each. During 1914, the first year following the publication of the *Guide*, for example, Mary spoke in Relief Society on the following topics:

> [January 15] Home Ethics "Personal pride in making one's own homestead clean and beautiful"
>> [February 12] The necessity of keeping record (genealogy)
>> [April 16] Home Gardening
>> [May 21] Planting Flowers
>> [July 16] Receipts for Canning Fruits and Vegetables
>> [August 13] Account of Conference
>> [September 10] Temple Work
>> [October 8] Power of Prayer
>> [October 15] Causes of Infidelity and Indifference to the Gospel of
> Christ

Finally, on October 28, 1914, "Mary S. Fowler introduced Miss Gertrude McShean who spoke on Home Economics—commencing with—home planning—house equipment—gardening—canning fruits and vegetables and meat—wheel tables—dish washers—steam canning—questions asked and answered." This is one of the few times an outsider was present to lecture on such topics, in this case at the behest of Mary Fowler. Once again, Mary provided a critical connection between her community and the outside world, where progress in the field of "women's work" was transforming that work into a science, worthy of study and expert advice. Relying on such expertise did not diminish Mary's own position within her community, but added to it by both providing additional resources from which her sisters could draw, and by highlighting Mary's own interconnectedness with others knowledgeable in these areas. In fact, Mary continued to lecture on topics related to health, child rearing, and "home economics," as well as religious subjects until her death in 1920.

The preceding list of Mary's lecture topics for 1914 confirms the fact that she was in the forefront of genealogy work in Huntington as well.

From that first mention of her discussion of "record keeping" in 1914, Mary assumed the position of one of the most knowledgeable and prolific workers in genealogy in her community. It was Mary who was chosen to give the monthly Genealogy lessons in Relief Society meetings; in fact, it became her most fervent work: Mary Fowler presented more than *twenty-seven* different formal lessons on genealogy in Relief Society meetings between February 15, 1915, and her death on October 29, 1920.

Again, Mary's genealogical discursive work reflects and exemplifies the concerns of the Relief Society itself.

> From 1914 to 1921 genealogy formed a prominent part of the theology course work [in the Relief Society]. Susa Young Gates, who since 1907 had been teaching genealogy in connection with the Church-sponsored Genealogical Society of Utah, adapted the lessons for Relief Society use.[97]

While Gates's lessons certainly provided Mary Fowler with useful material to include in her talks for the women of Huntington's Relief Society, it is also clear that her own genealogical investigations provided specific and detailed references she could draw on in these performances.

From the genealogical records copied carefully in her own handwriting from the Fowler family Bible, now lost, to the personal histories of ancestors she traced as carefully and thoroughly as she could, writing their stories in her own journal, Mary Fowler expressed an enthusiasm for and dedication to genealogical work that went far beyond the mere preparation of "guided" lessons on such topics for the Relief Society.[98] She became an expert in this area, and much as she had offered her expertise in health, "home ethics," sanitation, gardening, biblical knowledge, and literature to her Relief Society sisters, Mary sought to bring this love of genealogical work into their lives. As a teacher and speaker she was really quite incomparable; it was unusual to find a woman expert in so many different areas, and even rarer to find one willing to share that expertise with others through oral presentation and discursive performance. As *Women of the Covenant* suggests,

> Some wards found it difficult to "secure efficient class teachers," reporting in many instances lessons were "merely read from the Magazine." Since 1902, when the mothers' classes had begun, only a small number of women had felt comfortable assuming the position of "instructor," the title suggested by the general board.[99]

Luckily for the Huntington ward, this was not the case. In Mary Fowler they found not only a knowledgeable teacher, but a most willing one. In fact, the kind of leadership Mary evinced, while remarkable, is also characteristic of the opportunities women found in associations all across

America at the end of the nineteenth and beginning of the twentieth centuries. Such associations like the Relief Society provided women like Mary Fowler with the opportunity to speak and to be heard. In Mary's case, we find a woman who explored virtually every opportunity to develop a variety of discursive modes of expression. Whether she was bearing her testimony or lecturing on appropriate canning techniques or the latest advances in genealogical research, Mary apparently performed equally successfully within the Relief Society context. Even before she left for Provo, Mary commented several times in her own diary about being "asked to speak" in Relief Society meetings. Her "sisters" frequently comment on her eloquence and the value of her speeches; for example, the Relief Society secretary writes that a lesson on "Genealogy and Literature conducted by Mary S. Fowler—a very interesting time was enjoyed"; and "Mary S Fowler spoke very interesting."[100] Mary herself reports on January 3, 1901, that "I made the assertion in fast meeting that to be able to speak intelligently we must study, which was quoted by Sister Howard in the next R.S. meeting & by Sister Nixon in fast meeting." We can also find indications that Mary became skilled in drawing her audiences into her performances and creating collaborative events in the process; for example, only a few months before Mary died, the Relief Society minutes note that "Sister Mary S Fowler led in discussion of croup and remedies for same—drawing out the ideas and experiences of members present."[101]

Learning from her earliest experiences working with her mother and the other women of Orderville in harvesting fruit, tending silkworms, and more formally speaking in church meetings, and drawing on more recent discursive strategies learned in her nursing school courses and in the publications of the Relief Society, Mary Fowler developed her own characteristic styles and strategies for effective public discourse. In fact, she became well known for this prowess and was a sought-after teacher even outside the Relief Society context:

> People of all ages came to her, but more often than not it was not just to enjoy a visit. They wanted something when they came. Young people had a way of seeking her when there was a speech to prepare or some other part to get ready for a church or community program.[102]

In all of this Mary Susannah Fowler's sense of mission and duty was paramount. Through her speaking, Mary could work collaboratively with her women friends and acquaintances to bring about God's kingdom. Perhaps that is why the last few years of her life were devoted so enthusiastically to genealogical work. In researching genealogies, Mary provided the foundation work for a central LDS practice, baptism for the dead.[103] In doing so, she again focused on that theme of interconnection so central to

her own self-conception. Through genealogy, Mary found a way to con-
nect with both her ancestors and with those who would follow her on this
earth. On October 10, 1916, she helped to establish the "Fackrell Family
Organization" and became its first "historian." Just as she nurtured the love
and connection with her own immediate family members, so Mary Fowler
sought to bring that same joy to genealogy. As her son Fred writes:

> During her life she was a lode star drawing to her the married children
> who sought to keep their own homes as near as possible. Eloquent testi-
> mony of the warmth and breadth of her understanding is borne by the
> attitudes toward her of the wives and husbands of her sons and daugh-
> ters. Without exception they felt closely drawn to her with a loyalty,
> devotion, and confidence that removed every vestige of the "in-law"
> element from their relations. She attended the birth of many of her
> grandchildren and remained a wise counselor to their parents.[104]

So, too, Mary Fowler's legacy is heralded in the stories of her grandchildren who speak and write of her with a certain awe and a determined
admiration. The kind of belief in interconnection that remained so perva-
sive throughout her own life reflects in the voices of her grandchildren,
great-grandchildren, and great-great-grandchildren as they tell Mary
Fowler's stories, write their own personal histories, and participate in the
annual picnics of that same Fackrell Family Organization she was instrumental in starting, thus building anew the genealogical record she first
began compiling so many years ago. By teaching her sisters in the
Huntington Relief Society to do their own genealogical work, Mary was
able to weave together her own sense of reciprocity and mutual interdependence among women with her strongest belief in the connection of
family—past, present, and future.

And so, it is not surprising at all that just four days after her death, a
poem appeared in the minutes of the Huntington Relief Society:

> Sister Aurelia Johnson read 'Sentiments of Love' from the Huntington
> Relief Society to our Beloved Sister and co-worker Mary S Fowler who
> passed away at the LDS Hospital after an operation October 29 1920

> Sentiments of Love
> From
> The Huntington Relief Society
> To Our Beloved Sister and Co-worker
> Mary S. Fowler

> Oft when loved ones called to leave us,
> Pass to shining scenes beyond,
> Question, why too, thus bereave us,

Plunge us into dark despond.

Thus our sister and God's daughter
Has been faithful in her trust,
For she's surely been an angel,
With the sick and fatherless.

Oft when darkness was upon us,
While multitudes were fast asleep,
She was seen by Heavenly watchers,
Assisting those who watch the weak.

Oft when lips were parched and burning,
When the heart was sad and sick,
She was there to quench the fever,
And to comfort those who weep.

And in other lives she labored,
Ever standing at the head,
That we may receive a blessing,
For work accomplished for the dead.

We will miss her true and tender,
But One whispers at our side,
"Service she has gone to render,
Wanted on the other side."

While we mourn, their welcomes greet her,
Hail to one so nobly born,
With what joy they flock to meet her,
She, for whom the mortals mourn.

"Cease your sobs, oh cease your weeping,
In your Savior now confide,
She is in the Lord's safe keeping,
Wanted on the other side."

Even in death Mary Fowler's deepest belief in the interconnectedness of community extends to her sisters in Huntington, allowing them, through her, to be connected even more directly with "the other side," where she waits for their arrival.

3

"And Gave You All My Care"
Folk Healing as Mormon Maternal Practice

> But oh alas for this worlds joys that come and go so quick.
> You sickened for all that I could do and grew so poor and weak.
> I fed and clothed you well my child, and gave you all my care;
> And while I cared for you my heart was filled with constant prayer.

In Mary Fowler's own diary and in the writings of her family and friends, the most consistently represented identity construction of her is that of folk healer.[1] As Mary's son Fred remarks in his biography of his mother, "Service to the sick seems to be the most frequently recalled and first-named memory"[2] of her family and friends. In fact, Mary's account of her daily activities is virtually always marked in some specific ways with references to her role as community healer. Like many women healers, Mary Susannah Fowler's traditional healing practices take place within the context of other domestic duties. As Marilyn Motz has suggested in her work on nineteenth-century Michigan women:

> Nursing the sick was seen, in fact, as a central aspect of the woman's domestic role, not only within her own household but among other kin as well. Caring for the sick served both to express and to symbolize the role of the wife and mother within the family. . . . Nursing the sick, then, was both an expression of and a metaphor for the feminine domestic role.[3]

For Utahn Mary Fowler, healing was an extension of the kind of daily work that she engaged in within her own home, part of the daily routine of cooking, washing, sewing, taking care of children, visiting with neighbors, attending church and other social functions. Healing, then, is not set apart, but instead is integral to the ongoing life of both Fowler's family and her larger community. In fact, the interconnectedness of healing with other domestic duties articulates a particular theme recurrent not only in Mary Fowler's life writing, but also in the narratives of other women healers as well.[4] The theme of interconnectedness that first emerges in the understanding of the particular folk belief in community discussed in chapter 2 actually becomes for Mary Fowler one of what Sharon Kaufman has termed "cognitive areas of meaning with symbolic force."[5] As such, the theme of interconnectedness functions to explain, unify, and give substance to who Mary Fowler is, how she sees herself and her community. This theme (and others related to it) has its source in the historical, geographical, and social circumstances in which Mary Fowler lived—nineteenth and early twentieth century Mormon America.

Within this context, then, Mary Fowler's self-identification and the identity construction of her friends and family weave the theme of interconnectedness as it relates the images, metaphors, and symbols of her narrative together around a central meaning.[6] In order to understand the intersection of these kinds of identity construction most fully, we can begin with some of those central metaphors, what James Olney terms "metaphors of self,"[7] that emerge as the threads of a thematic and semiotic reading of Mary Fowler's life fabric.

Many folklorists and anthropologists interested in healing practices center their analyses on the historical or social or psychological factors operating within the distribution of the folk knowledge of healing. However, in her work with the folk medical practices of North Carolina healers, Karen Baldwin has suggested that it is just as important to examine the aesthetically highlighted narratives of women healers in terms of their symbolic meanings.[8] By examining metaphors operating within the diary of Mary Fowler and within the writings of her husband, children, and the members of her larger community, we may begin to understand the kinds of interconnectedness existing, not only between her traditional informal healing and Mary's other domestic activities, but also symbolically between the other most significant arenas of identity formation and reconstruction.

Carol McClain has pointed towards the importance of the metaphor of healing as nurturance, specifically maternal nurturance, when she suggests that indeed there exists a kind of cultural equation between maternal nurturance and domestic healing, and that through her healing practice the woman healer actually re-creates particular domestic relationships.[9] For Mary Susannah Fowler, the metaphoric fit between woman as mother and woman as healer is best demonstrated in the absolute seamlessness of her narrative rendering of the activities of individual days. Her diary entries for January 5–8, 1900, for example, reveal how making her son a shirt fits quite neatly in between sweating Sister Robins and making poultices for Brother Wilcox's sick babe who was having fits:

[January 5, 1900] Pa went to Scofield. Sewing. Sweat Sister Robins with hot mud. [January 6, 1900] Still sewing. Sister Norton helped me again. I trust I can return her compliments some time. Sweat Sister Robins. [January 8, 1900] Cloudy. Sweat Sister Robins. Made Asa shirt. Went to Bro Wilcocks and made some poultices for their sick babe. It is having fits.

Later, on January 15, knitting her son Arno's mittens and visiting the ill Brother Chase are juxtaposed with only a period in between: "Cloudy, has been for several days. Knitting Arno's mittens. Went to see Bro Chase. he is just as gentle and good when sick as when well." Being mother, nurturer, and healer are very simply part of the same vocation. As Barbara Ehrenreich and Deidre English point out in *For Her Own Good: 150 Years of the Experts' Advice to Women*, traditionally in America:

> The art of healing was linked to the tasks and the spirit of motherhood; it combined wisdom and nurturance, tenderness and skill. All but the most privileged women were expected to be at least literate in the language of herbs and healing techniques; the most learned women traveled widely to share their skills. The women who distinguished themselves as healers were not only midwives caring for other women, but "general practitioners," herbalists, and counselors serving men and women alike.[10]

Mary Fowler was such a woman healer. In a tribute to Mary after her death, Mrs. Ivy Brasher of Huntington wrote: "In the care of babies she was unexcelled. She was more than a nurse, she was a Doctor. She was a loving mother, a devoted wife, a thorough Latterday Saint and a faithful friend. May the Lord Bless her memory."[11] Such sentiments summarize the healer as nurturing mother metaphor used by many other acquaintances to capture the essence of Mary Susannah Fowler. This metaphoric relationship between nursing and maternal nurturing is certainly not novel. In fact, in the nineteenth century Catharine Beecher and Harriet Beecher Stowe explicitly outlined the nature of such a relationship when they wrote:

> God himself made and commissioned one set of nurses; and in doing this and adapting them to utter helplessness and weakness . . . he made them to humor the caprices and regard both reasonable and unreasonable complainings. He made them to bend tenderly over the disturbed and irritated, and fold them to quiet assurance in arms made soft with love; in a word, he made *Mothers!*[12]

In the nineteenth century, healing was the domain of women only within the family, and while women frequently nursed their neighbors, especially during childbirth, such care was always provided in a familial setting—not a hospital or professional clinic.[13] In fact, in nineteenth-century America, "healing was female when it was a neighborly service,

based in stable communities, where skills could be passed on for generations and where the healer knew her patients and their families."[14] As
Lamar Riley Murphy has pointed out, there were virtually no trained doctors among the earliest immigrants to America, and domestic healing practices flourished in the colonies. It was during the eighteenth century that
the situation began to change with the development of a new medical
"elite." Throughout the eighteenth and early nineteenth centuries, then,
domestic healing coexisted with professional medical practice and "ideas
about lay and professional responsibilities—as defined by doctors *and* by lay
people—remained fluid and mutually tutorial."[15] Medical practitioners
believed that a significant part of their enterprise was to actually *enhance*
women's role as health care givers within the family context.[16]

Mary Fowler's healing practices were firmly situated within the
familial networks associated with Mormon communities.[17] In fact, the
extension of the family through Mary's role as nurturing community healer occasionally came in conflict with her own maternal role. When her
daughter Laura was a victim of the 1918 influenza outbreak, Mary was
nursing her ill child when

> an acquaintance who lived on the other side of town came and pleaded
> that his baby was dreadfully sick and he had been advised by the one
> overworked doctor in the community to "go get Mrs. Fowler." When it
> was explained that she was nursing her own sick daughter who should
> not be left, he sobbed that he couldn't go home without her; he was sure
> that his baby would die. With this appeal she went with him, leaving the
> daughter in the care of her father. Three days were spent with the child
> which recovered. A few minutes were taken occasionally to come back
> to see that her own daughter was getting on alright.[18]

In their capacity as nurturers, women healers were often most knowledgeable about herbal cures. A basic understanding of botanic medicines and
other home remedies were available as part of common domestic manuals,
even those written by professional physicians.[19] Along with cooking directions, nineteenth-century recipe books also commonly included various
cures; Lydia Maria Child's *The American Frugal Housewife*, published in 1829,
for example, provided a number of recipes for common herbal remedies.[20]

So closely connected was the popular image of woman as nurturer
and healer that many patent medicines, especially during the late nineteenth
century, were advertised as being the "secret recipes" of women. Lydia
Pinkham's Vegetable Compound, for example, an alcoholic base combined
with various herbal ingredients, was marketed as a cure for various disor-
ders of the female reproductive system with advertising headlines promoting the product because "The Doctor Did No Good," and "Woman Can

Sympathize with Woman."[21] In both the *Deseret News* and the *Emery County Progress*, papers Mary Fowler would have read regularly, such advertisements appeared in virtually every edition, furthering the popular conception that Utah women healers were also health care experts.

Recognizing the importance of women's traditional nurturing role in nineteenth-century domestic health care, doctors sought to "educate women about health matters and join them in creating a health care partnership characterized by mutual cooperation and deference."[22] Health care handbooks written and disseminated by doctors sought to inform both female domestic healers and male physicians about health issues traditionally within the domain of women:

> Though the precise connection between advice literature and actual behavior is very difficult to establish, it is clear that maternal health guides promoted changes that eventually had enormous consequences for women's roles in the sickroom, the family, and the society. Physicians— most of them men—and eventually other professionals would define appropriate childhood and familial roles and behavior, while mothers would be charged with putting those ideas into action. During the first century of this crusade, however, women played an indispensable part in this role definition, because most physicians had so little experience with infants and young children that they could not stand alone. Women had roles of undeniable importance, both in real life and in advice literature.[23]

Such advice literature, both that produced by physicians and the domestic manuals written by women, promoted the understanding that through controlling their domestic environment women also played a crucial role in the prevention and causation of disease.[24] As an "American Matron" writing in the 1811 *Maternal Physician* put it, "a mother is a child's best physician, as *it is better by care to prevent disease* than to be ever so well skilled in curing it."[25]

Catharine Beecher's *Housekeeper and Healthkeeper* is a fine example of the ways in which popular literature, in this case a domestic manual, promoted this particular role of woman as nurturer and healer. Interestingly, in this manual Beecher also connected the business of health and hygiene with religious devotion, suggesting that disease itself was attributable to religious neglect because "laws of health are the laws of God, and when you disobey them you sin against your Heavenly Father."[26]

It is especially interesting, then, that Mary Fowler believed so strongly in the virtue of cleanliness. Virginia Rogers, Mary's granddaughter, remembers that her sister Rae told her that "Grandmother Mary had a thing about cleanliness. One time she was nursing someone and sent for Ammon to bring her food from her own house because that family wasn't clean enough for her. She had lots of things all around, kinda cluttered, but she was immaculately clean."[27] That belief in the importance of cleanliness was one Mary shared with other women as well. On March 18, 1909, Mary used a Relief Society meeting to discuss cleanliness with the women in her ward; the Relief Society minutes read: "The meeting was then turned over to Sister Mary Fowler to conduct the lecture on general nursing, commenced by explaining the things that a nurse should be prepared in, to perform her duties abely. cleanliness was then taken up and very good instructions given, questions asked and answered." And three years later on February 15, 1912, the Relief Society minutes note that a talk on "Home Sanitation" was presented by Mary S. Fowler. For Mary Fowler and other Mormon women healers such a conception of cleanliness, health, and disease and the role of nurturing women in domestic healing provided additional verification of the connections between religious piety, domestic duty, and healing efficacy.

This metaphor of the healer as nurturer is also closely connected with another trope that is central especially to the articulation of identity of women healers as they construct narratives of their lives and in the process forge their own concepts of self identity: women healers as mediators. Certainly Mary Susannah Fowler sees herself as a mediator, drawing meaning and balance and a kind of resolution from any number of significant oppositions—cultural, environmental, personal. In fact, Mary Fowler exhibits a range of mediating potentialities that many women healers share, although the categories of mediation necessarily are constructed in socioculturally specific ways for each healer. Mary Fowler's position as mediatrix involves the representation and rearticulation of the tensions between traditional healing practices and the "new" medicine, physical health and spiritual health, the "natural" and the "cultural," life and death, the individual and society, and domestic and public spaces, among others.

HEALTH CARE AND MORMONISM: THE CONTEXT OF MEDICAL MEDIATION

In order to understand the kinds of mediation Mary Fowler effected with regards to the tensions between traditional medical practices and the "new" medicine practiced by physicians and surgeons at the beginning of the twentieth century, we first need to examine the cultural context within which such an opposition arose, particularly with respect to Mormon attitudes towards health and healing.

In the early nineteenth century, when neither a medical degree nor a license was required for the practice of medicine, and when "quackery" was still rampant, medical professionals sought to enlighten the general public about the causes and treatment of disease, hoping to create a mutually cooperative approach to healing. They believed that by combining the experiential knowledge of domestic healers with the professional expertise of trained physicians the very best in medical care could be provided. However, the desired spirit of cooperation did not always result in deference towards physicians and the adoption of subordinate and supportive roles by the general public. When the general public lost confidence in doctors subscribing to rudimentary diagnoses and ineffective chemically produced medicines, they turned to a number of medical sects representing different philosophies of healing that challenged professional physicians. "Outrage against regular medicine mounted into a mass movement against medical professionalism and expertism in all forms."[28]

Perhaps the most influential early philosophy in this movement, the Thomsonian method, was first presented by Samuel Thomson in his *New Guide to Health* published in Columbia, Ohio, in 1832. Promoting the use of herbs, hot baths, and dietary moderation, Thomsonian medicine flourished during the mid–nineteenth century by providing a far milder alternative to many of the other medical practices of the time. Medical historians have attributed the immensely popular success of Thomsonianism to "contemporary medical inefficacy and the democratic temper of the times."[29]

This healing system would become the main basis of the working class and feminist alternative to regular medicine. In fact, Thomson's system was based in knowledge of folk medicine and domestic practice that he had learned as a boy from a female lay healer and midwife named Mrs. Benton: "Thomson's system was little more than a systematization of Mrs. Benton's combination of herbs and steam, which in turn was derived from Native American healing lore."[30] The Thomsonian method, the goal of which was to enable the democratization of health care, became the core of the popular health movement in nineteenth-century America. As such, it was scoffed at by many orthodox physicians who "tried to dismiss it as the embodiment of crude popular delusions. For them it was a manifestation in the medical arena akin to the religious enthusiasms of the day, such as the Millerite movement and Mormonism. . . ."[31]

Interestingly, several prominent early Mormons were themselves among the disciples of Thomsonian medicine, and they probably influenced Mormon founder Joseph Smith's own advocacy of this particular medical sect. However, Smith had other more personal reasons for eagerly embracing this particular concept of healing. As a young boy recovering from typhoid fever, Joseph himself had been misdiagnosed by a physician who claimed Smith had sprained his shoulder. After several weeks of intense pain, Joseph was finally correctly diagnosed with an infection that had caused a serious sore to develop in his shoulder. The physician at that point drained the sore "upon which it discharged fully a quart of purulent matter."[32] Even more dramatically, Joseph Smith's brother Alvin had been given a strong dose of calomel for colic by a doctor. The medicine caused a stomach obstruction that eventually led to the young child's death from gangrene.[33] These and several other less traumatic, but nonetheless trouble-some, incidents caused Joseph Smith to become highly suspicious of med-ical practitioners, and they help to explain the way in which he eagerly embraced Thomsonian medicine.

Smith's translation of the golden plates into the Book of Mormon includes an early reference to the importance of herbal medicine that aligns well with Thomson's teachings:

> And there were some who died with fevers, which at some seasons of the year, was very frequent in the land; but not so much so with fevers, because of the excellent qualities of the many plants and roots which God had prepared, to remove the cause of diseases which was subsequent to man, by the nature of the climate.[34]

Encouraged by Joseph Smith, Brigham Young, and other leaders, many Mormons embraced the Thomsonian method. Foremost among them, perhaps, was Priddy Meeks, an unschooled herbalist who developed his own philosophies of healing based firmly in Thomsonian medicine. Meeks, like both Smith and Young, connected herbalism with God's bless-ings; in his journal Meeks wrote: "We attended the sick both night and day and our success was marvelous, because the Lord blessed the medicine we used, it being such He had ordained for the benefit for His Saints, using no poison, no bleeding nor starving of our patients, but everything we used was in harmony with their food."[35]

After converting to Mormonism in 1840 at the age of forty-five, Meeks and his wife Margaret journeyed across the plains to Salt Lake City with one of the first Mormon pioneer companies, arriving in October of 1847. After a few years spent in central Utah, in 1876 the Meeks family moved to Orderville to join the United Order. At that time Mary Fackrell was just fourteen years old. It is of particular significance that Priddy Meeks was the primary medical resource in Orderville, Utah, while Mary Susannah Fackrell Fowler was growing into a young woman with a particular interest in and gift for healing. Certainly, her own healing techniques, remedies, and philosophies were developed through Mary's association with Priddy Meeks. Meeks's influence on Mary Fowler and on other members of the Orderville community determined to a great extent the nature of the "fit" between the herbal medicine he practiced and the dietary regulations and faith-healing beliefs of their Mormon community. As Meeks later wrote:

One main object I have in view is to turn the hearts of the Saints to the Word of Wisdom[36] that the wisdom may be sanctified in the hearts of the Saints to the exclusion of the popular physicians and their poison medicine of the present day, and simplify everyone among the Saints to one name for each article, with one meaning to that name that children may not err thereby, ignoring all the customs and fashions and technicalities of the dead languages that has caused the death of thousands of our dear friends, and obey the word of the Lord by using these herbs that He says He has ordained for the "Constitution, Nature, and Use of Man."

Also to simplify the practice of midwifery down to its natural wants; and what are its natural wants? Nothing but to have the obstructions removed, and you cannot prevent delivery only at the expense of life because it's the law of nature which is the law of life, which is the law of God, which is immutable. . . . [37]

These observations support the fact that herbs used both in healing disease and in the practice of midwifery fit well with the Word of Wisdom revealed to Joseph Smith, who by the time of the revelation was a strong believer in Thomsonian medicine. In fact, Smith often spoke directly about the importance of herbal applications. In "setting apart" Ann Carling as a midwife while still in Nauvoo, Illinois, for example, Joseph Smith laid his hands on her head and told her that she would be successful in caring for the sick if she would use herbs exclusively in her work. Years later in Utah Carling would become known as the "herb doctor."[38] Writing about the early Mormon midwives, Claire Noall puts Carling's work within a broader context: "The Word of Wisdom, righteous living, and the use of herbs as remedies for disease and a means of sustaining health were far more important to Mormons than the 'poisonous medicines prescribed by doctors.'"[39]

The connection between a belief in the curative properties of herbs provided by God and the espousal of Thomsonian medicine firmly grounded the healing practices of Priddy Meeks in the belief system of the Mormon community of Orderville. Drawing on the herbal remedies suggested by Thomson himself, especially the use of lobelia, Meeks not only worked to keep his community healthy, but he also trained many members of the United Order in the use of various herbs, both those identified by Thomson and readily available and those growing within the specific region of southern Utah. Meeks had previously helped to organize the Council of Health in Salt Lake, and his duties with the council in the early days of settlement included going out to "scour the canyons every Wednesday in search of roots and herbs to present to the Council the next day. . . . It was a speedy way to become acquainted with the flora of the country and the virtues and properties of each plant."[40]

Priddy Meeks's own daughter, herbalist Ellen Meeks Hoyt, whose mother was the well-known midwife Mary Jane McCleve Meeks, suggests that her father often sought to draw on connections between Mormon history as presented in the Book of Mormon and the use of regionally specific herbal remedies, and thereby strengthen the veracity and efficacy of his own herbal practice. In one example, Ellen Meeks Hoyt suggests that when the Lamanites and Nephites, who according to the Book of Mormon, inhabited areas of North and South America before the time of Christ, went into battle against each other, "many of them [the Nephites] were wounded and badly in need of some kind of remedy. Their battles were fought as far north as these very hills, and the warriors were cured with the same herbs that grow around us today. Thistle is for courage; sage to offset poison."[41] In telling this story, an addition to the doctrinal narrative, the Meekses dramatically place their own use of the very herbs that cured and brought solace to their religious forebears firmly within the larger belief narrative of the LDS Church. In doing so, their own medical knowledge can no longer be viewed as simply one of the many alternatives to institutionalized medicine, but rather as a God-sanctioned practice that has been effective, both physically and spiritually, for centuries.

In adopting the Thomsonian method for her own healing practices, Mary Susannah Fowler in many ways seemingly set herself in opposition to the institutionalized medical establishment. The scarcity of physicians in the southern Utah communities in which she lived made it not only acceptable but often critical that the practitioners of botanic medicine, nurses and midwives, were most often the ones available to care for the communities' medical needs. As Ehrenreich and England suggest, "In Thomsonianism women could find a dignified and neighborly system of care for themselves, plus public validation for their traditional role as healers for their families and friends."[42] For those who sought Mary Fowler's healing practices, often her care was far preferable to that of the "official" physician.

Within her own family, Mary's husband Henry Ammon grew to believe in the power of her healing ministrations far more than he trusted the physician's medical knowledge, as we have seen in chapter 1. Prone to both illness and accidents, Henry Ammon frequently notes the efficacy of his wife's care:

> Edson D. Porter and I were making a corn crib. We had some boards to rip so we took them to Delawn M. Cox's shop to do it on his lathe. While adjusting the machinery my jumper sleeve caught the saw and pulled my wrist onto the saw and cut my left hand more than half off. Several of the cords were cut into, and one of the bones also. . . . Inasmuch as it was my left hand and I had become a good violinist, the thought that I would

not be able to play any more was a sore trial to me. . . . My wrist and hand healed much better than anyone looked for and I have the use of three fingers to play the violin with. I will say that there was no doctor in that part of the country so Mary dressed the wound. I was never so peevish and cross in my life before nor since.[43]

On another occasion, Henry again needed to draw on the expert medical attention of his wife:

I have been very unfortunate in meeting with accidents. One nearly cost me my life. I ran a pocket knife through something I was working on right into my right leg above the knee and blood poisoning set in and was very serious before it was checked by my wife, Mary. She seemed to be a natural doctor. During the first seven or eight months of my mission Eliza, my second wife, was afflicted with Sciatic Rhumatism in one of her legs and was laid up most of that time so she could not leave the house, but she recovered long before my return home due to the expert nursing Mary gave her.[44]

On yet another occasion, Henry fell through the floor joists while plastering the schoolhouse in Milton, Utah, breaking his ribs. Henry's account reveals his belief that the medical doctors did nothing really to save his life, and that it was his wife Mary and the prayers of the church elders that kept him from dying:

The Dr. from Morgan was called in and he bandaged me up. I was put on a cot and sent home in a baggage car, reaching Provo about 10:00 P.M. I was carried three blocks from the depot to our home. I was in a very bad condition. Peritonitis had set in and when Dr. Dayler was called in, an hour later he did not give me until morning to live, but Bishop Berg and Brother Ahlander were called in and administered to me. Mary worked over me constantly night and day until she reduced the swelling and had me on the road to recovery.[45]

Later in his life Henry writes about the way in which Mary's diagnostic expertise and healing techniques again superseded the care of medical "professionals" and saved his life. After being taken to the hospital in Salt Lake and operated upon for gallstones (an operation Henry maintained he did not need), complications developed:

Through the neglect of one of the nurses, I got pneumonia about two weeks after the operation and nearly passed away. If my wife, Mary, had not been there I surely would have done so. She first went to one and then another until she convinced them I had pnuemonia and then they got busy right away doctoring me for it.[46]

Mary Fowler's reputation as an effective healer spread among her own family and within her larger community. There are numerous accounts of incidents in which medical doctors gave up the hope of saving a patient's life, only to have Mary accomplish the seemingly impossible. Both her grandchildren Milton Roper and Virginia Rogers tell the story of their grandmother saving the life of a baby in Huntington who is still alive today. Milton Roper's version of the story recalls:

> Now they tell a story of some woman who had a baby that was just get-ting over some disease and she come down with pneumonia. Everybody including the doctors was sure that the baby was gonna die. The baby went into convulsions and they called for Mary Susannah, "Run get Mary, hurry!" As soon as she took the baby in her arms, the convulsions stopped. When the mother or somebody else'd take the baby, the con-vulsions started again. She had to stay there holding that baby and com-forting her until she was completely over the convulsions. But she saved the baby. And the baby is a woman that lives here in town now; her name is Della Alger.[47]

And granddaughter Eudora Clements recalls the fact that when she became desperately ill as a child, instead of taking her to a doctor, her par-ents took her immediately to her grandmother Mary:

> When I was a baby I got really sick. My parents were living in a coal camp. I got so sick they thought I was going to die, so they took me down to Huntington to my grandmother and she worked with me. They thought I was dead, but she saved my life.[48]

Frequently, then, Mary Susannah Fowler and other women healers were called on either in place of or in addition to the medical profession-als. Most often it appears that, in southern Utah at least, folk healers were seen to be in complementary rather than adversarial relationships with physicians. Mary Susannah's granddaughter Rae Spellman recalls that "[Mary Susannah] learned a lot from the doctors she worked with. And she would occasionally go to Salt Lake to learn more. And then sometimes she got information by mail. She was constantly wanting to learn more and to know how to take care of people better."[49]

It was late in the nineteenth century that medical information actu-ally began to be more widely available in Utah. After Drs. Ellis and Margaret Shipp had returned to Salt Lake City from medical school in Philadelphia, with their husband Dr. Milford Bard Shipp, they began to publish a magazine in 1888 called the *Salt Lake Sanitarian*. This journal pre-sented some of the latest medical techniques and remedies, making them available to both physicians and herbal practitioners around the state. This was certainly some of the "information" Mary Fowler received "by mail." By 1890, the antiphysician attitudes of the Mormon hierarchy had become considerably relaxed, yet it is noteworthy that the *Sanitarian* still recognized the power of faith to heal and did not advocate the services of physicians as a substitute for administering to the sick.[50] It also continued to stress the responsibility of the people for maintaining their own good health and warned against "dosers and druggers," thus continuing to suggest conservatism in the use of traditional herbal remedies at the same time it helped publicize the "rapid strides that are being made in the selection and uses of remedial agents in disease."[51] Yet as late as January of 1900, Mary Susannah still maintained a somewhat skeptical attitude towards these "rapid strides"; on January 9, for example, she writes in her diary: "The smallpox is in the country. Many are being vaccinated, some with quite serious results. Pa don't favor vaccination. We will not have it done here."

HERBALISM AND SPIRITUALITY

Of the many herbs native to Utah that were used most widely by Priddy Meeks and his followers, as well as by other Mormon herbalists, one of the most prevalent was "Brigham" or "Mormon" tea. This tea, which was brewed from a reed-like jointed grass abundant in Utah and in the Southwest, especially along waterways, got its common folk name from an incident described by Austin and Alta Fife in *Saints of Sage and Saddle*. Brigham Young was called in to bless a woman who was near death. Looking out the window onto the mesa near the central Utah home, Young described a particular bush to the woman's husband:

> "You go out there," he said to the husband, "and behind the rim of that mesa you'll find a big canyon whose floors are covered with a bush about as high as your knees. Gather it and make a tea for Sister Jones and she will be healed."
>
> The husband was perplexed: this was President Young's first visit to that section of Utah. "But Brother Brigham," he inquired, "how do you know? Have you been out there?"
>
> "No!" he replied, in the tone a father might use to satisfy a child-ish question, "but I know it's there. I've seen it!"
>
> Ashamed of his moment of skepticism, the farmer leaped upon his horse and rode to the spot that Brigham had pointed out. He gathered up an armful of the shrub and sped home to brew the tea, as he had been instructed. His wife was healed almost instantly. Ever since, the Saints in the area have made yearly harvests of the herb and have used it to cure almost every type of affliction.[52]

In fact, Brigham Tea contains the chemical ephedrine which acts as both a decongestant and a stimulant. Again, the connection of herbal reme-dies with religious blessings in the narrative is foremost, not the suggestion of particular pharmaceutical properties—only in this case, the blessing was mediated by Brigham Young, the Mormon prophet and president.

It was BrighamYoung, also, who pointed toward the efficacy of combining botanic medicine with the Mormon religious practice of anointing
and laying on of hands in praying for the sick: "It is God's mind and will
that every father and mother should know just what to do for their children when they are sick." When children are sick, he suggested, "instead of
calling for a doctor, you should administer to them by the laying on of
hands and anointing with oil, and give them mild food and herbs and
medicine that you can understand."[53] At this time in the early history of
the church and certainly during the days of Mary Fowler's practice as a
healer, women were very much encouraged to wash and anoint the sick,
and especially to anoint women preparing for childbirth. In fact, Joseph
Smith himself said when questioned about the appropriateness of women
acting in this capacity: "If the sisters should have faith to heal the sick, let
all hold their tongues. . . .Who are better qualified to administer than our
faithful and zealous sisters whose hearts are full of faith, tenderness, sym-
pathy and compassion? No one."[54]

Mary Susannah Fowler's diary amply supports this activity and
demonstrates her own capacity to combine her skills as a healer who relies
on herbs and mud sweats with her religious and spiritual commitment to
performing the appropriate rituals. Early in September 1900 she notes that
she had spent three days with Sister Lenard, who was quite ill, giving her
mud sweats. Later that same month she writes: "Between Sunday School
and Meeting went with the sisters to wash and anoint Sister Lenard." And
on June 4, 1900, her diary states: "Called to assist in washing and anointing
three sisters. Ettie Norton and Laurie Wimmer preparatory to confinement
and Mary Brasher for barrenness. Took part with all." Census records and
Mary's own diary confirm the success of the first two rituals, and the third
ritual must have been effective as well, since Mary Fowler was Mary
Brasher's "nurse when three of my babies were born"![55]

Attitudes towards health within the Mormon communities in which
Mary Fowler lived support her ability to draw together the realms of physical and spiritual healing. Her recognized roles as healer and as leader of
women's groups within her religious community come together to allow
Mary the position of mediatrix, effectively bringing these two domains
into congruence. The cultural narratives described above also suggest that
members of Mormon communities in Utah actually saw no separation
between spiritual and physical healing; the two were necessarily part of the
same process. Mary Fowler's own spiritual fervor, then, contributed significantly to her abilities as a healer within this particular cultural context.

Throughout Mary's diary we find references to healing practices and
to prayer closely related. One entry for February 15, 1900, includes these
comments: "Went home with sick headache. Laurie heated dirt and put to

my feet and stomache and back. That helped me, but oh how sick still! When the children had prayers they prayed for me. Asa leading in prayer and I was soon easy enough to go to sleep. I know that I was blessed in answer to prayer." Even the Thomsonian sweat practices suggested by Priddy Meeks could not heal Mary's headache completely; it is the relationship between physical and spiritual healing that allows Mary Fowler to bring her own suffering under control and it is this same relationship that she offers to those she works to heal. Mary's sister Olive Fackrell Norwood provides just such an example:

> Another time when we lived in Huntington, Ronald [her son] who was about eight years old, was taken ill very suddenly in the night. My sister Mary stayed to help take care of him in the day time, and we'd take care of him at night. Mary was a good nurse. The doctor did not think he would live. One day as Mary was leaving to go home, Dr. Hill asked, "are you going home?"
>
> She said, "I thought I would."
>
> He said, "You better stay, it's a matter of a short time." He said it would be all over by morning so Mary stayed with us. Then she called in six or eight of the most faithful sisters in the ward. We held a prayer circle. I was struck very forcibly by the words of one sister as she prayed, "Father, we do not ask for this blessing because of our worthiness, but because we are mothers." We at once noticed that Ronald began to breathe easier and to our happiness he was restored to us.[56]

It is precisely this connection between her individual spiritual self and her Mormon community that best demonstrates a complex of relationships requiring Mary Susannah's mediation. As a healer, she consistently represents the social community to the invalid, and her healing both restores individual health *and* brings the ill person back into the arms of that social community. In this role, Mary often brings emotional comfort and sustenance as well as healing herbs and Thomsonian medical techniques. Not only does she help to bring those on the brink of death back to life, but upon occasion she helps to ease the transition to death for the deceased's family members left in this world. On March 25, 1900, for example, she writes: "Sat up nearly all night with Emma Ingle Powel and her little dead babe." And in the entry for January 29, 1900, we find her calling on Sister Robins who is described throughout the diary as constantly needing to be the recipient of sweats; this time, however, her visit is interrupted by a request that she go immediately to the house of another woman who was in need of emotional support at the death of her brother:

> this morning I called at Sr. Robins & while there was sent for to go to Sr. Gardners. She had just rec'd word that her only remaining brother Sam Chase had died of appendicitis. Staid with her a while then brought

Main Street, Huntington, Utah around the turn of the century. Photo used by permission, Utah State Historical Society.

her home with me. Tried to comfort her the best I could. Rec'd a letter from Pa's sister Harriet giving an account of the death of her darling child Ethel, four and a half years old. My heart aches for that poor bereave mother. Every child she has born for seventeen years has died. Sr. Wall & Hunter came to see me in regard to the improvement class.

Again, in mediating between life and death, this woman healer also acts to draw the grieving sister back into the social community, to not leave her alone in her time of need, and instead to take her to her own home, the two-room mud-floored cabin filled with eight children. In the midst of giving support to Sister Gardner, Mary Fowler expresses her passionate empathy for her own sister-in-law Harriet who has lost every child she has delivered for the last seventeen years. The fragility of life is palpable in this entry. And yet, perhaps even more remarkable is the direct announcement that even as she deals with death all around her, she is visited by two other women to discuss the activities of their reading group. One can imagine that Sister Gardner might have been swept up in all the activity of Mary Fowler's household, a dramatic enactment of the juxtaposition and mediation of the forces of life and death. These examples also demonstrate, as Kathryn Sklar has pointed out, "that women's illnesses and the solicitous attitude they aroused in other women created a sense of female solidarity and an opportunity to express affection to other women."[57]

Perhaps that sense of female solidarity gained through participation in the healing of another is what also underlies the fact that Mary Fowler became not only healer but confidante to many women in the communities in which she lived. Mrs. Laura Brown, for example, the mother of the infant Della who Mary Fowler saved from the convulsions induced by pneumonia, says that "Sister Fowler was a ministering angel. When she was holding the baby it would not have any convulsions, but the minute she stepped out another convulsion would seize the baby. . . . After the baby got well I used to come to Sister Fowler with my problems. I talked to her while she worked, and I always felt better when I went home."[58] Mary's daughter-in-law Jessie Manwaring Fowler expressed similar feelings when she reflected on her own relationship: "Mary had truly been a guiding light, a friend and a confidant. My dear mother lived so far away, I had really become dependent on Mary Fowler for advice and assistance through any crisis, such as any daughter would ask of her own mother."[59]

In other ways, too, Mary acts to unite the individual's experience of life and death with the understanding of the social community. After several diary entries chronicling the illness of Sister Ettie Norton's child, Arvilla, Mary writes that on May 7, 1900, "Word came that little Arvilla Norton was dying over to Grangeville. Made me feel dark and nervous. Took my work and staid with Ettie N. A warm day." Then on June 25,

1900, Mary notes that she was "Present at the birth of Sr Norton's little girl. I will wash and dress the baby." After attending to the needs of one child only to lose her to death, Mary Fowler acts as midwife to Sr. Norton as she delivers another daughter into the world. In washing and dressing the baby, Mary brings the baby into the social family of this Mormon community as well. Here again, Mary Fowler's role as healer positions her in the midst of the ongoing continuum of social concerns; her healing is not a separate "work," but rather a piece of the entire social fabric. It is no surprise, then, when we read on May 9, 1900: "Knitting. Was photographed with Ladies of the Club. . . . Sr. Woolman, Arvilla's grandma, sent me a dress pattern and a nice note recognizing my labors with her sick granddaughter." This interconnectedness is represented over and over again throughout the diary; on April 10, 1900, for example, she writes "Hard frost this morning. Attended business meeting of the club. Called at Sr. Bruces who is sick. Also showed Sr Cox how to make a coat." As the diary entries also suggest, Mary Fowler not only mediated between individuals and the larger society, but additionally, that mediation is often accompanied by the bringing together of natural and cultural forces. Two of the last entries quoted, for example, include weather reports juxtaposed with references to healing within a sociocultural context. This relationship between the natural and sociocultural is far more significant than these brief entries might intimate, however. Rather than simply being notations of recorded weather conditions as is the case in many women's diaries from this period, the specific references to clouds, warmth, snow, or sunshine that either begin or conclude most of the entries in Mary Fowler's journal stand as indexical referents to the necessary interconnections between the natural and cultural worlds she moves between. For Mary Susannah Fowler, the natural world was both source of healing herbs and medicinal remedies and significant metaphor for her own relationship with her God and her community. Perhaps this is no more clearly evidenced than in her own diary entry for December 12, 1899:

> The ground & everything else is covered this morning with a beautiful thin coat of pure white snow come to fill its wonderful mission of beautifying, purifying and gratifying before sinking away into the earth, there to give life and health to vegetation by its magical presence or running in the tiny rivulets to the great rivers & there rushing to perform its part in making the "mighty ocean." I think I would look in vain for a better example of unselfish usefulness.

Here Mary Susannah draws on her poetic gifts to implicitly compare the "unselfish usefulness" of snow to her own goals as a healer. Just as the snow performs its mission on earth in "beautifying, purifying, and gratifying," just as it "gives life and health," so too she strives to perform these same functions within her community.

This diary entry is also exemplary of the continued descriptions of weather throughout the diary that reveal just how in tune Mary Fowler was with the natural world. And even more importantly, it is through Mary's own ability to recognize, grow or gather, and use vegetation, herbs, and even the earth itself in her own healing ministrations that she restores members of her family and the larger community to health. It is Mary Susannah's own knowledge of the healing properties of the natural world that allows her to restore health and balance to those who either do not possess that knowledge or are too infirm to use it. Her abilities to use mud sweats and to make pills and poultices from herbs allow her to effectively mediate between the natural and cultural worlds both for herself, for her family, and indeed for her entire community.

Throughout Mary's diary there are references to the collection and preparation of herbs for her to use in healing. On July 22, 1900, when she was visiting her sons at a sheep camp, Mary writes, "Eben, Harry and myself gathered medicinal herbs, and pretty flowers." On the 18th of December 1899 she notes that "after the children were off to school I prepared herbs to make bitter pills. Did a little sewing in the evening. Eben, Asa and I made pills using melted honey to stick them with." And when it is impossible to gather herbs herself, she sends her children to purchase them, as she notes on December 1, 1899: "O what beautiful weather. Arno still a little better. Laurie doing a little washing with Ettie N. Rey has gone to Castle Dale to get Peruvian bark, Flax seed and Lemons for Arno," who had been sick with pneumonia. And today, the one recipe for an herbal remedy that is still used within her family is the one Virginia Rogers helped me to prepare in August of 1996 described in chapter 1. Combining herbs readily available in her own garden and other household items, Mary Susannah passed along to her family a recipe that is much more difficult today to reproduce. And even though Mrs. Rogers warned me of the "awful taste," she treasures her grandmother's remedy and dispenses it with pride.

Along with the preparation and use of herbal remedies, Mary Fowler also relied on "sweating" her patients to achieve particular results. Such "sweating" is a direct adoption of Thomsonian principles; according to Thomson, all illness came "directly from obstructed perspiration, which is always caused by cold, or want of heat. . . . to restore heat to its natural state [is] the only way by which health [can] be produced."[60] In order to cure the patient, it was necessary to "increase the internal heat, remove all obstructions of the system, restore the digestive powers of the stomach, and produce a natural perspiration."[61] To accomplish these goals, Mary Fowler "sweat" her patients. Sometimes, as her granddaughter Rae Spellman relates, the sweating was done with hot water: "When I was little I had a cold or something. Anyway I was pretty sick and grandmother got water and put it on the stove until it was really hot and then they put me in it and put a blanket around me to keep the heat in. In those days they did a lot of things they learned from the Indians."[62] Often, however, the application of hot mud was called for in healing particular illnesses, as several preceding entries from her diary indicate. Again, Rae Spellman provides some insight into this medicinal practice: "Oh, they had their ways of picking the mud. They didn't just use any old mud. It took somebody who knew where the right mud was and then they would put it hot on a person." Another granddaughter, Eudora Clements adds that

> she would get the mud hot in the oven; that's the only way they had of getting it hot and then put it on the person who was ill. She [Mary Fowler] felt like when people got sick, like with the influenza, there was a lot of poisons in the system and the hot mud would cause them to sweat out those poisons. She used that to treat rheumatism, and you know that heat would make the rheumatism better. And she used it for all sorts of other things, like influenza.[63]

Still another relative, Mary's niece Eula Fackrell Carlson, suggests that "they heated mud on the stove in a pan. They also got liquid mud from hot places in the earth, but you had to have specific knowledge of the places to find it. Then you put the hot mud on, as hot as you could stand it, and let it stay until cold. It was used in localized areas mostly, like on a shoulder. The mud would hold the heat."[64]

As her descendants point out, it was necessary to have knowledge not only about how to administer the hot mud, but also about where to find it. That kind of esoteric knowledge was often gained either from other Mormon healers or from "the Indians." In Mary Fowler's case it was probably from both sources. The *Emery County Progress* for Saturday, November 30, 1901, states in a report from the town of Huntington: "Frank Otterstrom, a young man living about a mile below here on the river has been quite sick for a few days. Dr. West, our 'mud doctor' has been attending him of late. He is reported better."[65] Although this is the only reference to Dr. West I've been able to find, his presence in the community is suggestive of the fact that others were practicing this particular method of healing, and certainly knew the location of the appropriate kinds of mud to employ.

Mary Susannah Fowler's interest in and concern for the natural world was not limited simply to the collection of herbs and mud for medicinal purposes. The kind of metaphoric relationship between her own personal identity and the natural world plays itself out again and again in her diary, in the reminiscences of her children, grandchildren, and community members, and in her poetry. One of the most intriguing of her interests involves the study of the stars. Her son Fred Fowler's recollections of his mother's interest in astronomy reveals that

> for this hobby she had to have company because all her life she had a certain dread of the dark. And so the interest of her husband was stimulated. The writer has a vivid recollection of the times when his parents' bed was made on top of the haystack or on the straw-covered shed over the stables where an unobstructed view was to be had and the stars could be studied during waking hours.[66]

Fred Fowler also indicates that his mother subscribed to sky maps so that she could follow the changing patterns of the constellations. As he suggests, "An intense imaginative interest in the stars was easily aroused in one of the make-up of Mary Fowler whose religious beliefs conceived God to be the creator of many universes, and whose design it is to help His spirit offspring to progress through mortal and immortal experience into eternal creatorship and godhood."[67] In other words, Mary's interest in the stars was not simply a "hobby" that she took up in her spare time, but it was directly connected to her religious belief system; understanding the movements of celestial bodies gave her greater understanding of herself and her place in the divine scheme. According to Mormon belief,

> In reality the greatest astronomers of all time lived in the early ages of the earth and received their knowledge by revelation from the Creator, Maker, and Organizer of all things. . . . But, as far as our records reveal, Abraham stands pre-eminent as the greatest astronomer of all ages. He saw, recorded, and taught the truths relative to the creation of the earth; of the movements and relationships of the sun, moon, and stars; and of the positions and revolutions of the various spheres in the sidereal heavens. . . . When the Lord comes again, he will reveal all things . . . then the perfect knowledge of astronomy will be had again, and the faithful will know all things about all the creations of him who is omnipotent.[68]

In aligning herself with Abraham in his great study of astronomy, Mary Fowler extends her own fascination with the natural world into the spiritual realm. According to Mormon belief, articulated in the Book of Mormon itself,

> This earth was not the first of the Lord's creations. An infinite number of worlds have come rolling into existence at his command. Each is an earth; many are inhabited with his spirit children; each abides the particular law given to it; and each will play its part in the redemption, salvation, and exaltation of that infinite host of the children of an Almighty God.[69]

Mary's desire to know more about the stars, her study of the celestial patternings from her shed-top bed, is a sign not only of her interest in nature, but of her fascination in learning the ways in which the natural world continually reveals more about the eternal.

By drawing her husband Henry Ammon into her astronomical endeavors, Mary Fowler is also once more acting the mediatrix. As Ammon hoists the bed up on top of the stable's shed to provide a viewing spot for their celestial explorations, Mary is able to draw him into her intimate relationship with the natural world. Just as the stars are patterned, so too is the couple's repeated exploration of the wonders of nature together, usually encouraged by Mary's energetic attention to the possibilities of bringing the powers of nature into the human cultural community. Henry Ammon's own missionary journal reveals just what an influence his wife had had on his own sensibilities. Sprinkled throughout the listings of proselytizing visits and notations of miles traveled are rich descriptions of Henry's growing delight in nature, and his own attempts to capture some of its wonder to send back home to his family in Utah. On April 2, 1901, Henry notes that "I got a small Box to put some shells and seeds in to send Home." Just a month later his attempts to capture Oklahoma's natural world and send it to Utah became even more daring as the following entries suggest:

> [May 30, 1901] thought of sending tortois home, but too expensive
> [June 6, 1901] After breakfast I boxed up the Tarapin in a Sardine Box and took it to the P.O. it took 16¢ postage. I hope it arrives at Home alive.
> [June 26, 1901] I got letters from the Office and one from Home with the news that all are well and the tortois reached there in safety and alive too Fred calls it a Tito bless his little heart I would like to see him perform over it.[70]

Henry's explorations of the natural world and his desire to share them with Mary continue. On July 7, he writes "I went to the creek nearby and gathered some pretty ferns to send home in my letters." And on July 26, "I got a small box from the store and Boxed up all the shells pebbles and little curiose I had gathered in the passed 4 months and mailed them Home The box weighed 8 oz and it cost 5¢ postage." While there is one entry noting that he mailed some shells to his second wife, Eliza (August 11, 1901: "I boxed up a pair of mussle shells to send to Eliza and wrote a letter"), it is clear that most of his collection of "curiose" was sent to Mary, a physical representation of the ways in which their relationship with the natural world brought the couple closer together across the miles. In this case, we find a kind of reversal of the mediation suggested above: while Mary is usually the mediating force drawing together and creating a kind of resolution between two (or more) different positions, here elements of the natural world are used as a medium of exchange, bringing together the two individuals whose lives have been separated in the cause of religious duty. The idea of mediation, then, becomes necessarily complicated in ways which reveal that far from being arbitrary, the mediation process is manipulable, elastic, capable of having the related terms shift to encompass ever creative possibilities.

In similar ways, Mary's own love of flowers and fruits, her embracing of the natural world within her own domestic sphere, is extended as she works to bring that world even more abundantly within the cultural spaces of her community. The intensity of Mary's connection with nature is best described perhaps by her friend, Elizabeth Brockbank: "Her love of flowers stands out very vivid in my mind. The ability to make them grow gave her a great deal of pleasure. She loved to dig among them. Every flower and shrub knew her and put every effort to grow for her. If flowers had a language she surely understood it."[71] As Mrs. Brockbank writes this tribute to her friend, she metaphorically replicates the kind of relationship Mary Fowler sought to have with the natural world; the ability to communicate and to make this world of nature comprehensible to others was as much a part of her role as healer as the specific herbs she fashioned into pills. Mrs. Brockbank adds that "every young person, old person, or little child that called on her must have a hand full of flowers and perhaps some seeds or plants to take home. She was very generous with them and many a flower garden in Huntington today has something that Sister Fowler has contributed." In this way, then, Mary Susannah integrated her visitors (the world of community and social responsibilities) with the order and beauty of the natural world that consistently supplied her with the remedies she used to keep those visitors in good health, or to restore them when they became ill or injured. The Relief Society minutes for the spring of 1914 support Mrs. Brockbank's observations: On April 16, 1914, a "talk on Home Gardening [was given] by Mary S. Fowler"; On May 21, 1914, "Sister Mary Fowler gave a talk on planting flowers"; and on July 16, 1914, "Mary S. Fowler gave receipts for canning Fruits and vegetables." In speaking of the importance of flowers, fruits, and vegetables to her sisters in the Relief Society, Mary Fowler again extends the understanding of nature beyond her immediate home, reaching out to her community, offering them the kinds of connections she has found so significant. It is this same connection I experienced for myself when visiting Mary Fowler's grandson Milton Roper in Huntington; he suggested that his granddaughter offer me carrots that she had just harvested from Mary's own garden.

In all of these ways, then, Mary Susannah Fackrell Fowler acts as both a nurturer and mediator within the community in which she practices traditional healing. Her own words, the words of family members and friends, and the cultural and historical background into which their words fit, suggest the powerful ways in which this woman healer establishes within the pages of her diary the presentation of a very particular kind of self, a self whose unifying, substance-giving theme may be seen as interconnectedness. It is precisely this theme that also becomes articulated in the variety of other discourses that seek to represent Mary Fowler, to construct her identity by focusing on recurrent motifs that each individual speaker or writer has independently identified as central to his or her conception of the "Mary I knew." The thematic focus on interconnectedness, whether in the act of nurturance or the act of mediating cultural oppositions suggests that this woman healer (and those who knew her) envisions her life as a continual process of establishing and reestablishing connections, and through these interconnections bringing the world into balance—for herself, her family, her church, and her community.

4

"We Knew 'Twould Entertain Us"
Literacy within a Community Context

> We'd not much reading matter
> none else with whom to chat
> & we knew 'twould entertain us
> & so we re read that.
> I don't mean that I read it
> you read to me you know
> while I cut out my patch work
> & you rested from shoveling snow.

One of the primary ways that Mary Susannah Fowler chooses to engage in the process of connection making is through her acts of writing; and it is through her writing that, at the same time, she continually constructs and reconstructs her own identity. These writings are the only way we have today of encountering the Mary Fowler who lived a hundred years ago *as she presented herself* publicly. So it is through these unmediated essays and poems that the conceptions of community and the value of interconnectedness are most fully realized in Mary's own metaphors of self. In order to better understand the context within which this writing was performed, though, it's necessary for us first to examine her communities' own graphic practices, both from an educational and from an aesthetic perspective.

FACKRELL FAMILY LITERACY

While scholars interested in the development of literacy historically have focused primarily on the formal educational practices of different cultural groups, it is just as important to examine "the cultural force of extracurricular educational practices," as Susan Miller has suggested.[1] For Mary Susannah Fackrell Fowler those extracurricular practices were most frequently found within the contexts of her family and the larger Mormon community. In both cases Mary Fowler was immersed in particular conceptions of the value of words that pervade her own discursive practices. Family stories about Mary's father, David B. Fackrell, consistently portray him as a self-made man of words. Laura Fackrell Chamberlain, Mary's sister, writes:

> David's school conditions were not very good at the time he was home in Vermont. On going to New Orleans at age fifteen, his schooling was very limited only attending a short time. He was very quick in learning and learned a lot from his favorite book, Webster's Dictionary. He was always adding new words to his already vast vocabulary and never was puzzled in spelling or giving a definition of any word. He gained under difficulties a fine practical education.[2]

Fred Fowler echoes those comments and adds: "Mary's father, although he had but a few weeks of formal schooling, was known as an authority on spelling and punctuation. During the years of his wandering he had evidently found much interest in reading."[3] When I discussed the nature and extent of the Fackrells' educational experiences with Lois Worlton, a great-granddaughter of David and Susannah Fackrell, she said,

> I think this was a very bright family. . . . So far as I can tell David Bancroft had only three years or maybe less of schooling, but one of his favorite possessions was a dictionary. And he carried this dictionary with him where ever he went, studied out of the dictionary. He was an expert speller. And he knew how to pronounce words.[4]

This interest in language apparently suffused David B. Fackrell's entire life. As Netty P. Fackrell notes, "David had 20 children and named them for the letters of the alphabet with their mother's maiden name for a second name."[5] Seemingly fascinated with the beauty of letters themselves, David selected his children's names beginning sequentially with the letters A through T! For someone with this kind of devotion to language, a formal education was simply not necessary.

In describing the source of Mary Fackrell's interest in writing, Lois Worlton went on to point out that Mary's mother, Susannah, was also self-educated, and that as a schoolteacher in Orderville she educated others as well: "that's one reason that these kids were so well educated, was because both their parents were. And I think they probably spent a lot of time teaching their children."[6]

Much of that teaching was accomplished through simply reading to their children:

> It is worthy of note that in the starkly limited home of her parents which started as a single log room with dirt floor and dirt roof, and with open fireplace and built in bunk bed, there were some books. Susannah loved

to read novels, an activity then frowned upon by church leaders; and Mary's father continued his interest in reading—an interest picked up during the days of his wandering.[7]

Although Susannah's experience of having her baby drown after she was distracted by reading with her women friends certainly attenuated her own practice of reading,[8] nonetheless "books were known in the home and book learning was respected."[9] Laura Fackrell Chamberlain recalls, "I was sent to school when I was five years old and learned to read. I liked so much to hear someone read or to read myself. My father would read to us in the evenings. When we could get stories I surely loved to hear them."[10] In these evening reading sessions, David Fackrell first introduced his children to literacy as social practice, an understanding that would underlie Mary Fackrell Fowler's own conception of herself as a literate woman for the rest of her life.

The Fackrell children, then, were taught the real joys of experimenting with language, of reading and writing, primarily by example. David Bancroft Fackrell's own self-taught writing abilities were displayed not only in letters to his family but also more publicly in published form. One of the few written reports detailing the progress of the Orderville community was provided by a letter David B. Fackrell wrote to the *Deseret News* in the early months of the United Order's settlement in southern Utah. This letter is still widely quoted in almost every study of this early Orderville experiment in communal living. The model of literate parents who had developed their talents as readers and writers *on their own* with little recourse to formal institutionalized education provided Mary Susannah Fackrell and her siblings with a perspective on the value of language, and also on both the possibility and necessity of the self-development of literacy. One particularly relevant example of the effect of her parents' emphasis on family literacy is Mary Susannah's own dedication to learning the Braille system as an adult in order to teach her sister Bertha, blind since infancy, the joys of reading and writing. As a 55-year-old mother and grandmother, Mary ordered the newly available Braille materials, taught herself the system, and invited her sister to come to Huntington and live with her for several months so that Bertha could finally learn to read. (See photograph, page 108)

THE ORDERVILLE COMMUNITY AND THE DEVELOPMENT OF LITERACY

Fortunately for the Fackrell children, their parents' real fascination with and devotion to the values of reading and writing were in concert with the Mormon community's strong emphasis on education. Among the first buildings constructed in Orderville was the schoolhouse. And unlike many

Mary Susannah Fackrell Fowler and her sister Bertha Fackrell. Note the Braille book in Bertha's hand, indicating the photo was taken after Mary Susannah had taught her blind sister to read according to the Braille system. Photo courtesy of Virginia Fowler Rogers.

American communities, Orderville, along with other Mormon villages and cities, valued education equally for both genders.[11] In fact, Joseph F. Smith had early on spoken about the "importance of the higher education and superior knowledge women should attain."[12]

Within the larger context of church-authorized attention to the literacy practices of its children, both male and female, the Orderville community sought to offer both institutionally directed and informal opportunities for learning. "Night school was held in a few of the homes. Capable men and women taught the fundamentals of schooling and drilled their students in phonics, spelling, pronunciation and penmanship."[13] Because of the scarcity of paper, slates were used for all written work and spelling matches were extremely popular.[14] In these spelling matches, and in the following description of reading pedagogy, we begin to find another clue to the development of literacy as social practice, not only within the Fackrell family but also within the larger Orderville community:

> For reading, instead of rushing over many pages for an assignment, we were given from five to ten pages and told: "Take your reader home; go into a room by yourself—stand, taking a position as if facing your class, and read the lesson five times aloud."[15]

Even though the students were instructed to "go into a room by yourself," the entire thrust of the assignment was for the students to practice reading aloud to a group of peers. Reading was seen not as a solitary practice, but as a social one in which the intent was to make the text understandable to an audience, albeit an imaginary one. Such an assignment reinforces the understanding of the social implications of literacy; reading becomes a way for knowledge to be shared and negotiated rather than hoarded and commodified. In this way, the particular concept of community practiced in Orderville is itself implicated in understanding the discursive practices of its inhabitants.

This emphasis on communal literacy becomes even more relevant when we read the following description of the grammatical pedagogy of Orderville's school:

> In the beginnings of grammar we were expected to watch for a misuse of words and phrases in and out of school and write down the incorrect use of words or phrases giving the names of persons thus using them; then we were to correct them. It kept us on the alert and furnished us with some good natured rivalry as well as constructive criticism and no little amusement when read in class. Each tried to present the longest list of mistakes. All were watchful not to make the same mistakes twice.[16]

The results of such praxis no doubt involved a tension between the competitive spirit of compiling the longest list of one's peers' mistakes and the cooperative impulse that worked towards the grammatical betterment of the entire community. As that tension played itself out inside the classroom and in other informal interactions, the social implications of literacy were displayed dramatically. In a very real sense, the power of the word—and the word used *correctly*—became a kind of social power, capable of both self-aggrandizement and humor, often at the expense of one's peers.

Another dimension of literacy as social practice can be seen in the informal extracurricular activities of Orderville's youth. For Mary Fowler and her friends, especially her young women friends, reading was a significant part of social activities. As Emma Seegmiller recalls:

> I usually did the reading when we got together in groups. During the Order girls as well as boys went into the fields to pick up potatoes and top beets and carrots. A good story was generally tucked away in my lunch basket. It was as important as the food. While we rested at the noon hour the story was brought out, often a detective story and you are aware how exciting they can be.[17]

The very language of Mrs. Seegmiller's recollection reveals the dialogic nature of the practice of literacy in Orderville. As she addresses her readers directly in the last sentence, reminding them of the excitement of good detective fiction, Mrs. Seegmiller reiterates the social nature of the very act of reading. For Mary Susannah Fackrell and the young people of Orderville, reading, writing, and speaking were all inextricably bound up in their own social identities and in interactions with their peers. In addition, for the women of Orderville, the communitarian life provided opportunities for reading that may have been more difficult to experience in other communities in America; as Emily B. Spencer writes from St. George, Utah—not far from Orderville—in an article for the *Woman's Exponent* in 1876:

> Women in many nations are but the pack-horses of men. Rude, uncivilized and barbarian, men lord it in idleness, while women labor to raise bread for them to eat. Women in civilized countries, of the laboring classes, have had many domestic duties to perform, which to them have generally been pleasant; generally I say, for I believe, as women educate themselves and move in a higher sphere of thought and action, the daily routine of household employments becomes irksome. But in the present state of society, how can they be carried on differently? . . . There is, it seems to me, but one remedy for the women; to unite their labors as the United Order can unite them, and as the Relief Societies have made a beginning, whereby there will be more time for intellectual improvement, than can be now taken in the majority of the households. I often hear the remark, "I really do not find time to read," and I have sometimes felt as if domestic duties were so urgent, in my own case, that I have to

forego the pleasure of reading and writing, although every odd moment is spent on one of those pursuits. . . . The every day practical duties of life should not be discarded, but every girl should be taught to perform them with ability, while at the same time they should not be the whole work of this existence. The dawning of a future era for women is lighting up the world, and women will rejoice to be emancipated from many cares that now hinder increased usefulness.[18]

Emily Spencer looks to the United Order to provide the time necessary for women to become emancipated from drudgery and sees their "increased usefulness" to lie not in homemaking chores, but in "reading and writing." The belief that the practice of polygamy allowed women greater freedom to develop themselves intellectually was widely espoused as a reason for polygamy to be considered a feminist cause by women in Utah. Emmeline B. Wells, for example, provides a typical statement of this position: "[Polygamy] gives women the highest opportunities for self-development, exercise of judgment, and arouses latent faculties, making them more truly cultivated in the actual realities of life, more independent in thought and mind, noble and unselfish."[19] To have their own lifestyle spoken of in terms of possibly providing a panacea to overworked women the world over offered inspiration to the female members of the United Order in southern Utah; it also provided renewed affirmation of their literacy practices and aspirations. By working together and sharing household duties, the women of Orderville created a social order that interestingly supported and encouraged a socially constructed literacy.

The very isolation and poverty of the Orderville community also contributed to this understanding of literacy as social practice. Because of an often dire financial situation, reading material was scarce:

Much reading was done, even though the reading material was limited. The Order took twelve newspapers which were passed from one family to another so they could all share them. It was the same with books; each one had the privilege of reading all that were available in the community.[20]

The Bible and standard church works, copies of Shakespeare's plays, and the writings of Dickens or Scott were among the few available books in Orderville.[21] But perhaps of even more importance to the community were the newspapers alluded to above. The *Deseret News*, Salt Lake City's premier newspaper, provided a link to the wider Mormon community and to the world; however, it was the church-published magazines designed for the guidance of its members that were most eagerly anticipated:

Even though money was extremely scarce, the Deseret News . . . and these magazines were subscribed for and eagerly read by the people of Orderville.

The following extracts were taken from an old journal found among the Ward Records:

"March 24, 1875—Wrote to Salt Lake City to see if we could get twelve copies Deseret News, thirteen copies Juvenile Instructor, and six copies Woman's Exponent and pay for them on the Temple or Tithing Office in St. George or at Washington Factory.

"April 14—Thirteen copies of Juvenile Instructor came today with the back numbers sent for. Want pay on Caanan Co-op herd or 20% discount on Washington Factory or Tithing Office orders.

"May 13—Sent a letter to Deseret News with $1.80 for postage on 12 copies of News, promising to get tithing order from St. George for subscriptions on same and forward it.

"July 23—Went to St. George Got receipts for $42.00 for Deseret News and $32.50 for Juvenile Instructor.

"August 22—Board meeting held at 5 P.M. $2.00 appropriated for two copies Woman's Exponent for six months."[22]

For an economically struggling community such as Orderville, these subscriptions quite obviously put a strain on the town coffers; however, the commitment of the Ordervillians to both literacy and knowledge of their church made such an investment of resources absolutely necessary.

The *Woman's Exponent* and the Development of a Writer

The effect such publications had on the development of Mary Fowler's own sense of herself as a woman of words cannot be overestimated. Certainly, the *Woman's Exponent*, which she read from childhood until its demise in 1914, was the most consistently influential reading material for her. First published in 1872, the *Woman's Exponent* was truly the voice of Mormon women, linking them to other women nationwide. Purporting to offer an "almost complete history of woman's work in Utah and matters pertaining thereto," the *Exponent* also connected the efforts of Utah women in the areas of suffrage, for example, with those of their sisters in other parts of the United States. The newspaper itself was a symbol of the independence and productiveness of Mormon women; in 1893 an article on women journalists in the *Exponent* claimed that it was one of only three papers west of the Mississippi River that was "edited and published entirely by women," including women typesetters. The *Young Woman's Journal*, which began publication in 1889, provided opportunities for women across the Mormon West to publish their own writings, and it offered literary advice as well. Writing about clubwomen across the United States, Anne Ruggles Gere points out:

The creation of centralized publications helped formalize the circulation of texts. . . . Both the *Young Woman's Journal* and *Woman's Exponent* enabled Mormon clubwomen to participate in textual exchanges that embraced their religious sphere but also extended beyond it. Although associated with the Relief Society and a reporter of its activities, the *Exponent* remained an independent woman-directed enterprise support-ed by subscriptions. Similarly, the *Journal's* close affiliation with the Young Ladies' Mutual Improvement Association did not, particularly under Susa Young Gates's editorship, preclude its including a wide range of club matters. both the *Exponent* and the *Journal* published frequent references to the activities of General Federation clubwomen in other parts of the country . . . as well as mention of being cited or "kindly spoken of" in General Federation journals.[23]

These women's journals, then, allowed the young Mary Fowler to enter into an even larger community of women than the ones she encoun-tered in first Orderville and then Huntington. By providing a vital link between women in Orderville, Huntington, and other somewhat isolated Utah towns and villages, the *Young Woman's Journal* and the *Woman's Exponent* expanded both the knowledge base and the social interactions of these women, even if those interactions were primarily via the medium of print. Literacy as social practice extended the networks of female resources in new ways, and for a woman like Mary Fowler, one of the most signifi-cant extensions was exposure to a wide range of women's writing and to discussions about the very act of writing itself. The *Young Woman's Journal* included long articles about canonized writers—Shakespeare, Milton, and Chaucer, for example, while the *Woman's Exponent* advised readers of rec-ommended books and articles considered both "excellent and useful" and "practical, moral and intellectual . . . written by such women as Lilian Whiting, Martha D. Lincoln, Maria Louise Poole, Mary E. Watkins, Fannie Fern, Bernice Harraden, and Sarah Grand."[24] At the same time that it made women writers the focus of interest, the *Exponent* sought to place these writers within the context of "books that can never . . . be surpassed. . . . the Bible, Book of Mormon, the Iliad, the Odyssey, Shakespeare, and Milton,"[25] thus, as Anne Gere points out, "borrow[ing] status through asso-ciation and expand[ing] the terms of culture."[26] This expansion also extended to an inclusion of poetry and essays by the finest Mormon women authors of the day: Eliza R. Snow, Emmeline B. Wells, Emily Woodmansee, Hannah King, and Hannah Cornaby, for example. In the work of these women writers Mary Fowler found exemplary poetry that she often chose to read aloud in Relief Society meetings, thereby sharing not only the value-laden content but also the formal features of the work itself.

Huntington Relief Society building that Mary Susannah worked so hard to fund during her time as Relief Society Counselor. Photo used by permission, Utah State Historical Society.

These writings, shared within the close context of Relief Society and MIA meetings, helped to create a community folk aesthetic that would continue to shape the verse written by Mary and her women friends in southern Utah. However, the women's writing recited in association meetings was not confined to Mormon poetry and prose. Both the *Exponent* and the *Young Woman's Journal* published writings by and about such prominent literary figures as George Eliot, Harriet Beecher Stowe, Louisa M. Alcott, Elizabeth Barrett Browning, Margaret Fuller, Elizabeth Wilcox, Anne Bradstreet, and Phillis Wheatley. These publications often ran articles or "notices" about the current work of women authors; for example, in the July 1, 1878, edition of the *Exponent*, a notice informed the readership that George Eliot was at work on a new book. Such communication placed the women of central and southern Utah, as isolated as they were, in contact with the pulse of literary developments, especially among women in America. It gave them the sense of belonging to a community of women writing. In addition, the *Journal* also regularly included more expansive articles on women's literary productions. In 1899, for example, the paper published articles entitled "Women's Literary Renaissance" and "Women in 18th Century Literature."

Most importantly, perhaps, these women's newspapers placed the literary efforts of the Mormon women of Utah distinctly within the circle of significant literary productions. Utah women were not marginalized by articles such as those referred to above, but rather they were drawn into conversation with the larger literary community of women. This was accomplished through the rhetoric of the editors. In May of 1893, Mrs. May Booth Talmage delivered an address at the World's Congress of Women in Chicago, Illinois, on the importance of literature and art in Utah. Intended to acquaint and impress those outside the territory with the intellectual and aesthetic sophistication of the women of Utah, the address was reprinted in the *Young Woman's Journal* the following year with a somewhat different rhetorical intent. In this case, the article was an encouragement to women writers of the Mormon West, and a reminder of the obstacles they had overcome to keep literature alive and flourishing during the pioneer period:

> In order that a correct estimate may be formed in regard to the facts which are to be presented, let me first remind you, that although nearly half a century has passed since the pioneers first entered the valleys of Utah, during many of those years the people were almost entirely excluded from the advantages possessed by the great world outside. Had not the roots of a strong, pure love for that which forms the beautiful in our lives been implanted in hearts determined to protect and foster them under all conditions, they must certainly have been crushed and blighted

beyond restoration by the stern hardships and chilling blasts of the life endured by our pioneers.[27]

An evaluation of the literary production of Utah women follows a discussion of art:

> Standing beside, and sharing the honors almost equally with music, is literature. The works of our prose writers teem with lofty ideas and noble sentiments, such as careful mothers can with safety and pleasure place in the hands of their daughters.
>
> 'Tis true the poems of our local writers are what might be termed sweet songs of the heart rather than the effusions of erudite brains, but for that reason they are more deeply appreciated. Within the pages of their representative paper, the Young Woman's Journal, edited by one of their number, our women and girls are encouraged to their best efforts in either branch of literature . . . and thus it is that in Utah, once so barren and desolate that a fortune was offered for the first bushel of grain that could be raised there, Literature and Art have lent their refining influences, have shed a halo of intelligent light upon the rugged cliffs and verdant valleys of our Mountain Home, and have greatly assisted in transforming the once barren desert into a veritable garden of roses.[28]

However measured this account of the intellectual dimensions of the literary production of Mormon women might be, it nonetheless highlights the position of women in "making the desert bloom like a rose" by preserving and producing literature of such nobility and sweetness that it was capable of transforming the environment in which they were obliged to live. And not surprisingly, the rhetoric of the desert-blooming rose metaphor was taken directly from both the Book of Mormon and the Old Testament, Isaiah 35:1, emphasizing again the connection between spiritual and intellectual literacy.

A year later in the first of a series of articles entitled "Journalism for Young Women" published in the *Journal,* Walter M. Wolfe provides even more effusive encouragement for women writers in Utah by placing their efforts within a larger historical and geographical context. Wolfe begins his discussion by framing his advice to young women writers with a historical look at the place of women in literature:

> From the days of Sappho, woman has had a conspicuous place in the world's literature. Long before the age of the Grecian poetess, the song of Miriam rang across the waters of the Red Sea, and the hymns of Deborah led the armies of Israel to victory. And yet woman's sphere has been circumscribed. Her poetic nature and finer sentiments were allowed to find expression in rhyme and rhythm, but in no other corner of the vast field of literature was she permitted to gather the laurels that were bestowed on her more favored brothers. When a woman of marked genius burst

forth upon the ancient world, she had either to court the odium that to this day attaches itself to the brilliant Aspasia, or else to endure the martyrdom of the Alexandrian Hypatia.

Today how different? Without laying aside one iota of modesty, dignity or womanliness, the woman of the nineteenth century, freed from the false conventionalisms that have too long bound her, is reigning in all the departments of belles lettre—in poetry, in fiction, in criticism and even in journalism.[29]

By first situating women's literary productivity as originating with biblical figures such as Deborah and Miriam, Wolfe contextualizes the poems, essays, and stories of nineteenth-century Mormon women within the larger framework of these spiritually significant productions. Even more remarkably, the author reassures his female readers that at this great historical moment at the end of the nineteenth century, they are able to attain a literary distinction denied their gender for centuries. However effusive this evaluation of woman's literary potential is, Wolfe is even more encouraging to women like Mary Fowler who live far from the bustling "action" of publishing houses and newspaper presses. For he goes on to suggest that

> it is a significant fact that, so far as woman is concerned, life in large cities is not conducive to the best mental effort. To put the proposition in another form, woman is more susceptible than man to the influence of environment. He can shut himself within four white-washed walls, bolt the door, darken the windows, and force his mind to place itself in precisely opposite conditions. In the smoky, stifling atmosphere of editorial rooms, he can write poetry about babbling brooks and green fields, but such poetry is born without a soul or heart. To a woman such work would be false. She needs more than fact, more than fancy for her creations. She needs inspiration. It is the divine heart that speaks in her. . . .
>
> Mountains and valleys, bounding waves and songs of birds, not the crush of ballrooms and the perfumed lies of an artificial civilization, awaken the dormant seeds of literary creation in woman's breast. They are just as necessary for the perfect ripening of literary fruit.[30]

For Mary Fowler and her sisters in Utah's Dixie, these words must have been tremendously encouraging. While today we might easily read a problematic essentialist and sexist subtext in the quotation above, certainly for these Mormon women the suggestion that their rural location was in fact an enhancement to their literary ambitions would no doubt bolster their own sense of poetic possibility.

Such encouragement couched in these general terms was amplified and made more specific by a range of articles in church publications that provided advice to writers in every genre. As early as 1876 the *Woman's*

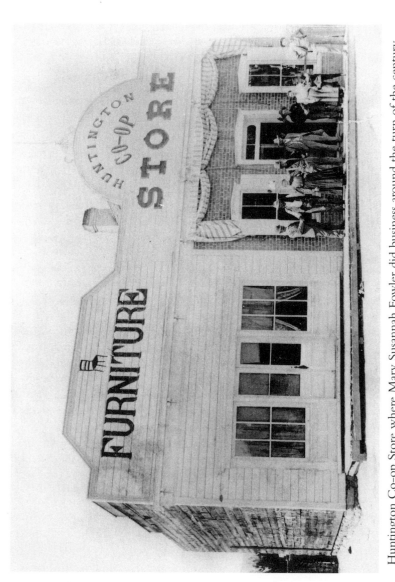

Huntington Co-op Store where Mary Susannah Fowler did business around the turn of the century. Photo used by permission, Utah State Historical Society.

Exponent published an article based on a "recent Woman's Congress" that began with a statement about the progress of women in literature:

> Through all the ages, exceptional women have been poets, historians, and novelists. But if we look back only for thirty years, we will realize that it is only in our own generation that women have obtained a recognized and thoroughly respected position in literature. The term "blue stocking" applied to all women who used the pen, did not lose its sting until a very recent period. And it was more than hinted that such women not only had ink-blacked fingers, uncombed hair, and slipshod feet, but that they must necessarily be neglectful of all recognized womanly duties.
>
> The field of literature is conquered for women. There are no longer bars or obstructions of any sort in the way. A woman who has anything to say, is privileged to say it; if it is worth hearing, the world will lend an attentive ear.[31]

The article then went on to include much more specific advice to women who desired to join the ranks of conquering poetesses and essay writers. For example, the author, E. B. Duffey, advised that

> the professional writer must compel the inspiration, or write without it. A woman who writes for a living must hold herself in readiness at any time and at all times. She must be ready to write upon any subject and in any style. She must send a poem by return mail, if required, or write up a whole geographical division, without previous knowledge of it, and with nothing but a guidebook and a dictionary of dates for references; and yet have her article interesting, and read as if unlimited information was withheld solely for want of space.[32]

Such preparedness inevitably results from adequate training and the article suggests that this training is necessarily based on "experience in life" that gives the woman writer truly "something to say . . . fresh earnest thoughts of her own, that the world will care to hear." Finally, Duffey suggests that the most important question is: "Does she feel an irrepressible desire to write? Can fancied want of time prevent her? Do difficulties of any sort hinder her? Can discouragement daunt her? If so the crown of authorship was never destined to rest upon her brow."[33] Ultimately, then, given adequate experience in life and having something to say that would interest others, it is the writer's unquenchable desire, a "powerful overwhelming impulse to write" that determines real success as an author. For a young woman like Mary Fowler, inspired perhaps by the opening paragraphs of this article to become one of the vanguard of nineteenth-century literary women, such advice offered a way to understand how writing might fit into her otherwise overly full life. In this context, writing was not simply something pleasurable in which to fritter away idle hours, but rather the result of fervent inspiration and undaunted courage to withstand all obstacles to literary fulfillment.

Other articles in both the *Woman's Exponent* and *Young Woman's Journal* focused on specific strategies for accomplishing the task of writing. While Walter Wolfe went on to write a series of articles in the *Journal* giving advice primarily concerning "women's journalism," other authors provided continuing suggestions regarding the process of writing poetry and fiction as well. Lucy Page Stille created her own series of articles for the *Journal* entitled "Helps for Young Writers: Some Concise Lessons in Composition," where she provided specific grammatical and structural advice.[34] Yet perhaps the most specific advice was given by editors interested in providing guidelines for young authors who might wish to publish in the *Exponent*, the *Journal*, or other church publications such as the *Juvenile Instructor* or the *Contributor*. Walter Wolfe himself echoes Stille's "Helps for Young Writers" when he focuses on the process of invention in writing:

> Even though she does not expect to become an authoress, every young lady among the Latter-day Saints has important literary duties to perform. In common with her brothers she will join the Mutual Improvement Association, and, when sufficiently mature, will become responsible for a certain portion of the work of organization and instruction.
>
> In the editing of the monthly paper or the preparing of an article for its pages we should be original. Our mothers before us and our daughters after us write on Virtue, Obedience, Charity and a score of kindred abstractions that have from repetition become most woefully monotonous. When the subject is announced we all know what is to follow, and when the paper is ended a sigh of relief always blends with the congratulatory smile.
>
> In such articles, as well as in testimony, personal experience is desirable, for, you may be assured that nothing said by you will interest others unless it is especially attractive to yourself. It would be a great credit to every daughter of Zion if she could commence her literary work in the Young Ladies' Association, and characterize that work, no matter how humble and unpretentious it might be, with the same enthusiasm and painstaking faithfulness that would characterize it if it were prepared for the *Young Woman's Journal* or the *Juvenile Instructor*.[35]

Thus, Wolfe tailors the comments made more generally by Stille to the concerns of the young Mormon woman author who writes for publication in the local Young Women's Mutual Association newsletter. Mary Susannah Fackrell Fowler must certainly have taken this advice to heart, for she continued to write essays for the Mutual newspapers throughout her life. The topics of such essays included warnings against such sins as evil speaking based on jealousy and anger and exhortations to young women to "honor your parents" and to maintain "originality of character." In an editorial for the first issue of the Huntington YLMIA's *Gem* she edited, Mary Fowler describes the mission on earth of her sisters as making themselves fit "to go back to His presence." Lest such writing fall into the pattern described by Wolfe as being "woefully monotonous," Mary does rely on personal experience to make her points most effectively and to bring these "abstractions" into a much clearer focus. For example, in the essay entitled "Originality of Character," Mary writes:

> Girls which do you think is the nicer, the honest whole souled girl, who is not ashamed to let her own ideas be known, and to do right merely because she knows it is right, or the one who is always paterning after someone else? In my humble opinion the original girl is far the nicer. It is often necessary for us to change our habbits & manners for better ones; but to me it shows a weakness, when I see a person trying to act or speak or dress like someone else whom she thinks pretty smart. This habit of mimicing even goes as far some times as our eating. Why I have even seen a girl leave the table as hungry as when she sat down, just because she had not the moral courage to eat what she wanted but must act as dainty as any one else at the table. I don't think I should tell you girls who that party was, because I would be heartily ashamed to have you think I was ever that foolish, but may be you have seen persons just like that yourselves. I think we might appear just as beautiful and just as refined without mimicing others at all.[36]

By couching this essay in terms of her own personal experiences, as well as by using dialogic direct address to her readers—the women of Huntington's YLMIA—Mary Fowler legitimized her own knowledge and experience as a kind of authority.[37] This assumption of authority through the voice of the essay also allowed for a kind of self-construction in which the reader learns as much about Mary Fowler as she does about the topic of originality of character. Quite appropriately, the essay form, assuming the authority of the personal, actually enacts what it seeks to convey—the importance of an individual woman's own self-fashioning. Within the context of her close-knit female Mormon community, Mary could experiment not only with the essay form, but with the assumption of authority in writing, as well as with her own self-construction. Taking Walter Wolfe's advice, she structures an essay by combining her own personal experience with an understanding of community values. At the same time, she elucidates and displays those values for other women and demonstrates her own process of growth. If Mary Fowler, the writer and editor, could come to understand her own foolishness in mimicing others, then most certainly others could do so as well.

In another article in his series, Walter Wolfe is even more specific about the invention process and the structuring of a narrative for publication:

> The story-writers and essayists who have a desire to write for the Young Woman's Journal, the Juvenile, the Contributor, or the News will find it helpful to "block out" a story in mind. Carry a notebook and jot down that which may afterwards become material for introduction or theme. Then, when the idea is clear, construct the skeleton. This will occupy your leisure moments for a month. The first attempt should be short, 1,500 to 3,000 words. In all details, make haste slowly. There is no golden road to success, but patience and perseverence will conquer all obstacles.[38]

Throughout Mary Fowler's journals, notebooks, and loose scraps of paper preserved by her grandchildren, she attempts to follow Wolfe's advice. At one point, she made notes in a fairly haphazard way for the essay she would compose and then deliver in a Relief Society meeting. In other places, we find jottings that indicate the development of an idea that is at first quite loosely conceived. Following the advice of a writer for the *Juvenile Instructor*, Mary even made lists of topics to be covered in letters to her husband while he was on his mission, checking off or marking through each topic as she completed writing the letters. As the *Instructor* pointed out,

> Foolish correspondence is a very useless thing, but good, sensible letters are always welcomed, and are very improving to the writer. It is a nice plan to note before hand the heads of the points you wish to take up on a scrap of paper. Then you are not so apt to forget things you wish to mention. When you have them put down, run along the lines and number them in the order you would like to mention them in your letter. This will help you to write in an orderly manner, and make your letter more pleasant reading. . . . Practice makes perfect in any line of business, and ease and grace in composition is of slow growth, and comes of great patience and much practice.[39]

Mary Fowler obviously took this advice to heart, and continued to practice moving towards the ease and grace of an accomplished writer. Her conception of herself was certainly bound up in this movement.

Primarily, though, Mary Fowler considered her writing talents to lie in the tradition of poetry, and the authors and editors of the church-sponsored journals also provided suggestions about the writing process involved in producing poetry. In a letter to a young female author desiring to be given guidelines for writing poetry, "Aretta," an obvious pen name assumed for a column in the *Young Woman's Journal*, suggests that the young woman should engage in the process of invention not according to a set schedule, but rather that she should "write when you feel so prompted, and do not always wait for time. When time comes spirit and desire may be gone." She goes on to say, though, that the beginning writer should "not be in a hurry to see your poems in print lest you may sometime wish, as others have done, to recall them when it is too late. When you are older and have studied more you will better understand why I say this."[40] This advice is echoed by an article in the *Juvenile Instructor*, "For Young Writers": "Write always the best you can, and lay away your productions carefully. If six months afterwards they seem as good to you as at first, send them to the printer, and see what he thinks of them."[41] This author also suggests that if the piece of writing is declined by the publisher, this may be even better than acceptance, because it will spur the young writer on to "fresh effort" and "more patient, faithful labor."

Occasionally, the editors provide even more direct suggestions for contributions to their magazines. In 1893, under the headline "Writers Attention," Susa Young Gates, the well-known *Journal* editor, is quite forceful in her directness:

> There is one word I want to say to every one of the contributors of the Journal. It is this: Please do not send me personal poetry. That is, verses written to Brother So and So, unless they be extra good or there be some principle or story in the lines. The public at large don't care whether Brother So and So went on a mission regretted by all who knew him or not. If you have some lesson to teach, some principle to evolve through your personal addresses in verse, then send them along. Again, I must from now on make it a standing rule to all contributors, that only such matter as is written especially for the Journal can be paid for. No matter whether in prose or poetry. I am very often glad to get verses and addresses read before Associations, or at parties, or to individuals. But such matter has served its primary purpose, and it could not be expected that writers should be paid for second-hand matter. It is like a milliner wearing a hat to a public place and then hanging it up in the store for sale. Please, my dear and valued contributors, do not take offense at these words, for it was absolutely necessary to speak them. Write for me just the same, or a great deal more; send me all the excellent addresses and poetry which has been written for this or that purpose. But make me a present of the second-hand matter, and when you want to receive wages for your work, do it first-hand and say so. Put at the top of your contribution the words, "Written for the Young Woman's Journal," if it is so, and you shall be paid in the modest way you have been in the past.[42]

Providing astute rhetorical advice regarding audience expectations and desires, Gates notes that the strictly personal content cannot be judged of interest or concern to general readers. In this discussion, Gates outlines the tension between the individual artistic impulse and community taste. If Mary Fowler had learned from other authors and editors to personalize the essays she composed so as to avoid monotony, from Susa Young Gates she learned to avoid writing poetry that could not expand the personal to the realm of community relevance. Additionally, Gates noted that authors of such writing, as well as of other previously performed pieces of work, would not be remunerated by the magazine. While such a decision was certainly monetarily advantageous to the struggling journal, it also reaffirmed the idea that women writers need be especially attentive to the principle of originality.

We might wonder why so many editors and literary advice givers (as well as individual writers like Mary Fowler) would consistently come back to this issue of originality. In this particular literate community of Mormon Utah, the fact that so much of the writing produced focused on gospel principles as they were to be worked out in the daily spiritual lives of the faithful contributed to the possibility of overworking familiar spiritual mandates and values to the point of tedium. This is a very real example of the tension between the conservative and the innovative at work in the folk aesthetic. What is particularly interesting here is that the folk aesthetic developed by individual Mormon communities across the Utah Territory was consistently informed by the professional poetic and essayist traditions of Mormon authors and editors in Salt Lake City, as well as by the works of nationally and internationally recognized writers published in the church-produced journals. Mary Fowler provides an excellent example of a regional writer at the center of such aesthetic tension, for she portrayed community-held values in a recognizable and aesthetically acceptable form, while also creating verse compelling enough to be published in journals originating in Salt Lake City. The constant interplay of a local aesthetic with more global considerations frames Mary Fowler's discursive practices in both prose and poetry.

THE LADIES LITERARY CLUB OF HUNTINGTON

Nowhere, perhaps, was the working out of this tension more noticeable than in the brief history of the Ladies Literary Club of Huntington. Through the readings selected by members of the group, the women of the community entered into a discussion of works that constantly drew their own folk aesthetic into dialogue with the literary aesthetic of the larger world. While this particular association was certainly not as long-lived as its sister clubs in Salt Lake, Huntington's club, under Mary Fowler's direction, exemplified the dialogic nature of literacy among the women of south-central Utah. Through ongoing discussions of selected pieces of literature and through the sponsorship of dramatic performances, Huntington's club allowed the women to begin to articulate the various possibilities available in aesthetic choices.

Certainly such choices were not made in a vacuum. The same journals that provided advice to young women writing for the Mutual publications cited above also frequently printed articles detailing the meetings of a number of women's literary clubs in Salt Lake City and Provo. Often these notices indicated the range of books discussed and the sentiments expressed by members of the club. In February of 1891, the *Young Woman's Journal* published an article on "A Successful Woman's Club" that detailed the Ladies Library Association of Kalamazoo, Michigan, the "oldest literary society for women in America,"[43] thus extending an understanding of the working of other clubs to those outside Utah.

Along with notices concerning literary club meetings around Utah, both the *Exponent* and the *Journal* gave advice concerning appropriate reading material, advice clearly taken to heart by Mary Fowler's reading group. Articles entitled "Acquisition and Use of Words," "In the Home: Books to Read," "Don't Read Trash" and "What Shall the Latter Day Saints Read?"[44] all set parameters for the maintenance of a wholesome intellectual life. In Utah, as in other parts of the United States, the question of whether novel reading was indeed "wholesome" became a hotly debated issue.[45] On the national scene, Catharine Beecher claimed that "fictitious narrative" made "vice and crime alluring," transmitted a false view of life, and persuaded readers to "abandon duty in search of unrealistic dreams."[46] For Susa Young Gates the issue was not a clear-cut one; under the "Editor's Department" headline in the *Young Woman's Journal*, she notes:

> There is so much harm arising from this habit of novel-reading that one is often tempted to cut the matter short, especially if such a person be lazy and disinclined to go into the merits of a case, that one feels sometimes like saying, "Oh, novel-reading is bad, and young people ought not to read them at all!" This will not suffice for me, however, for I have found in my experience, both with myself and with the many young people who come under my care and advice, that it is much better to tell them the whole truth, and to make them intelligent observers and actors than it is to attempt arbitrary measures with them.
>
> The fact of the matter is, that so far as I am personally concerned, I have read so many novels, and having been just as much benefited as I have been harmed by them, I have therefore studied into the causes of good and evil concerning novels. The whole thing is capable of being reduced to some sort of a science, and there is a possibility of showing young people the good and the bad in this as in almost any other recreation. . . . There are as certain laws that underlie the influence of novels upon the human mind, as the laws of medicine or diet. If you eat certain kinds of food they will produce certain effects upon the body. Just as surely, if you read certain kinds of books your mind will be affected in a

certain way. . . . Still, broadly speaking, proper mental food will make a
man full of good and truthful thoughts.

There is so much harm done by these trashy novels. It makes me
shudder to think what some of the daughters of Zion read.[47]

Several paragraphs later we come to a description of just what a
trashy novel consists of, in Gates's estimation, and then what other options
the novel reader has in making choices:

... she spoke only of lords and ladies, of rich and refined people, and she
always gave the impression that the only happiness on earth would be in
finding an English lord, with a handsome face, a sinful past, which he always
gives up solely and wholly because of the heroine, who is always pretty and
winning, and then some way they marry and live happy ever after.

Such stuff and nonsense. If girls would read such books as Walter
Scott's novels, Miss Muloch's, Charles Kingsley's, George Eliot's,
Thackery's and in short read only those which have a pure and intelli-
gent tone, they would not have such silly ideas about love and marriage
as many of the girls about me do. . . .

Miss Chapin was asked what kind of books were good for girls, and
what they should avoid. She replied, that a book that made you feel as if
you wanted to be better, and to do your life work in a more dignified
and pleasing way was always good. But if, when you arose from the
perusal of a novel, you felt dissatisfied with your life, with your sur-
roundings, and especially with the work you ought to do, you may be
sure such a book is bad, no matter by whom it may be written.

And if you want to keep up with the times, you must read the best
novels, as well as the best histories. I don't know of anything sweeter nor
purer to put into the hands of young girls than the stories of Louisa M.
Alcott.

The girls, however, need not go far into the world for reading matter now. I think our own people are producing some of the purest and
best literature. It may not be polished with the smoothness and elegance
of rhetorical mastery; but it contains nothing that will injure and very
much that will elevate and refine.[48]

Within these few short paragraphs, the essence of what might be
termed a nineteenth-century Mormon aesthetic has been defined. It is an
aesthetic based not primarily on rhetorical elegance or stylistic smoothness,
but rather one grounded firmly in the desire for purity and spiritual refine-
ment. Although the *Journal* and the *Exponent* consistently encouraged the
development of a variety of rhetorical skills in young Mormon women
writers, as illustrated above, the editors and regular contributors also
acclaimed the higher literary good to be one based on the values their
community held dear. Over and over again, discussions of the selection of
books focus on this particular principle; for example:

Here, then, is the test of healthy literature—the book that "hath not the spirit of Christ is none of His." By this test, what books are we called upon to lay aside and disapprove? All trifling and prostituting books should be shunned.

The aim of reading is not to nourish sickly sentiment, to cause men to whine and laugh, but to labor and worship among eternal realities. All books which aim to crush the religious element in man, quench the sense of moral obligation, rupture the tie which connects him to the Eternal, in whatever form they appear, they may come in the garb of philosophy, wit or eloquence, we must repudiate all that do not breathe loyalty and reverence to God.[49]

Within the confines of such guidelines for the selection of texts, Mary Fowler chose readings for her book group. The only reference in her own diary to such a selection is that dated April 3, 1900, in which Mary notes that she "selected sentiments from Byron's poems for Ladies Club." Clearly she is keeping to the prescriptions suggested in the *Journal*. Perhaps an even more revealing diary entry, though, is one referring to her son Arno's selection of reading material: "Arno bought a book 'Stories and Speeches of Lincoln,' refused to buy story of James boys. I feel grateful for his choice."[50] For Mary Fowler, aesthetic considerations primarily based in content rather than stylistics became most significant. Unfortunately, no minutes exist of the meetings of Huntington's Ladies Literary Club, and we aren't able to discover either the ways in which selection of texts were negotiated within the group or whether there was any discussion, for example, of the relationship of style to content in the texts they chose to read. What we do know is that even though there appears to have been little danger of "prostituting" texts being selected by this particular group, the church authorities quite expeditiously forced the disbanding of Huntington's club. Interestingly, it was a visiting church authority from Salt Lake who identified the "danger" such a club might pose to the community, and not the local bishop—who knew the women involved and who had supported the formation of the club as well as its thespian offerings.

In this respect, Mary Fowler and her Mormon sisters in Huntington were not that different from women across the United States who decided to advance their intellectual development by forming literary clubs, a decision that caused immediate and fervent opposition. Immediately after the founding of the New England Women's Club in 1868, for example, the *Boston Transcript* warned its readers: "Homes will be ruined, children neglected, woman is straying from her sphere."[51] And in Utah, even women who belonged to literary clubs themselves cautioned about the ill effects such clubs could potentially bring.

At least two years before the organization of Huntington's literary club under Mary Fowler's direction, the *Young Woman's Journal* published a discussion of club life across the country, and specifically in Utah, that might certainly have served as both an impetus and a warning for the founding of local societies throughout the new state. In her column "With the Editor," Susa Young Gates paid homage to the club movement, but warned that club life should not detract from a woman's responsibilities to her own religious organizations:

> Of all the movements which characterize this latter half of the nineteenth century, there is none more portentious and interesting to the student of sociology than the association of women in clubs, societies and conventions. . . . Many of our girls, who have some chances of education, as soon as they have tasted the sweets of knowledge, are wild with the intoxicating delight, and they forthwith vote meetings a bore, their Mutual Improvement Association slow and insipid and nothing short of Browning Readings and Longfellow Clubs will feed their highly intellectual cravings.[52]

Expressing the same concerns about literary clubs as Catharine Beecher had voiced concerning novel reading, Susa Young Gates cautions Mormon women that to participate in study clubs to the detriment of maintaining active membership in LDS women's organizations was not to be tolerated. Perhaps this warning, along with the decline in membership in women's organizations churchwide, contributed to the disbanding of Huntington's literary club two years later.[53]

Whatever the real combination of reasons for its dissolution, the brief life of Huntington's Ladies Literary Club did provide Mary Susannah Fowler with the opportunity to try out her own aesthetic criteria in the selection of texts for the group she had organized. Grounded in her early reading of canonical texts, in the advice of journals produced by fellow women members of her church, and in a belief that "what is spiritual good is what is truly beautiful," Mary Fowler not only chose material to be read and discussed in her reading group, but also continued to develop her own community-based folk aesthetic, an aesthetic that informed her own writing throughout her life.

5

"I Love Thee, My Muse"
Folk Poetry and the Construction of Identity

My true friend & helper, tis such I would choose
To call thee, & own that I love thee, my muse.

The community-based aesthetic that informed Mary Fowler's own writing throughout her life is precisely what distinguishes "folk poetry" from other kinds of literary productions: it is poetry written for a close community of peers and deeply rooted in the concerns that belong to that community.[1] What makes folk poetry different from "elite" published poetry is precisely the fact that the aesthetics that govern its production are negotiated within the close group in which the poetry is written and shared. While there was a time when folklorists might have considered poetry "folk" only if it were orally produced in the tradition of the Yugoslavian epic singers, for example, we now understand that certain written forms display many of the same characteristics as those epics, and that the similarities lie in the fact that community aesthetics shape the formal articulation of themes relevant specifically to the poet's community. In actuality, such a distinction between folk poetry and elite poetry is not a simple one, especially in nineteenth- or twentieth-century America.

Certainly in Mary Fowler's case, her exposure to the literary productions of the larger literary world outside Orderville and Huntington, Utah, through the newspapers and journals she read complicate such distinctions and blur the boundaries between folk and elite. And while the emphasis here on the ways in which Mary's poetry responded to the aesthetic values and judgments of the people in her community suggests its folk roots, I'm fairly sure that Mary herself was never particularly concerned with which of these categories her work might be considered under. For her, the important thing was to write and perform poetry that articulated common concerns in a manner that both expressed her own beliefs and values and at the same time reinforced her connections to the Mormon community.

Given both Mary Fowler's literacy background and her unswerving belief in a particular kind of Mormon community, it is not surprising—in fact it is particularly appropriate—that she chose to write poetry displaying precisely the kind of interconnectedness she sought in her own life. The over sixty-five examples of Mary Susannah Fowler's poetry still preserved display a remarkable dialogic character that truly exemplifies the very nature of the genre of folk poetry. Not only do her poems draw on the linguistic and poetic conventions of her community—not only do they focus on topics central to the cultural concerns of her family and friends—but the very contexts in which she writes, and the formal features that define her writing, suggest this same intense focus on the importance of interconnections.

FOLK POETRY AND THE EXPRESSION OF COMMUNITY VALUES

In formal terms, the poetry that Mary Fowler wrote was composed in concert with the aesthetic sensibilities of her community. Although this aesthetic is not one that might be judged particularly favorably by many well-educated readers today, it was importantly developed within the particular context of rural Mormon Utah in the late nineteenth and early twentieth centuries. Most of her lines were arranged in stanzas of either iambic tetrameter or iambic pentameter, following the most familiar rhyming patterns available in the popular press in Orderville and Huntington. Drawing on the cultural resources available to her, Mary Fowler created poetry that was grounded in biblical allusion, canonical texts, and contemporary Mormon writing. Following the lead of Mormon women poets like Eliza Roxcy Snow and Susa Young Gates, Mary composed verse that attempted to celebrate conventionality rather than avoid it. Frequently, she read her poetry aloud, so she could appropriately emphasize syllables that sometimes varied slightly from what might be considered accepted meter. In scanning the lines of the entire corpus of her work, it becomes clear that Mary Fowler wrote what might be called a "loose line," one that exhibited a great tolerance for innovative stresses. In addition, she often called upon poetic conventions of contracting words to help the meter along, and frequently the contractions were strikingly original constructions. Yet always the most salient compositional principle seemed to be making her writing both aesthetically pleasing and understandable to her audience of peers.

Interestingly, as I read more and more of Mary's poetry and learned more about her life and the communities in which she lived and wrote, my own poetic aesthetic began to be altered.[2] Poetry that I had judged to be "pretty bad" when I first read it now appeals to me in ways I could never have predicted. Somehow understanding, and in some ways entering into,

Mary's community—albeit from a distance both historical and intellectual—has allowed me to suspend my own culturally produced aesthetic
judgment, if only in the particular context of my construction of Mary
Fowler's life. Perhaps this, too, is a consequence of reciprocal ethnography
that has the power to transcend cultural and historical differences. While I
suspect that not many readers of this book will experience this particular
aesthetic transformation, perhaps contextualizing the writing process here
will help us to better understand the very nature of community-based aesthetics, not only with respect to poetry but in relation to other vernacular
artistic productions as well.[3]

WRITING AS SOCIAL ACTION: COMMISSIONED POETRY

For Mary Fowler, writing poetry was not something to be done in a solip-
sistic, internalized way. Her writing itself was a social act. Like the English
folk poets described by Roger Renwick and the Canadian writers examined by Pauline Greenhill, Mary Fowler wrote poetry that was "intended
to inform, to persuade, to manipulate, or to affirm the relationship of *com-
munitas* with and among significant others."[4] In fact, much of Mary's poetry was composed at the request of others. Although, like most folk poets,
she was not known primarily as a writer, Mary Fowler was nonetheless a
well-known and admired poetess within her community. Frequently she
was asked by her peers to produce poetry for special festive occasions rang-
ing from Relief Society anniversaries, to the visits of church dignitaries, to
the celebration of birthdays and the mourning of the deaths of children.
Mary's poetry was related intimately to the community's ongoing social
life; indeed, it marked and characterized significant moments in the stream
of community events.

Perhaps the most visible social occasions for which Mary Fowler was
charged to provide verse were the anniversary celebrations of the women's
organizations. The poem "Our Mission," written and performed on February
15, 1889, for the Relief Society's anniversary, in many ways marks Mary
Fowler's immediate acceptance by the community of Huntington, which she
had joined just three months earlier. That she was asked to write this poem
after so short a time speaks to Mary's impressive abilities in developing the
interconnectedness she so prized. The first few lines of the poem demonstrate
as well the socially significant stance the genre is capable of articulating:

> Our Mission
>
> Our Mission dear sisters is not far extended
> Tis at home with our families, near home with our friends
> Tis not mongst the nations this is not intended

But yet to vast labors our mission extends
Our sons and our daughters need teaching and training
They need all the care that we mothers can give
To aid them in banishing sin but retaining
Their souls purest freedom by which they may live
Think you 'tis our mission to teach them each fassion
Which babylon sends they must surely take up?
Think you we've no power to hinder the passions
Which if followed will end in old miseries cup?
I will tell you dear sisters the time is here with us
When we must be doing our missions to fill
When we must be grasping the chance ere it leaves us
To keep/save our good name for we can if we will.
What mission more noble more grand or aspiring
Than that which by Father to us has been given
We've the choicest of treasures, those which if desiring
We may see be exalted with power in Heaven.

Instead of reciting the glories of the accomplishments of the Relief Society that she had so recently joined, Mary Fowler takes the opportunity to exhort her sisters to rejoice in the "mission" that exists for them at home, not away in the mission fields of Oklahoma or England. Most significantly, in the very first line of the poem she addresses her Relief Society sisters directly. She formally structures the poem in dialogic terms, drawing her listeners and readers into the intimacy of conversation by the immediacy of direct address. This dialogue is characteristic of Mary Fowler's verse, and it most significantly displays and celebrates the possibilities of poetry to express the interconnections so vital to her experience within this Mormon community. As she questions her sisters about the way they view their mission and responds with her own thoughts on the matter, Mary re-creates a dialogue within formal generic constrictions, articulating her own hortatory position. In this way, the poetic form itself exemplifies that which she is advocating—both in her poetry and in her life.

A year later, when again she is asked to write a poem for the anniversary "by invitation," Mary is clearly more familiar with the community, more a part of its ongoing life. She speaks directly to members of different ages, and refers to community experiences understood by all:

We've met to celebrate the day
When we were organized
As helpers in a noble cause.
This theme we all have prized.
A fitting time for us to meet!
The starting of the year:

It seems to animate the soul
With [line torn and missing]
We love to see you older folks
The merry band that was
Join in the laugh, the song, the dance,
And help to aid the cause.
You've born your burdens long and well.
They have been heavy too!
And as we see you here tonight
We feel, May God bless you!
The middle aged, and younger ones,
How will we love to come;
And mingle in the pleasures here,
Where 't seems so much like home.
'Tis one short year since thus we met
Times seem about the same.
Yet many changes have been wrought
Since we together came.
One year ago friends met with us
Who now are far away.
Who knows but they're with us in thought
Our aniversary day.
Some of our band have left their homes
Opressions yoke to flee
Though loyal people in the cause,
And worthy to be free.
We've met with trials this past year
We meet them all our days
Lifes changes brings us care with joy
The rose brings thorns always
But trials show our real worth
In this our God is good.
We see His ways are always just
when rightly understood.
With all we've blessings every day
we should be thankful for
Tis hard for us to realize
how we dependent are.
Yet if we bravely bear the cross
not choosing which 'twill be,
We'll win the prize and wear the crown
in Heaven where all are free.
I hope I may be pardoned now
for using precious time
For something that is worth no more

> than this my wandering rhyme.
> I'd like to take a noble part,
> I would Indeed I would.
> But now my muse dont serve me well.
> I did the best I could.

Except for the last two four-line stanzas, Mary addresses her sisters directly by age group and at the same time uses the inclusive "we" to describe group experiences. In this way, Mary Fowler's inclusion within the group of Mormon women in Huntington is made even more complete. A little more than a year after her arrival in the community, Mary speaks not only at the invitation of the group but as one of them. The trials and successes of the community are her own, and by using the first person plural she is able to convey this sense of interrelationship most effectively.

However, in the last stanzas Mary assumes her own voice, and the tone of that voice is especially worth noting. After celebrating the collective "we," Mary now reinforces the authority of that collectivity by asking to be "pardoned now/for using precious time /For something that is worth no more /than this my wandering rhyme." In other words, she seeks in these last lines to downplay her own individual creativity and thus focus attention back on the group. Such self-effacement is characteristic of much folk poetry; as Pauline Greenhill suggests, "Folk poets notoriously, even definitionally, attempt to deflect texts away from themselves."[5] In this case, Mary Fowler's disclaimer by means of blaming her "muse," may also have been at the same time a (somewhat) disguised bid for recognition.

The attempt to offer such disclaimers is continued a year later when Mary Fowler again is called upon to produce a poem for the Relief Society anniversary. This poem (which won't be quoted in its entirety) begins:

> Written for the RS aniversary.

> It is with fear and trembling and feeling my weakness
> I stand in your presence dear Sisters/tonight/today
> I have earnestly sought for the aid and assistance
> Of Father to dictate what/e'er I might write/I might write or say

Again, Mary's self-effacing stance suggests that she is herself incapable of creating real poetry, but that, in this case, she will rely on God to dictate the words of her verse. Interestingly, this poem, copied into "Mary Fowler's 2nd Book of Origanal and Selected Pieces," is written in a manner that indicates two possible versions. If the poem were to be performed during the day, it would be read one way; if it were to be recited at night, the alternate version would be used. This emphasis on the performative aspect of this poetry cues us to the fact that self-deprecation is far more understandable in a verse spoken before one's peers than in a poem published in written form. In this case, Mary Fowler assumes responsibility to her audience for both the authorship and the performance of the poem. Both poet and poem are judged by the aesthetic standards of the community during such a performance. This is not simply a gender-specific disavowal of poetic worth, but more, perhaps, a kind of hedging against too demanding an aesthetic critique. Or, alternatively, the disclaimers might be offered ironically, since she is aware of her own poetic capabilities and knows her audience will react positively to them. In all probability, the lines of disclaimer were written and performed for a number of different reasons. Most importantly, though, by offering those disavowals Mary expresses the same humility she continually calls for in her poetry, a humility especially prized by this community of women.

Whatever the complexity of reasons for the disclaimers almost always included in Mary Fowler's publicly performed poetry, it is clear that the preponderance of the symbolic weight of these poems lies directly upon descriptions of events and topics of community concern. In drawing attention away from herself as poet and towards community-focused topics, Mary's use of direct address is particularly effective.

The same strategy of employing direct address that so effectively involves the listener or reader in the Relief Society anniversary poems is used yet again in "Mother's Counsel," a poem written in 1889 "by request for the Primary Association":

1   Listen sisters while I tell you
What my mother told to me
When I was a little lisper
Pratling idly round her knee

2   Said she "pray to God in Heaven
He will hear your humble plea
He will answer in His wisdom
No matter what your lot may be."

3   I have found in all my life time
All my pains and pleasures too
When I heeded Mothers council
That her words to me were true.

4   Pray to Father little children
Pray to Him both old and young
Ask Him to protect and bless you
And help you to guard your tongue

5   And you'll find in all life's changes
He will ever be your guide

In your joys as well as sorrows
He will not forsake your side.

6   Thank Him too for every blessing
He so kindly gives to you
And to show that you are grateful
Be at all times just and true.

On this occasion, though, Mary Fowler chose to address two slightly different audiences. She begins by speaking directly to the sisters who teach the Primary children and then shifts later to talk directly to the children themselves. It is fairly clear from the short, iambic verse written in *abcb* rhyme that the poem is intended to be understood and taken to heart by both the children and their teachers. In fact, because the verses are numbered (a practice Mary employs in other poems intended to be sung), it is likely that this verse was created to fit a tune well-known in the community.

By using her mother's words as indirect address within the poem, Mary is able to extend the principle of interconnectedness even further by demonstrating that her own relationship with her mother provided her with an understanding she is now able to share with both the teacher-mothers and the children they are devoted to instructing themselves. The web of interrelationship through generational ties draws close a community that shares the same strong Mormon values, even though Orderville and Huntington are separated by hundreds of miles.

The Versification of Intimate Connections

Mary Fowler was also asked to write for individuals within the community, and these poems display the same emphasis on interrelationship and mutual dependence, whether they are addressed to her sisters or to male citizens of Orderville or Huntington. In the following example, Mary writes, and apparently performs, a poem on the occasion of a birthday in Huntington:

Brother Chase's birth day

'Tis a pleasure we don't often meet with
To be priveleged to mingle today
To show our respect and devotion
To Father and friend in this way.

You have toiled up the hill of lifes morning,
In faith you have crossed the divide;
And now among friends who esteem you,
You toil down the warm sunny/cool shady side.

We would that your future be pleasing,
And that you be spared long on earth,

As a blessing to friends and to kindred
Who honor the day of your birth.
And when our course here has been finished
And we have been called to ascend.
May we then be worthy to mingle
With our beloved father and friend.

Again, the importance of the relationship within the community is stressed in this poem, where a tension exists between the desire for Brother Chase to live a long life so his friends can have the blessing of his company on earth and the longing to be united with him again in heaven.

The significance of mutual interdependence displayed in poems such as these is demonstrated more specifically in the poems Mary Fowler was commissioned to write by individual women. Such requests for her poetry indicate the extent to which Mary's poetry was prized especially by her women friends and how, despite the humility expressed in the verses quoted above, she assumed a particularly powerful role within the community as she expressed the range of feelings and beliefs shared by her Mormon sisters.

Mary Fowler was asked by the women of Huntington to write poems for the most intimate occasions. On December 10, 1890, she wrote the following poem "according to the request of sister M—— J——" for another birthday, this time M. J.'s husband:

I wish you a happy birthday and many many more
May this new year bring you much joy with plenty for your store
And may your family be blest with health and comfort too!
May you be led in righteousness in all you say and do.
Of course some times this life is hard, and trials cloud the way
It takes much courage to press on, we have to watch and pray
I'm tempted oft in trials hour wrong things to say and do.
My lot some times seems very hard so far away from you.
If God had in His mercy given me more children to rear,
How changed had been my lot today, oh yes how much less drear!
But though this has not been my lot and has me sorely tried,
Dear husband don't blame me for that nor cast me to one side,
May you be blest with all good gifts. And at all times own Gods hand.
That one day as a saviour you may on Mt Zion stand!
May we while passing through that state of sin and death prepare
Our hearts to meet in that blest land, is constantly my prayer.

The intimacy of this poem lies not only in the fact that it is written at the request of a wife for her husband's birthday, but even more significantly, it is the expression of a woman who clearly is separated from her husband and suffers from the fear of abandonment, both physically and emotionally, because of her inability to produce children. The incredibly personal content of this poem seems to belie the fact that one woman actually requested another to pen these words. In assuming the voice of the "speaker" of this poem by choosing to write from the first person perspective, Mary Fowler addresses the absent man directly as "dear husband," asking him not to "cast *me* to one side." Here, a woman who has borne eleven children assumes the position of her friend who has obviously had trouble conceiving. These birthday lines reveal more about Sister M. J. than they do about the one to whom the poem is addressed. It is certainly a testament to the nature of the intimate relationship between the poet and her friend that Mary Fowler reproduces this poem in her "2nd Book" and disguises her friend's identity by using only initials.

Such intimacy among friends also underlies the poems Mary is called upon to write for women whose children are either desperately ill or recently deceased, as in this poem "written to Ralph in behalf of his Mother":

One year ago my darling boy I took you in my arms.
And how I prized each breath: thought I earth hath no sweeter charms.
None but a mother e'er can know how my heart leapt with joy
When first I knew you lived and breathed my little baby boy.
And when you grew to notice me, and smile and coo so sweet,
I was more than paid for all my pain, My bliss was most complete

But oh alas, for this worlds joys that come and go so quick.
You sickened for all that I could do and grew so poor and weak.
I fed and clothed you well my child, and gave you all my care;
And while I cared for you my heart was filled with constant prayer.

That He who hears the ravens cry would heal my little son,
His wisdom deemed it otherwise Thy will not mine be done.
And I who with my feeble sense thought I'd known so much grief.
Was doomed to suffer that much more that all erst seemed but brief.

For months my babe you were so weak at times I thought you dead,
And you were ten months old before I saw you raise your head.
Yes loved one you are one year old and still how weak you seem,
I scarcely can believe my eyes, it seems a cruel dream.
Your sickness has if that could be brought you more near my heart.
And in my love it seems you are of my own self a part.
My darling boy if I could see you strong and well again
It seems all other crosses I could bear and not complain,
God grant that this my fondest wish may soon be realized
If I may have this precious boon it will be gratefully prized.

Within these lines, Mary Fowler's own motherly sensibilities are shared with the friend whose young son is so close to death. It is as if the two women become one mother through the compositional process.

Sometimes, however, the mothers Mary wrote for were not fortunate enough to even be able to hope that their children would recover. Drawing on her own experience with the tragedy of a child's death, Mary Fowler is able to call forth the emotions surrounding such a sad event. While a poem Mary Fowler wrote for her friend Minerva Black isn't included in the "2nd Book of Origanal and Selected Pieces," where she copied many of her verses, we do have Mary's own diary entry for February 10, 1901, that describes the situation: "By request of its Mother wrote lines on the death of George & Minerva Black's baby. There have been eight deaths during this winter."

As a woman whose vernacular verse was highly valued by the community, Mary Fowler was called upon again and again to provide poetry for both public occasions of community import and to help others voice their often intensely personal joys and sorrows. The women of the community, especially, asked for Mary to share her poetic gifts most frequently. Through her poems, through the very act of writing and then often performing her verses, Mary Fowler was able to create anew bonds of friendship and to continually refocus attention on the significance of interconnections between community members. At the same time, Mary also found time to write poetry for her own purposes, and, not surprisingly, these verses also centered on the importance of her own personal connections with family and friends.

Personal Poetry and the
Thematics of the Interpersonal

Whether they were autograph-book verses, poems written for Christmas or New Year's, birthday wishes for family members, or letters in rhyme to loved ones far away, Mary Fowler's writings were primarily concerned with her own interpersonal relationships. Through those relationships, and the verses that continually reaffirmed and elaborated upon them, we can better understand the personal construction of the woman we know as Mary Susannah Sumner Fackrell Fowler. As Pauline Greenhill reminds us, "In communicating with others, folk poets say a great deal about themselves."[6] In Mary Fowler's case, the concerns of the community are her concerns and the distance between author and audience is perceived and presented as virtually nonexistent. The interconnections so prized by Mary Fowler are precisely the reasons for this perception of unanimity of vision. While the focus on community values is certainly characteristic of much folk poetry without respect to cultural or geographical context, this particular poet so enthusiastically embraced the folk idea of

Henry Ammon Fowler, Mary Susannah
Fackrell Fowler, and their four oldest chil-
dren. Photo courtesy of Virginia Fowler
Rogers.

interconnection that her vernacular verse reveals how this particularly
intense concept acted to construct and be constructed by her.
Interconnection, then, becomes a primary thematic focus for the topics
Mary addressed in her poetry. As such, these topics fall within what Roger
Renwick has termed "frames of reference of both culturally normative
content and culturally normative ethos."[7]

What is particularly interesting in this respect are the topics *not* generally addressed in Mary Fowler's verse. Unlike her prose essays, the content of Mary's poetry almost never focuses on specific virtues valued by the
community. While her essays often instruct and model such behaviors as
originality of character, obedience, and reliance on the power of prayer,
Mary Fowler's poetry displays a completely different rhetorical stance, one
which replaces the didactic with the interpersonal. While folk poetry in
other regions and within other cultural contexts frequently has been seen
to function in terms of providing information and/or persuading others

Christian Otteson children, Huntington, Utah, c. 1898. George Edward Anderson photo, used by permission, Utah State Historical Society

about culturally problematic concerns, Mary Fowler's poetry, instead, consistently seeks to reaffirm the interconnections so valued by both her community and herself. Wherever issues arise with respect to the development and maintenance of personal interrelationships, we might expect to find a poem written by Mary Fowler articulating her own perspective and providing personal examples to illuminate the topic. Most interestingly, though, neither her practices as a folk healer nor her role as nurturing mother receive much attention in Fowler's poetry. In trying to locate even a couple of lines to function as an epigraph to chapter three, I became frustrated by the virtual absence of references to health and healing. Likewise, there are no admonishments to her friends regarding their motherly duties, rarely a reference to her own techniques of mothering. It is as if these topics were so much a part of her very being that they needed no further articulation in words shared with others. Or perhaps it was simply that Mary chose to focus on those aspects of her own experiences in which her community's strong belief in mutual interdependence was somehow either called into question or demanded further elaboration.

In the poems Mary wrote for Christmas and New Year's to family and friends, the importance of interrelationship and mutual dependence is a frequent focus. During the year 1891, Mary composed several poems to mark the transition from one year to the next; each of them included an emphasis on the significance of friendship in community. For example, in writing to her husband's sister Harriet early in 1891, Mary includes in her wishes for the new year the line, "May the friendship be yours that you have ever prized; And every fond wish of yours be realized." At the end of that same year, she penned a Christmas greeting intended for a wider audience, but it included the same focus on interconnectedness:

Christmas Wishes

I've planned and been thinking I've thought and I've planned;
I've used my best efforts with brain heart and hand,
For those whom I love, both afar off and near,
To give them this morning a wee Christmas cheer.
I wished this but find it has been quite in vain,
For I've been unable this wish to obtain.
I find a good wish all I have to impart,
I hope you'll accept from a warm sincere heart.
My wish, Merry Christmas to each one and all.
May it bring happy cheer to the large and the small.

In her poverty, Mary is unable to offer any gift other than her words. It is significant that in giving these she draws together all those dear to her, both "afar off and near." That same year she sent this poem to an aunt and uncle:

A letter to Aunt E Lawler

We are nearing the dawn of another new year.
My hearts filled with good wishes for those who are dear.
And way down in my heart where 'tis warmest and true,
Is reserved dearest Auntie a snug place for you.
And you, uncle accept of my hearty good will.
May you both be quite happy this year in life's mill.
May heaven send to you its rich treasures of love.
May He comfort your hearts with His light from above.
My Dear Uncle and Aunt may you live long on earth.
And may all of Christ's teachings to you be of worth.
Please remember me kindly to those dear to you.
Oh how often I think of and pray for them too.
May our lives all be such while we're living down here;
That we'll meet when we've passed to a holier sphere.

In this poem, though the title suggests it was primarily written for her aunt, not only does Mary call her uncle and aunt by terms of genuine affection, but she also asks to be remembered to those "dear to you," remarking that she thinks of and prays for them, also. Most importantly though, the verse ends with a wish that they will all meet in the next life.

Again, the ultimate desire is to be reunited with loved ones after death in accordance with Mormon doctrinal belief. Each of these greetings reaches out to family members in an all-inclusive way that seeks to eradicate the physical distance between them. At the same time, Mary reminds both herself and her family and friends that ultimately death will most certainly come, and with it the danger of a potentially permanent separation. Additionally, then, she reinforces the belief that it is only through a life lived well on earth that they might be reunited in a relationship that breaks the strictures of time and space in that "holier sphere." For Mary Fowler, the key to the everlasting interconnection she so desires is precisely the spiritual life that is the essence of the sense of community. A separation that necessitates the sending of Christmas and New Year's greetings through the mail, as painful as it may be, becomes merely a trial to be endured in order to reach the possibility of permanent interrelationship.

THE AUTOGRAPHIC IMPULSE

In even the shortest of the poetry—rhymes composed for autograph books that appear to have been tremendously popular in both Orderville and Huntington—Mary Fowler demonstrates a dual concern for both this ideal of community and for her personal relationship with those for whom she writes these verses. Copied into her own "2nd Book," the following verses are labeled simply "Autographs" and their intended recipients remain unnamed:

> If I am worthy here to write I trust that this will prove
> A token of remembrance 'twixt me and one I love.

> Of our sentiments brother please accept
> O'er looking their plainness or any defect
> The truest of comfort in them may you find
> May they also remind you of friends left behind.

> How could you think me such a heartless thing
> As to forget the one I fondly love
> Whose voice has made my very name more sweet
> Whose welfare's blended with my every move.

> Whatever may come in future time
> *May my fate be always linked with thine.*

> I desire to see you happy in this life
> And blessed as daughter, sister, Mother, wife,
> I sincerely hope your future may be bright
> New pleasures surround you and your cares be more light

Yet I wish you greater gifts than these to the faithful given
They are courage, wisdom, knowledge, strength and a crown of
gems in heaven.

Of course, it is in the very nature of autograph rhymes to describe the affection between writer and recipient, so it is not surprising that the tone of these verses is focused so intently on the description of friendship's goals. The last entry especially, though, suggests that in wishing for her friend to be blessed as "daughter, sister, Mother, wife," Mary Fowler is focusing attention specifically on all those relationships most central to a woman's life. It is *in relationship* to those most significant others that a woman is truly blessed. Additionally, we again find that it is through a life well lived that one might truly enjoy in heaven the permanence of those relationships so prized on earth.

It appears to be the case that autograph books were compiled most frequently in Mormon Utah either for birthdays or for when a member of the community was departing to relocate or to fulfill a church mission. Both Mary Susannah and Eliza Fowler wrote in the book Henry Ammon Fowler used to collect sentiments from his friends just before his move from Orderville to Huntington. In this case, Henry Ammon selected an old notebook, previously used by his father as a journal, for this purpose. While Eliza's entry was quite brief, Mary chose to wait until they had actually arrived in Huntington to enter her lengthier personal sentiments:

Homage to the higher ranks belong
Engaging them in honors formal cool
Not to the humble sounds grand riches gong
Round happy homes where love and sunbeams rule
Yes give to such their pride tis grandest show
And let them love it for it will not last
More heart felt lasting joys be thine below
More real joy than worldly show can cast
Or worldly riches bring. Be there the seed
Near whose enduring lovely ever green
Flow purest streams the grandest wealth indeed
On ever till it reach the Eternal stream
With jealous eye tis natures gift to each
Long have I viewed thee always found thee true
Earnestly, fondly I hope that we may reach
Reward with the faithful united with you.
Only the truest love will endure the rude storms of life.
Mary S. Fowler

Just as she chose to focus her Christmas and New Year's greetings within the framework of a hope for eternal interconnection, so, too, did

Mary Fowler choose this same theme for the poem that would represent her in her husband's autograph book.

THE POETICS OF SEPARATION

Whenever separation from loved ones was either imminent or intensely recalled (even on festive occasions such as Christmas), Mary wrote poetry that focused on the genuine possibility of relationship without separation, a relationship that could only reach fulfillment after death. The whole issue of separation, of travel away from her community, whether that travel be by a friend, a family member, or herself, was almost always cause for Mary Fowler to write poetry. In fact, other than festive poetic offerings on birthdays, the personal verse that Mary wrote to friends was almost always occasioned by travel or separation. For example, while she was visiting Orderville a couple of years after moving to Huntington, two Orderville families she knew well moved away. Mary composed this poem for them:

> Parting Lines to W. Carroll & E. D. Porter & Families
>
> Among the many crosses of this life
> Is parting from the friends we long have loved
> And though we deem tis Father wills it so
> We will miss you who have in our circles moved
> We will miss your kind examples in our school.
> We will miss your teachings and your presence to
> And in all our entertainments howe'er good
> We know that we shall miss and think of you
> And may you find as true and loving friends
> In any place you choose to make your home
> May pleasant scenes surround your paths in life
> Nor unnecessary trials to you come.
> It may seem like this is an outward form
> These wishes have been given of oft before
> But this is truely and sincerely from our hearts
> May Heavens choicest blessings on you shower.
> And for the seeds you've sown so richly here
> May you reap harvests bothe in Heaven and earth
> For each and all of you we ask the same
> May goodness e'er apreciate your worth!

Even though Mary herself had left Orderville, she continued to write poetry mourning the loss of others who chose to move elsewhere. Interestingly, she did not indicate in her notebook whether or not the poem was commissioned by someone (or some group) in Orderville. The use of the first person plural might indicate that this was the case; however, in every other example of a "requested" poem a notation indicated such a commission. Whatever the motivation, whether personal or at the community's request, the poem's significance lies in Mary's choosing to focus yet again on the theme of separation and to link it to the spiritual life.

Perhaps Mary's own separation from her parents and the community in Orderville was so painful that for the rest of her life this particular theme kept emerging as a way to understand and make sense of it. In fact, although the extensive prose account of the Fowlers' journey from Orderville to Huntington is certainly the lengthiest piece of writing Mary Fowler ever produced, it is in a poem she wrote on this occasion that she actually reveals most clearly her own sense of interconnection with the community and the deep sense of loss she experienced in moving away:

> It is now my lot to roam,
> From my dear Long Valley home.
> And to leave the friends I loved
> in child-hood days.
> Yet my heart will ever yearn
> for the happy times return
> that we lived and loved.
> in child-hood's happy ways.
>
> Many friends, I yet may find,
> That are just as good and kind;
> But those of my youth
> they never can replace.
> And no matter where I bide;
> Whether joy or ills betide
> I will not forget the friends
> of child-hood days.
>
> Oh my home, my dearest home
> Now the time to part has come
> Yet I'll prize the recollection
> And I'll sigh for thee
> My dear Long-Valley home.
>
> There, I leave my mother true,
> And my dear old father, too,
> All my brothers and my sister
> there do dwell.
> It may not be otherwise,
> I must leave these many ties,
> Yet my heart is with my home
> in Orderville

As the months, and years go bye
And new friends do come my way;
Will they find a vacant corner
any where?
Will they ever think of me,
When no more my face they see,
Will they miss me
in the silent hour of prayer?

In this poetic version of the experience of leaving the only real home and community she could remember, Mary Fowler evokes the painful leave-taking she was experiencing, and rather than looking forward to their eventual reunion in heaven, she wonders at the end of the poem whether her family will even miss her as they kneel to pray. Her own sorrow is palpable in these lines, one of the earliest examples of Mary Fowler's poetry that still remains today; it may very well have taken the rest of her life for Mary to be able to rewrite her own sense of loss in words she addressed to other leave-takers through the years. In that revision, the significance of family as emblematic of community joins with the recognition that one must necessarily be spiritually tried and tested through loss; thus, in this poem we also find the beginning threads of several recurrent themes that are interwoven within the framework of a lifetime of poetic renderings.

TRIALS OF THE HEART

Throughout the majority of the verses written by Mary Susannah Fowler, the dual themes of the significance of family and the necessity of enduring trials in this life are juxtaposed continually. This conjunction of thematic foci begins early in Mary's writing endeavors when she confronts her husband's travel to avoid the federal agents searching for polygamists and her own family's move to Huntington. Surely the intensity of the closeness Mary experienced within her own biological family and within the larger Orderville community contributed to the wrenching sorrow she experienced in moving away. Throughout her life the poetry she wrote especially about her own mother continued to resonate with the intensity of her affection and with the sense of loss she felt whenever they were separated. In this poem composed for her mother's first birthday after the move, Mary enters into a conversation with her mother where she is able to tell her so many things she has been unable to say in other ways at other times:

Mothers birthday

1   Mother dear my thoughts are with you
Though my home is far away

How I long to see you mother
On your fifty third birthday

2   Long this was my blessing Mother
To each day behold your face
Now in pleasure pain and sorrow
There is none to fill your place

3   While those happy days were with me
I very much your worth did prize
But your love & tender counsel
I could not half realize

4   One day comes then goes forever
Others come to fill its place
And each rings fond mem'ries Mother
Of your kind and loving face

5   How you've striven to bless and comfort
How with heart felt earnest prayer
You have eased pain lightened sorrow
What is like a mothers care

6   Would to God we all might be there
And assemble on this day
Father Mothers brothers sisters
Honoring her whose locks are gray

7   From the sacrifices suffered
From the care to others given
Winning love from those around her
Making her a home in Heaven.

In this tribute Mary Fowler is able to bring together the unconditional love she feels for her mother with an understanding that she must, like her mother before her, suffer in order to love fully. This idea of sacrifice pervades not only Mary Fowler's writing, but her life as well. Just a few months later, the intensity of the loss she experienced in this separation from her mother finds expression in another verse:

O why did they part me from thee

Dear Mother my heart aches I'm sighing
I yearn for the happiness past
For tender and loving expressions
For kindness which always would last.
Why Mother did I ever leave you
And drift out upon lifes rough sea
The fates that are hov'ring around us

O why did they part me from thee

Why should the years change & grow harsher
As swiftly they pass from our view
Why dont all bring a share of contentment
Like those when I lived there with you

O mother if years could make fonder
The hearts that are linked with our own,
If they'd make us more kind and more patient
And were harshness among us not known
How 'twould lighten our pains and our heartaches!
How pleasantly moments would fly!
How little would poverty try us!
And jests from outside we'd pass by.

You can't take me back again Mother
Though you list to my piteous cries
For I would not & could not even sever
The least of our family ties
I must live on content with my portion
Give my babies the care which they need
And repay their sweet loving caresses
E'en though my poor yearning heart bleed.

Torn between her desire to return to her mother's tender care and the necessity of taking care of her own children, Mary conveys the profound sorrow she experienced through this separation. It is a sorrow Mary continued to express throughout her life whenever the anxiety of separation from her mother became overwhelming. If her mother became ill, her concern found an outlet in poetic form, as in the following example in which her mother seems to be able to communicate with her through prayer:

I have grieved since Mothers illness
Grief which no rest would allow
Now there comes a gentle whisper
Peace—your Mother's better now.
I am greatfull, blest assurance
Precious birth—so calm and still
Coming in the mornings quiet
I opine it is her will.
She has known how I would worry
And how anxious I would be
When the word came of her illness
And I'm sure she prayed for me.
Yes she's prayed as I have heard her
Often when she used to pray

And the blessing came and found me
Tho I am so far away.
Brought me comforting assurance,
And relieved my soul of pain
For I feel my Mother's better
And we yet may meet again.

Once more the "comforting assurance" of a mother's love brought Mary the peace of mind she had sought. In this case, the connection with her mother is accomplished through spiritual fidelity and the belief in an all-powerful God. Immediately following this entry in her "2nd Book," however, the following undated poem reveals that faith and prayer did not always provide an immediate "balm" for Mary's broken spirits:

A letter, dear Mother, please write one to me
Oh how my heart yearns for a letter from thee
A letter dear Mother. O can you believe
How fondly I cherish those I do recieve.

Away from the ties which by nature are formed
I feel that I'm in the great war all unarmed
The pathway before me is filled with sharp briars
I'm tried as it were, in the furnaces fires.

But however gloomy my lot here may be,
Tis brightened when I get a letter from thee
And tho when you write you speak not of my woe
Your words like a balm to the wound quickly go.

And then I feel stronger to do what is right
As you have well fought and most won the good fight
I know Im a coward, I dare not to tread
Where missiles are flying always round my head

And when in my weakness I'm tempted to fly
And like the base traitor my colors deny
I feel like renewing and dare not to flee
If comes that sweet missive, a letter from thee.
I'd like to be faithfull, you know, mother dear
All truth, all correct-laws, I fain would revere
I know when this battle for right shall have passed
We'll be at that haven of rest which will last.
Then write a good letter, dear Mother, to me.
It brings such a wealth of sweet solace from thee.

It is only through her mother's words of encouragement that Mary believes she can endure the trials with which she is continually faced. The significance of words, their ability to provide a real connection with one from whom she has been separated, their effectiveness in salving the hurts she has suffered, is reiterated throughout the verse. For Mary Fowler, words have a God-like power to bridge the awful separation and bring peace to her troubled soul. In fact, the first letter from her mother after Mary had left Orderville inspired a verse that celebrates the connection across the miles made possible through the written word, and at the same time, the poem also begins to suggest the origin of the trials that Mary and her Mormon sisters and brothers suffered:

> My letter
>
> Mr. Postman you sent me a treasure
> When I sent for my mail yester night.
> 'Twas a letter from home and the dear ones
> Whom I left with tears diming my sight.
> 'Tis the first I have had since I left them
> And it told how they all get along
> Tis indeed a good kind loving mesage
> From some of the best of lifes throng.
> It told sir about my good father
> Who has gone for a season to stay
> With his friends in a much cooler climate
> For his home is too warm now a days.
> And from one of the dearest of mothers
> There was many a kind loving line
> Telling how she was lonely with out me
> And how for her children she pined
> And how through a dream though so simple
> She was strengthened and comforted too
> And felt not to grieve for her children
> I think that a blessing dont you
> And it told Mr Postman of others
> So good and so dear to my heart
> It told of my brothers and sisters
> With whom I regretted to part.
> And could you believe it Postmaster
> Those heartless officials of law
> Have taken my own sisters husband
> To lock him in fellonies jaw.
> Don't you think Mr Postman these fellows
> Must suffer for what they have done
> In robbing those good wives and mother
> Of their dutiful husband and son.
> If all had been well 'twere much better

But I'm glad of these lines anyway
From the home I am proud to remember
And will be to my dying day
Now I want to thank you good Postmaster,
For giving this treasure to me
For I realy do want to thank some one
And I dont know who else it may be
But they say there's a God up in Heaven
Who gives us the things which we need.
And may be He'll smooth the rough places
And comfort the hearts which now bleed
And I think I'll thank Him too for sending
The letter from loved ones at home
And I'll ask Him to guide and protect them
And turn to some good every moan
Now I think you deserve some good blessing
For giving this treasure I do
And if there's too many blessings for my folks
I hope He will give some to you.

In this lengthy verse, Mary Fowler is able to draw together the good-
ness of God in providing the letter and the comfort of her mother's words,
even as those words spoke of the trials her family encountered through
embracing God's principle of polygamy. It is primarily this issue, the terrible suffering Mormon women and men had to endure because of their
practice of polygamy, that defined many of the poems Mary wrote during
her life.[8] In this case, her mother's words brought the news that her father
had fled to a "cooler climate" to escape the federal marshals and that her
sister's husband, Thomas Chamberlain, a bishop in Orderville, had been
arrested and imprisoned in "fellonies jaw" for his beliefs. The lines concerning the way in which the "heartless officials of law" robbed "those
good wives and mother" of their "dutiful husband and son" and Mary's
own desire that these men should "suffer for what they have done" no
doubt reflect the confusion and terror enveloping the women of
Orderville and Huntington as their husbands and fathers were arrested and
taken away.

LIVING THE PRINCIPLE:
SEPARATION THROUGH INTERCONNECTION

Mary Fowler herself was already familiar with the trials of living the
principle. Shortly after Henry Ammon married Eliza Norwood, his second
wife, he had been forced to flee Orderville to escape arrest. The following

poem, written on a loose piece of foolscap and dated April 1888, was found along with other examples of Mary's poetry omitted from her "2nd Book":

It does seem very cruel that you should have to hide
As if you had been stealing & feared you would be tried
For you to leave your dear ones & asume another name
Does look as if old Satan might soon His fellows claim
And when you have been driven from home so far away
How shall we do without you who'll be our shield & stay
Who'll guide our erring footsteps who'll bless our children
A Fathers loving council & teach them how to live
And you'll be sad & lonely when you are forced to roam
From loving wives & children from all that makes a home
There must needs be offences but woe unto the one
By whom they come for judgement will be poured on them
I will repay the sinner this God hath truely said
Tis better that ye suffer than be in darkness led
This looks clear in some cases but then it seems to me
If I'd the reins of Judgement I soon would set you free
The sobs of loving children nor sighs of parents dear
From those who had been severed you'd never have to fear
But yet one must not murmur for if it be Gods will
'Twill make us purer better though tis a bitter pill,
And then the wicked portion must brimming fill up
That God may send His judgement & misery they sup
So fare thee well dear husband may the gospels peace attend
Your every thought & action that God may be your friend
And may you not lack comfort from good friends true and warm
And may those wicket spotters not do you any harm.

God's trials and his friendship meld together in this verse written just before her husband fled the "wicket spotters" who sought out polygamist husbands. Just a few short months later, Mary again wrote words of encouragement to her husband who was still in hiding:

Fight on
June 10th

Courage husband be thou brave fight on
Be thou not the tempters slave   " "
Though the world does mock & frown
And Satans power would pull you down
Though they might stamp you as a clown
                    Be brave fight on
Do not weary in the chase fight on
For thy foes will miss their base   " "
Heaven can break this gloomy spell

> Let the days of good deeds Tell
> Remember all will yet be well
> Fight on fight on
> When sore trials throng thy way fight on
> Peace thou not to watch & pray   " "
> Let thy voice extend in prayer
> Set it not on worldly care
> Heavenly treasures thou shalt share
> dear one fight on

The separation that occasioned this writing was only the first of many for Mary Susannah and Henry Ammon Fowler. Ammon was frequently away on construction work, or shearing sheep, or helping in the mines to make enough money to support his two families. The longest separation, though, was during his church mission to the southeastern states and Oklahoma Indian Territory from October 1900 to November 1902. Although Mary Fowler certainly encouraged her husband to go on this mission, the poetry she wrote during his absence reveals that same longing and fear of separation. On November 23, 1901, less than a week before her husband's birthday, he was clearly much on her mind:

> One desire
>
> 'Tis nearing bedtime and my work's put away;
> The children have now quit their evenings play.
> The wee ones are cosily tucked in to bed,
> The days work is done and the prayers are all said.
> Just one thing i'd like ere the eve does depart;
> 'Tis to press my dear husband once close to my heart,
> Give him one loving kiss and hearty good night;
> Then I could sleep soundly until morning light.
> Yet as duty calls him awhile from his home,
> I'll wait for him fondly until his return.
> And to Fathers keeping him I will commend;
> And ask Him to bring him to us safe again.

By poetically commending her husband to God's fatherly keeping Mary was able to sleep soundly.

During those two years, Mary found that poetry provided a way to express the connection between her love and the trials she and her husband were forced to endure. Six days after she penned the preceding lines, Mary composed this verse for her oldest son Arno to "recite on his pa's birthday," and it is written as if Arno had composed the lines himself:

> Ammon's Birthday.
>
> 'Twas on this day some time ago
> A spirit came to earth

Embodied with mortality
Loved as of priceless worth.
His parents who were kind and good
And loved the gospel too
Were stricken in the prime of life
And passed beyond our view
And now the boy that came to earth
A few short years before
Was with two sisters left alone
And scanty was their store.
Deprived of parents kind advice
In recklessness he roved.
Just so he lived and had some fun
He cared not where he moved.
Yet Providence is very kind
And did not once lose sight
But prompted him to shun bad ways
And do that which was right.
His early youth was very hard
But not content with that
Good uncle Sam has now seen fit
To give a harder rap
Than death in nat'ral form could be.
He is the cause to sever
The ties which Father had ordained
Should e'er remain together.
This man who first was innocent
Then grew to break the law
Has sev'ral foll'wing in his path
'Tis him whom I call pa.
Whatever comes I hope he'll stand
And claim the side of truth
For his example's what we'll be
When we've passed erring youth.

Even when serving a church mission, Ammon is portrayed as a law-breaker because of his belief in living the principle of polygamy. In writing this poem for her son to recite on his absent father's birthday, Mary Susannah weaves the web of sacred interconnections between family members and the trials that must be endured in family's name. Her words in her son's voice resoundingly echo these themes both in content and performance.

Only two days later, Mary reveals that her husband's return, eagerly anticipated though it was, might occasion additional sorrows. Although none of her other writings—not her diary, not her prose essays, and certainly not the minutes she took in Relief Society meetings—refer in any way to the strain of living in a polygamous relationship, Mary Susannah

Fowler's poetry is suffused with the pain of this nearly intolerable situation, even when her husband is far away from both his wives and their children:

I am waiting husband waiting
Waiting for your coming feet.
Yes I'm waiting fondly waiting
Waiting your loved form to greet.

I am watching down the roadway
As I've often done before
And I breathlessly am list'ning
For your coming as of yore.

Ah, I'm waiting dearest husband,
Yet there comes a pang of woe;
With the pleasure there's a heart ache
Many of the Saints may know.

For is there not one who'd greet you
Yet whose heart is torn with grief
Who was wont to bid you welcome
And with me our husband meet.

Yet to me the fate seems cruel
That bids loving ones to part.
Though I'm longing now to meet you
Pain with pleasure fills my heart.

While I wait my soul is yearning
Hoping that we'll all be true;
That when passed these seens of trial
We may live in joy with you.

Mary's own yearning to see her husband upon his return from his mission is tempered in this verse by her concern for her sister-wife Eliza. Since the federal marshals were ever vigilant during this period, Eliza could not go with Mary to meet their husband, and in this poem Mary declares that "pain with pleasure" fills her heart at this predicament. In the last two lines we again find her belief that if they each live a truly spiritual life, enduring whatever trials may come, they will all be able to live together "in joy."

Nowhere else in all the volumes I collected during the course of this study could I find a reference to Mary's true internal feelings about her sister-wife, except for an interesting two line reference at the end of a poem omitted from her "2nd Book." This poem, obviously composed when her husband was away (probably on his mission), is addressed directly to him and discloses more intimate thoughts than she usually allows in her poetry.

For example, after describing how she had been thinking about their times together in the past, Mary writes:

> Some how I am longing for pleasure
> Not just like we have here to day
> I just long for a friend who can love me
> In the old quiet true child like way

Yet several lines later her reverie is interrupted and she concludes with the following stanza:

> I was going to write this here letter
> as long & as good as could be
> but Eliza just now past the window
> & scared it all right out of me.

Her intimate thoughts disrupted by her sister-wife, Mary abruptly concludes her poem; over one hundred years later we will never know whether or not she ever shared these thoughts with her absent husband.

These two poetic references are the only direct indications of Mary's own feelings about her sister-wife in spite of the fact that Mary addressed another poem to her sister-wife when she visited Orderville after their move to Huntington,[9] in spite of the entries in their husband's autobiographical writings concerning Mary's nursing of Eliza during his absence, and in spite of the minutes of the Relief Society that indicate their mutual participation in meetings over a number of years. As brief as they both are, the poems suggest a tension between the outward acceptance of, and genuine participation in, the principle of polygamy and the internal struggle in which one might have to engage to overcome any personal hesitancy in that acceptance and participation. Mary Fowler was able to overcome her fear of separation, her concern for her family's often dire financial situation, and her worries over the possibility of her husband's arrest through the strength of her own spiritual beliefs. Mary understood that her mother, father, sisters and brothers, her friends in both Orderville and Huntington, her husband and her sister-wife were all united together in a spiritual community of Saints chosen by a loving God who allowed them to be tried in order that one day they would be joined together forever. This faith was the sustaining force in both her poetry and her life.

Poetic Self-Construction and a Community's Values

This idea of community extending far beyond an earthly life must necessarily inform our understanding of Mary Fowler's self-conception as daughter, sister, wife and—perhaps, most of all—mother. In Mary's own writings we discover the interconnections of lives woven together here on earth are revealed as permanent relationships only insofar as they are created on the loom of a continually tested spiritual fidelity. Nowhere do we find that testing through almost unbearable trials more dramatically demonstrated than in the poems Mary Fowler composed on the deaths of her own children. Although separation from parents and siblings, and the concerns over her husband's safety in his absence, prepared her in some strange way for the ultimate separation from her own babies, the trial of their loss tested Mary Fowler's faith in the deepest of ways.

In her self-construction, Mary Fowler clearly placed the greatest emphasis on her own motherhood, for in that role she increased the Kingdom of God. In doing so, she strengthened the very community to which she was so committed. Even though she did not write many poems about her role as a mother, each birth was the occasion for a celebration, and each new life provided poetic inspiration, as in this brief verse composed for her daughter Laurie Ellen on July 19, 1888:

> Though noble, blue-eyed elf, thy mother's pride
> All gems of earthly hue grow dim by thy sweet side.
> Thy sunny little face, all round, does light impart,
> Thy mother's comforter, with place in papa's heart.
> Could earthly gems procure this tiny, precious pearl?
> Not all earth's wealth could buy our darling little girl!
> Sweet child, may all the gifts which eyes could ever see
> Be fitted for thy form and given unto thee.
> God keep thee from all harm, and in His grace and love
> Give honor where there's honor done, and life for heaven above.

So meaningful were the connections between Mary Susannah and her children, so complete her trust in God to keep them safe, that when a child died, she was emotionally devastated. In particular, the loss of Susannah, the child named after her and after her mother, provided the crucial test of how capable Mary Fowler was in bringing her own spiritual beliefs to bear on this most difficult of separations. On March 12, 1890, Mary wrote:

> Our own Sweet Anna we love you still
> Though you've passed beyond our view
> And our hearts are pained; yet we own Gods will
> For darling He gave us you.

> And four short months you staid to bless
> Our home with your sunny face
> My heart aches darling, though you'r at rest
> For nothing can fill your place.

> I long so to hold you once more to my breast!
> To feel your warm breath on my cheek!

Your sweet little cooing would lull me to rest
But now my heart feels like 't'would break.

Your sweet little spirit is waiting for me
Where all is so Heavenly fair
And for my erring footsteps a light it will be
For I know I shall meet you there.

Here, Mary is able to say with authority that she will meet her child in heaven, and this statement gives evidence to her belief that enduring terrible trials is necessary to reach the true interconnectedness of an everlasting spiritual community. It also indicates her ability to conjoin two different understandings of God, one whose "grace and love" kept her other children from "all harm," and one who allowed the death of this youngest child.

Six months later, she revisits both Susannah's grave and her own understanding of this spiritual trial:

Susannah

It seems such a little while darling,
Since death came to our peaceful home,
Robed us of our sweet little flower
And left us in sadness to mourn.
I know that God called thee my darling,
Yet, Oh how my heart throbs with pain
When I think my little Susannah
Can't come to me while here a gain.

'Twere cruel to ask thee my treasure
To come to this world ful of woe,
And leave thine associate seraphs,
To comfort my heart here below,

So Father will Thou be my comfort,
My guide and my strength and my stay,
Prepare us to enter Thy Glory
And live with our darling I pray.

Although this verse begins addressing the daughter who has died, Mary Susannah Fowler eventually shifts the addressee to God himself in the last verse, as she asks him to allow the rest of her family to "enter Thy Glory" and be reunited with her baby daughter. The separation from her child, even when understood as temporary in the light of the promise of eternal connection, remained a painful one throughout Mary Fowler's life. Yet it was through that personal pain that Mary was able to write verses for other mothers who had lost children of their own.

In the assumption of responsibility as the voice of her community, especially the women's communities of Orderville and Huntington, Mary

Fowler drew on her own experiences to explore and expound upon the most deeply held cultural beliefs. The very ideal of a community—constructed not upon politically ideological bases, but rather on spiritual imperatives—found voice in the verses Mary produced throughout her life. A close examination of her poetry reveals that such a notion of community encompassed Mary's understanding of the necessity of enduring earthly trials in order to celebrate the perpetual peace of the heavenly extension of the Mormon community on earth.

In constructing an identity that changed as her own realization of these spiritual perspectives grew, Mary Fowler articulated in her poetry not only a strong sense of her community, but a shifting awareness of her own interconnectedness within that community. Through her participation in women's associations, through her work in anointing and healing the sick, and especially through the words of her own poetry, Mary Fowler participated most fully in not only the trials through which spiritual fidelity is forged, but in the knowledge of an everlasting community with those she loved. The very metaphors of self that came to symbolize Mary's own identity construction found expression in poetry that both embraced the values of her Mormon community and marked her presence within that community as one who helped to create and negotiate its mutual interdependence and sense of interrelationship. How startling then it is to find on the last page of "Mary Fowler's 2nd Book of Origanal and Selected Pieces" this poem:

> My true friend & helper, tis such I would choose
> To call thee, & own that I love thee, my muse
> How oft when my heart's filled with sorrow & grief
> Thou dost in thy kindness, come to my relief.
> And heavily press me to sit down and write
> The comforting sentences thou dost indite
> I know thou wert sent from our Father above
> And greatfull I am for this mark of His love.
> When sorest of trials have come unto me
> I've found none to comfort & soothe me like thee
> Should happiness some day drive from me the blues
> I yet will proclaim this, I love thee my muse.

Even as Mary Fowler continually asserts the importance of interconnection with family and friends, in the end she acknowledges that when truly tried, it isn't her mother or her husband, or even a woman friend, but the poetic "muse" whom she finds better than any other to "comfort & soothe" her. The spirit within her, sent from "Father above," is the true mark of God's love in her life. In Mary Fowler's ability to write and perform poetry we find the clearest articulation of the most meaningful connection of all—the connection that allows the individual to find expression and give it voice within the context and constraints of her own community.

6

"Your Words Like a Balm"
A Matrix of Discourses

But however gloomy my lot here may be,
Tis brightened when I get a letter from thee
And tho when you write you speak not of my woe
Your words like a balm to the wound quickly go.

As I read the range of discourses that enabled me to piece together an understanding of Mary Fowler's ideas about community, her dedication to healing within that community, and her own poetic renderings of the sense of interconnection she so valued, I found myself selecting those representations of family and friends that seemed to best articulate the woman I had come to know. In short, I found myself constructing Mary Fowler, or rather a version of Mary Fowler that suited my particular purposes. As a folklorist, I was interested in the aesthetic performances revealed in the words of Mary's own diary, as well as in the words of her husband, children, grandchildren, and friends. As a cultural historian by interest rather than academic training, I also wanted to understand Mary Fowler's life within the particular cultural context in which she lived. However, as I read more and more of the variety of discourses that constructed and reconstructed her life history, I began to realize that the interpretive truth of Mary Fowler's life does not lie in the "objective" events that comprised it, but rather in that continual construction and reconstruction of her identity by herself, her family, her community, and now by those who read each of these discourses. The extraordinarily expansive matrix of discourses that I drew on in compiling the brief historical narrative of the first chapter provides us with any number of different constructions of the identity of Mary Fowler, polygamous wife, healer and nurse, folk poet, church leader, mother, community member. And, yes, even that brief history I wrote as an introduction becomes a part of the ongoing reconstructive process. As readers, you, too, are engaged in the process of piecing together your own understanding of just who Mary Fowler was—and is.

The juxtaposition of the various discourses within the preceding chapters reveals two related understandings: first of all, by juxtaposing a range of written and oral genres of life writing with very different rhetorical and performative possibilities, we realize more fully the complexity of constructing a life based on these discursive fragments; in the process, we understand the relative strengths and limits of each of those discursive practices much more clearly. Through multiply discursive constructions, then, we as readers come to understand better both Mary Susannah Fowler and the genres of life writing that present her history.

Life Writing

In fact, life writing may be viewed from a number of different critical perspectives. First of all, it "may be viewed strictly as a limited and limiting genre, as it was in the eighteenth century."[1] During that period, life writing was simply the equivalent of biography, which often included autobiography and "*perhaps* other kinds of autobiographical writing."[2] Another definition of life writing suggests that it is a less exclusive genre of personal writing that not only includes biography and autobiography but also "less 'objective,' or more 'personal,' genres such as letters and diaries."[3] Finally, life writing may be seen as inclusive of any genres in which "the author does not want to pretend he/she is absent from the text."[4] From this perspective, life writing genres would also include their fictionalized equivalents. In this way, as Marlene Kadar suggests, "life-writing becomes both the 'original genre' and a critical comment on it, and therefore the self-in-the-writing."[5] This expansive definition of life writing is impressive and quite clearly applies to the materials that present the life of Mary Fowler, yet I believe Kadar's definition can be broadened even more, if our goal is to understand the real complexities of constructing such a life. We must read the nuances of the *interaction* and *collaboration* of the multiple constructions of Mary Fowler that become central to our own understanding.

One example from Mary Fowler's own writing helps to demonstrate this point. When Mary Susannah Sumner Fackrell was a young child, her family experienced a particularly moving and influential tragedy. As Mary Susannah's own daughter, Laura Ellen Fowler Roper, tells the story, her grandmother Susannah Sumner Fackrell often was present when

> the neighbor ladies used to gather for a rag or sewing bee and always enjoyed eating dinner together. One time when they were assembled at Susannah's home she was busy serving dinner, which included tea. The Saints had been counseled to quit drinking tea and coffee, but it was hard for those who had always drank it. When Susannah was ready to sit down to eat she thought of her sixteen month old baby boy and asked where

he was. A search was made and he was found drowned in the spring not far away. She took that as a punishment for serving and drinking tea and never drank any more after that.[6]

One afternoon as I searched every issue of the *Young Woman's Journal* for articles on literacy practices in Utah during this period, I discovered quite by accident the only published poem of Mary Susannah Fackrell Fowler. Published under the pseudonym Cyrenia (after her brother Cyrenus), more than thirty years after the tragedy presented in the preceding narratives, this poem provides another perspective on the troubling events:

My Reasons for Not Drinking Tea

"Why don't you drink tea, my dear sister?
Come have a good cup now with me.
I've drank it for years, it don't hurt me;
And 'twouldn't hurt you to drink tea."

"Don't urge me to drink it, I pray you,
If I do take this 'tis my first.
I have a good mind now to tell you
A tale I have seldom rehearsed.
"You know in revealed 'word of wisdom,'
We're taught, among other things, tea
Is not good for drink; but that is not
The whole of my reason you'll see.

"I once had a dear little brother,
The purest and prettiest elf;
I've never yet seen one so charming
Though I have a few boys myself.
"My mother drank her tea in those days.
'I can't do without it,' thought she,
'For work I must, daily and hourly,
Yet I feel that I ought to quit tea.'

"She struggled against the impression,
Yet tried to feel just as she should.
Thought she, 'when my work's not so pressing,
I will quit, that will do the same good.'

"Thus 'twas when one day ma took baby
And went to see Aunt Mary Ann;
Her baby was sick, and she said, 'do
You know I've been thinking Susann—

"'If I would quit tea, that my baby
Would be well and hearty again.
If I thought that,' said ma, 'I'd quit it
And that right away, Mary Ann.'

"She stayed there awhile, then went homeward,
Still feeling, 'I ought to quit tea.'
But thinking, 'I'll wait, till my baby
Is well, and as strong as can be.'

"Well, father came home from the Muddy,
And mother was busy of course;
For she was preparing to move there
And that hid all other remorse.

"One day ma was fixing dinner,
When baby came bringing a chair,
And asked her to sit down and take him
So cute, she could hardly forebear—

"But said, 'run and play mother's baby,
'Tis done all but fixing the tea;
One minute sweet darling then baby
May come and have dinner with me.'"

All true to that sweetest of natures,
He went as my mother had bade,
And taking the cup from the table
Straight down to the spring those feet strayed.

"When mother was ready she called him;
No answer, the truth flashed like wild;
'O run to the spring he is drowned! O
My God! O my baby, my child!'

"What need of my telling it farther?
He drowned, O how cruel! who dreamed
Of him being snatched in a moment
By death, who so full of life seemed?

"The tea didn't do it they tell me,
'Twould have happened like that any way;
To me it seems closely connected—
Don't urge me to drink it I pray.

"I was but a child when that happened,
My mother has not drank it since.
She doesn't say, 'daughter don't use it,'
The incident did me convince.

"And while I can labor without it,
As well with my brain and my hands,
There's no need of straining my conscience,
Or breaking my Father's commands."

The same basic rendition of the narrative occurs in both Mary Susannah's poem and the transcription of the oral narrative of her daughter that was quite obviously a retelling of a prose version by Mary Susannah. Interestingly, though, a first-person account of the incident by Laura Fackrell Chamberlain, Mary Susannah's older sister and Laura Ellen's aunt, reveals a somewhat more complicated picture:

> When I was about twelve years old there was a story paper, *The New York Ledger*, being printed. It was expensive so four families of us took it together. Our mothers and we girls used to get together sometime to read the stories. We would take our work and take turns reading. It came to my aunt and we went to her home so we would not miss the continued stories, as it had to be passed on that day. One day when we had been there we hurried home to get dinner. My mother was so busy that she did not notice that the baby, a beautiful little boy sixteen months old, had gone out. When she missed him she told me to run to the spring where we got our water. She thought of that the first thing. The baby was there and I got him out.
>
> I will never forget that time. It was awful. My mother blamed herself that she was not doing right. Her sorrow was terrible. She never read any more novels or drank tea or coffee, but tried to live as near right as she knew.[7]

These three different versions of an incident that occurred during Mary Susannah Fackrell Fowler's early childhood actually suggest a number of different motifs that recur in almost every discursive rendition of her life: the significance of family and community, especially a female community; the importance of religious dictums in a life well lived; the fragility of life and the daily presence of illness and/or death; and binding them all together, a recognition of the weightiness of "the word." The various versions of the story of Susannah Fackrell's tea drinking (and perhaps novel reading) leading to the death of her child become significant in the ways in which, *read together*, they suggest how Mary Susannah Fackrell Fowler drew on her own family history to support a value-centered view of the world. This example illustrates dramatically the necessity for allowing all the retellings, every reconstruction of this life, to reverberate with each of the other renditions.

Such a juxtaposition of versions alerts us to the problem of trying to historically reconstruct the "one true" Mary Fowler. Drawing on the critical stance of Suzanne Bunkers and Cynthia Huff in *Inscribing the Daily: Critical Essays on Women's Diaries*, we can see that Mary Fowler's diary needs to be considered "within the context of traditional definitions of autobiography and postmodernist challenges to these definitions."[8] Traditionally, historians and literary critics alike have sought to represent the "true self" in writing biographies or presenting historical autobiographies for the public.

Yet, postmodernist theory provides us with alternative notions that "ideas about the 'self' are constructs rather than eternal truths; that the canon can be revised to consider any text as a representation of reality and identity; and that writing the history of any set of conventions that we identify as a genre is a dialogue between the present and the past."[9] The assumption is that these texts may be read as kinds of signification, as linguistic representations constructed from the many discourses available at any particular historical moment.[10] This is precisely what occurs in the play of texts that construct various Mary Fowlers in different historical moments. The "self" both positions itself in the discourses available to it, and is produced by them.[11] Mary Fowler's choice of writing both diaries and poetry allows her to position herself in particular ways. At the same time, she is produced by those same discursive forms, as well as the multitude of others mentioned above. Her "self," in other words, is exactly that locus, that position where those discourses intersect with each other.

It is the *reader* of the various discourses who engages in the interpretive act of piecing together those modes of signification, just as Mary Fowler might have pieced her rag rugs—not in an effort to produce a seamless whole—but in order to delight in noting the way certain texts are illuminated by others, or to discover discursive discrepancies, just as the very best rugs play with the juxtaposition of color and material. For in the same way that Mary braided the wool scraps, so, too, the reader might use Francoise Lionnet's controlling metaphor of *metissage* or the "braiding" of cultural forms in the act of continuously reconstructing a life such as Mary Fowler's.[12]

The very act of reading these multiple discourses as they intersect or ignore each other poses particular adventures for the reader. Marlene Kadar suggests that "life writing can be used not only to privilege previously neglected selves, but also to constitute a rallying post or reader position from which to see the constructed self in the text"; and, as she observes elsewhere, the reader does not face the task of judging the text according to how "realistic" the autobiographical truth may be, and therefore how good or bad the life disclosed, but rather "the involved reader takes great pleasure in inventing a persona for himself or herself as he or she reads."[13] In this way, life writing is truly collaborative: as a reader and listener I reconstruct Mary Fowler's self at the same time I am reconstructing my own identity as reader, listener, and writer, as woman and mother, as friend and confidante. Such collaboration is, as Jane Marcus argues, a reproduction of women's culture as conversation: "If we agree that the [autobiographical] writer resurrects herself through memory, then the reader also resurrects the writer through reading her. . . . [This collaboration] does not occur in the male model of individualistic autobiography, where the reader is not expected to take such an active role."[14] Whether that reader is male or female, the "conversation" between

Mary Fowler and the reader, the collaboration between the reader and Mary's husband or granddaughter, allows an evolving understanding of both this turn-of-the-century poet and healer and of the reader him- or herself.

Each particular genre involved in this discursive matrix of significance represents particular challenges and rewards to the reader. Some of the discourses available to the active reader of Mary Fowler's life—the Relief Society and Mutual Improvement Association minutes, the memoirs of Mary's contemporaries in Orderville and Huntington, the records of the United Order, and Mary's own poetry and essays—have appeared as the "building blocks" of the various constructions of Mary Fowler's life throughout the preceding chapters. Here, I want to focus particularly on the problems and rewards of reading those discourses that are intentionally directed towards the production of a life history (or at least part of a life history) of Mary Susannah Fackrell Fowler: her own diaries, her husband's missionary diaries and autobiographical life histories, the personal life histories of family members, life histories of Mary herself written by her children, and oral narratives of her grandchildren.

DIARIES

The reader of diaries, especially women's diaries, must necessarily assume an unusually active role. The obvious difference in the "plots" of diaries and those of most other narratives is that "the novelist, poet, oral storyteller, or writer of an autobiographical memoir knows what happens next and directs the reader's response at every point. Most diaries, on the other hand, are a series of surprises to writer and reader alike, one source of the immediacy of the genre."[15] A number of contemporary diary theorists have pointed toward this dynamic between the known and unknown as a central feature of diary writing and reading. As Harriet Blodgett puts it: "For the reader, suspense is indigenous to the diary form and gives any diary a quality of tension not unlike the suspense of reading a novel or play . . . the comparative concision of most diaries and the diarists' selectivity . . . oblige the reader to stay imaginatively alive, to fill in around the mere framework offered."[16]

In fact, the editors of many women's diaries find that the texts they work with provide just such a "mere framework." For example, Laurel Thatcher Ulrich has suggested in her groundbreaking analysis of the diary of Martha Ballard that the "diary does not stand alone." It simply lacks sufficient detail to make itself coherent to an unknowing reader, who is unable to identify the people, the places, or the events within the diary without additional information provided by the other diaries and private writings, wills, tax lists, deeds, historical records, town meeting minutes, medical treatises, novels, and religious tracts.[17] Similarly, when I first read Mary Fowler's diary I was "hooked" as much by what I did *not* know as by what I was able to learn from those few pages. The entries were often so terse that they seemed to be comprised according to some secret code; it seemed impossible for a reader outside Mary Fowler's immediate community to really understand these entries without extratextual information. And yet, finding that extratextual information became an all-consuming passion for me as reader. I can remember, for example, the frustration I felt, holding the pages of Mary Fowler's diary for the first time, wondering what was meant by the phrase "sweat Sr. Robins"; this frustration is described in detail in chapter 1. Margo Culley suggests that my experience is not unique when she writes that "one source of the engagement of reading a private periodic record is precisely this activity, which can be akin to putting together pieces of a puzzle—remembering clues and supplying the missing pieces, linking details apparently unrelated in the diarist's mind, and decoding 'encoded' materials."[18]

While women's diaries are frequently cryptic in the brevity of their entries, certainly the extent to which any individual diarist's words need to be decoded by the reader varies tremendously; in part, that variation can be attributed to differences in anticipated audience. Several contemporary scholars have suggested that women wrote in their diaries in the nineteenth and early twentieth centuries simply when they didn't have anyone else to talk to. While that may have been the case in some instances, there are a wide variety of other reasons—and other audiences—for diary writing during this historical period: to provide travel notes and homesteading information for future travelers, to satisfy personal literary ambitions, to leave something for one's grandchildren to treasure, to give evidence of one's gentility as a lady who could write daily, or to respond to religious dicta, to name just a few.

In fact, the American diary itself has its roots in the genre of spiritual autobiography, "a form that is used to chart the progress of the pilgrim's soul toward God. This is a function the diary may still serve today for some individuals."[19] Here, too, the Calvinist tradition encouraged self-examination and exposure of one's self to God. An individual's written record of her life aided her in assessing her progress toward salvation.[20] During the late sixteenth and the seventeenth centuries the formulaic diary of conscience had been introduced; kept by both male and female covenanters, as it would be later by Quakers and Methodists, this form encouraged religious soul searching and served as "the ancestor of the personal diary preoccupied with the inner life."[21] Certainly this conception of the chronicling of inner spirituality has been foremost in the Mormon encouragement of journal keeping that still exists today.

Beginning in the nineteenth century, Mormons, believing that they were indeed the Latter-day Saints and that they were living an important mission at a very important time, kept diaries to record their part in the endeavor. They sought to record the ways in which they as individuals were helping to bring about the Kingdom of God, even in their daily activities. In addition, they wanted to keep these records for their descendants, who might then be able to understand the role their family played in the early days of the LDS Church, and to acknowledge the contributions that their family had made to the Mormon mission. In this respect, diary keeping by the Mormon faithful was also influenced by church authorities, whose own often extensive diaries served as models. Joseph Smith himself wrote,

> Long imprisonments, vexatious and long-continued law suits, the treachery of some of my clerks, the death of others, and the poverty of myself and brethren from continued plunder and driving, have prevented my handing down to posterity a connected memorandum of events desirable to all lovers of truth; yet I have continued to keep up a journal in the best manner my circumstances would allow, and dictate for my history from time to time, as I have had the opportunity so that the labors and suffering of the first Elders and Saints of this last kingdom might not be wholly lost to the world.[22]

In fact, church doctrine also contributed to the emphasis on record keeping of this sort. As Joseph Fielding Smith wrote in *Doctrines of Salvation,*

> The Lord has always impressed upon his people the necessity of keeping records. In Adam's day, we are informed by Moses, the Lord commanded that records be kept. . . . And so they were commanded to keep records. They were not only commanded to keep a record of important *events,* but they were also to keep a record of their *families* and preserve it that it might be of benefit in time to come.[23]

Certainly, well-kept diaries and journals might be seen as a significant part of this focus on family as well as official church records. Nineteenth-century Mormons also had other reasons for keeping diaries: like many other rural groups who depended on each other for support in barn building, agricultural endeavors, et cetera; diaries were used as a kind of unofficial record of the services they had provided for others and what others had done for them.[24]

For Mary Susannah Fackrell Fowler, however, the encouragement of her church to keep a journal was only one of several possible reasons for engaging in writing a diary. Although Mary Susannah never explicitly stated her reasons for diary keeping in her extant writings, other nineteenth-century women diarists actually acknowledge that they are writing with a particular audience in mind. For example, Texan Henrietta Embree's diary for May 18, 1858, suggests a number of potential audiences and reasons for writing:

> I have nothing in my journal interesting to be seen, but then if my friends wanted to see or here find it ready why should they not, I have no secrets in it, I expected for it to be seen I intend to take it to Kentucky with me for my Relatives, I thought it would give them some idea of a life in Texas, they could judge for one year of my life, I also thought it would be interesting to read myself in later years.[25]

Another Texan, Susan Newcomb, writing less than a decade later expands on this last reason in her own diary entry for June 14, 1867:

> I am writing these things just to keep practise, and perhaps I would be glad to see these scribblings twenty years hence if I should be so fortunate as to live that long. They would call to memory the days of my youth, the days that I spent in my cottage home far in the west, on the frontier of Texas, the only settler of Throckmorton County.[26]

Three years later Newcomb expresses a slightly different perspective when, after reflecting on how terrible the coming year would probably be, she writes on January 1, 1871:

> I think it advisable to brace ourselves up and prepare for the worst, but others may look at things in a different light. How ever I have a right to express my opinion any way I choose on this paper, for I dont suppose it will ever be read. It isn't for the public.
>
> Perhaps someone will see it when I am numbered with the dead; but then I will not know it, and as a matter of course I'll not care, and surely no one would ridicule the writings of the dead. I may like to look over this old journal sometime, but it will be of no importance to any one else, until my boy is old enough to read and understand.[27]

Susan Newcomb then works out within the first few lines of the 1871 diary the fact that her words may well be read by others in the years to come, certainly by her son, and that even though she is ostensibly writing only for herself and not "for the public," there is an understood silent audience waiting to respond in the future.

Unfortunately, other diarists, like Mary Fowler, are not so clear about their intended audiences. The best clues we may have to the possible relationship between writer and assumed reader/audience lies in the text itself—not only in terms of content, but stylistically. The more consciously aesthetically marked and crafted the diary is, the more likely it was intended for a wider audience than the writer herself.

Attention to aesthetic highlighting can be subjective at best, however. For the most part, many women's diaries are presented in a mostly prosaic, straightforward style. Louisa Bain, a nineteenth-century diarist, called her own diary "dry facts, no feelings," and though her diary does include some expression of emotion, she is indeed far more focused on factual observations. Harriet Blodgett notes that Bain's label "could be affixed to the large number of diaries that are bare-bones records."[28] Certainly, Mary Fowler's diary is one of them.

Stylistically, Fowler's diary might be described by what sociolinguist Basil Bernstein has called a "restricted code." Such a code is comprised of "unelaborated prose, few modifiers, concrete language, an emphasis on 'how' instead of 'why,' and implicit rather than explicit emotion."[29] Bernstein suggests that this restricted code tends to be used by and among people who share strong common bonds. In the case of Mary Fowler, however, and other diarists who write mainly for themselves, the restricted code is employed even more selectively in ways that sometimes make the code's restrictions initially decodable only by the author herself. For example, on Sunday, October 21, 1900, Mary Fowler wrote only: "attended S.S. and meeting." Although the Sunday date might immediately cue the reader that this reference might have something to do with church attendance, the specifics of the reference are initially somewhat obscure.

Such a style is no doubt also directly connected to certain structural features of this particular discursive form. Estelle Jelinek suggests that

> rather than the progressive, linear, unidimensional works that men wrote—chronicles, *res gestae*, intellectual histories—most women's self-portraits are cast in discontinuous forms and disjunctive narratives. Diaries, letters, and journals . . . are accessible forms for women whose emotional, intellectual and practical lives are fragmented by domestic responsibilities that leave them little leisure time to contemplate or integrate their experiences.[30]

Jelinek's observations about the connections between the formal stylistic features of women's writing and the realities of those women's fragmented lives have been echoed by a number of feminist historians interested in reclaiming women's voices and writing women back into history by attending to these "nontraditional" literary forms. They suggest, for example, that diaries offered a kind of writing practice, one that allowed the expression of a sense of self organized relationally. Diaries were flexible enough to "allow for the discontinuity, gaps and silences that were an inevitable part of female life."[31] Suzanne Juhasz notes that "in their form, women's lives tend to be like the stories that they tell: they show less a pattern of linear development towards some clear goal than one of repetitive, cumulative, cyclical structure. One thinks of housework or childcare, of domestic life in general."[32]

Certainly these observations are relevant to this study as well as to the numerous other projects that have sought to make connections between diary style and women's disjunctive lives. However, the case of Mary Fowler affords an additional perspective. Although Mary Susannah certainly fits the picture of a woman whose life was necessarily disrupted continually by the exigencies of nurturing family and friends, the restricted diary form she chose to embrace mirrored her own life's structure. Nonetheless Mary Fowler also found the time to write extensively in other genres, most notably poetry. While her abbreviated diary entries suggest the writing of a woman who simply had no uninterrupted time for composition, other discourses demonstrate that she was actually able to find numerous occasions to compose in poetic form. What this suggests, of course, is that the formal restrictions of the diary were ones that Mary found acceptable, even particularly appropriate, for particular discursive goals. For Mary Fowler, and I suspect for thousands of women like her, the journal served most importantly as a record of her own life, and style was incidental, not a generic imperative.

The very physical diary itself provides clues to this connection between audience, purpose, and rhetorical style, for

> the ideal way to study a diary is to have the manuscript itself in your hand because all the material aspects of a diary create important impressions. Is the cover ornate? Are the edges gilt? Does it have a lock? Or was the writing done on the least expensive of notebooks whose covers have barely survived?[33]

While much of Mary Fowler's collection of poetry and essays is carefully copied into a hardbacked red book suitable for saving, her diary appears in a foolscap, paperback notebook that is often used for other purposes—lists of things to do, notes on church conferences, lists of money owed. Not only are the covers not ornately gilt, but in the case of the last extant portion of the diary, the cover has been lost completely. For Mary Fowler, the connection between the simple, sometimes cryptic style and the material notebook in which her diary was kept clue the reader that her diary was probably kept primarily for herself, as a private document.

There were, in fact, occasions on which Mary's own poetic impulses emerged in her diary writing, although it was certainly an unusual occurrence. The epigraph to this book, also quoted in chapter 3, is perhaps the best example of Mary's poetic sensibilities emerging in her diary. Although such ebullience and metaphoric detail is unusual in Mary Fowler's diary entries, this particular example demonstrates that the absence of such detail in other places in the diary is not due to lack of rhetorical ability, but rather is an intentional discursive choice made by the author. Such a choice is not unique to Mary Fowler. Elizabeth Baer, for example, describes the Civil War diary of Lucy Buck, which most frequently echoed a similarly straightforward, prosaic style, but did have days on which her prose style is "self-consciously poetic and romantic."[34] Even in their usual concern with daily record keeping, these women occasionally found it necessary to use poetic discursive forms. In those places in the diaries we find an elaboration of particularly significant themes. In the example above, Mary Fowler articulates most clearly her belief in the model of nature for revealing what might be considered her own life's guiding principle, that of "unselfish usefulness."

The very dailiness of most of the diary entries, however, is what "matters to most women; and dailiness is by definition never a conclusion, always a process. The classic verbal articulation of dailiness is, of course, the diary."[35] In the nine months of the first extract we have of Mary Fowler's diary, she rarely missed a day of recording. Sometimes the entries were extraordinarily brief, as in the entry for November 30, 1899: "Ettie better, went to sr G's." Yet, the important thing is that the entry was there. In this respect, Fowler's diary keeping might be evidence of Margo Culley's assertion that "keeping a diary, one could argue, always begins with a sense of self-worth, a conviction that one's individual experience is somehow remarkable. Even the most self-deprecating of women's diaries are grounded in some sense of the importance of making a record of the life."[36]

And that record most often was composed of the details of domestic life. As early as the seventeenth century both English and American women's personal diaries were comprised largely of these domestic details, and that continued to be the case through the nineteenth and well into the twentieth century.[37] Mary Fowler's diary, for example, most often focuses on such details as chronicles of domestic work accomplished: "Wash day. Mary Brace helped us. Laurie staid out of school" (December 15, 1899); healing and nursing: "called on Sr. Gale who has a broken arm & worse than that a boy in jail. Took her some pills. She was glad to get them" (December 19, 1899); concerns about her children: "Rey's birthday. Seventeen yrs old and very little larger than Asa who is twelve. But he is a good boy and I trust he will be larger soon" (December 14, 1899); and records of the weather and of financial transactions: "Snow three inches deep" (December 17, 1899), "Thermometer at zero" (December 22, 1899), and "Arno came home. He paid $30 on wagon, gave me $5" (June 24, 1900).

Along with the inscription of daily events, some nineteenth-century women used a particular diary code to keep track of menstruation, and others found their journals useful places to jot memory aids.[38] Mary Fowler's list of topics to include in her letters to Ammon while he was on his mission (cited in chapter 4) is a fine example of the incorporation of a different kind of memory aid in a diary.

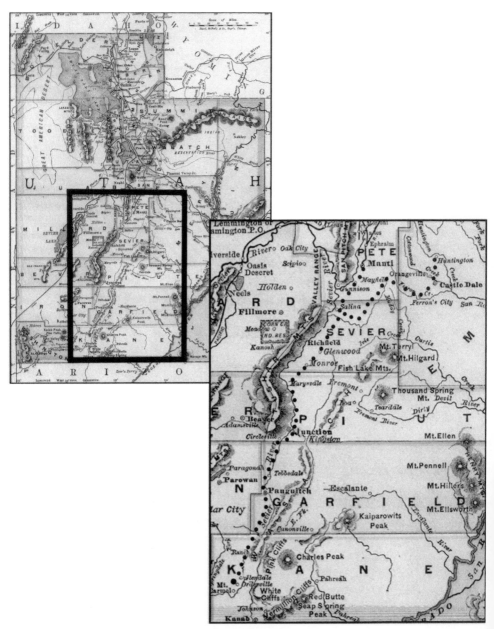

Map of Utah produced for the *Encyclopaedia Britannica*, c. 1888. Enlargement indicates the route taken by the Fowlers and their party as they moved from Orderville to Huntington, Utah that same year.

Mary Susannah and Henry Ammon Fowler traveled along the
banks of the Sevier River on their journey between Orderville and
Huntington, Utah. Photo used by permission, Utah State Historical
Society.

Such attention to the details of daily life pose a particular challenge
to the reader. "There are few beginnings and ends; it is all 'middle,' and one
tries to read forward and back at the same time, groping through the baf-
fling, too-great intimacies of private writings."[39] Such moving back and
forth actually challenges one's sense of time.[40] In part, that challenge is due
to the very nature of the concept of daily writing itself, for "even the
phrase 'keeping a diary' suggests resistence to time, change, and ultimately
death. . . . the essence of the impulse to keep a diary is captured in 'I write,
therefore I am.' And will be."[41]

Any time there is a major disruption in a woman's life, any time there
is an occasion which creates a sense of discontinuity of self, of change,
keeping a diary can be an attempt to preserve a continuity that may seem
broken or lost. It is no wonder, then, that Mary Fowler's most extensive
piece of writing, one clearly based on daily accounts, chronicles the most
significant move of her life from Orderville to Huntington in 1888. It is
also not surprising that the only fragments we have left of her diary, the
only ones we actually can confirm the existence of, detail the period both
immediately preceding her husband's mission and the time he was away.
On both of these occasions, Mary Fowler's life was disrupted in significant

ways, challenging her sense of self, her sense of the person she had been and the person she was becoming. In addition, they highlight the force of separation on Mary's own deep sense of interconnectedness.

The piece of writing that details the trip from Orderville to Huntington is the opening entry in a large, red, bound book entitled "Mary Fowler's 2nd Book of Origanal and Selected Pieces." Although it is written in the past tense, more in the fashion of a memoir, the detailed account is so specific that it must certainly have been composed from daily entries in a now long lost diary:

It was a fine day the thirtieth of Oct. 1888, that the time came for me to bid farewell to my dearly loved home in Orderville. With aching heart I bade adieu to my brothers and sisters (my parents being absent) and many dear friends, took a last look at the old home, and started with our family (who were as loth to part with home as I was) and some others for Huntington. Harriet Eliza and my self walked across the heavy sand and came up with the wagons just above the Esplin farm. Ere we left the dear place I picked up a little peble which though tiny and simple, is to be placed among my keepsakes. We came as far as the Factory that night. Our family was kindly entertained by my brother in law, Bro Chamberlain and family. Isaac Allen and family prefered to camp at the wagons, and Albert Allen and family went on a mile farther to Willis Webbs place. Next morning we got a fair start, but found our loads to be too heavy for the teams, consequently we had a great deal of walking to do. I took my baby and one of my little boys and went ahead of the teams in order to see Sister Louisa Spencer, I found her self and husband at home; and they expressed many good wishes for us on our journey and in our future home. We traveled to with in a mile or two of the divide that night and camped. J. Adair camped with us and he also gave us a mutton. As it looked some like raining we tried to prepare for it, and after evening prayer we retired for the night. Some of the beds were made in the wagons, others under the wagons and one bed was entirely without shelter. As we had expected it did rain and rained very hard. Those on the ground got soaking wet and muddy while those in the wagons did not entirely escape the wetting and were very tired, from the efects of uncomfortable positions and being kept awake. When morning came we found we had not been at all prepared for camping in a rain storm. Many of the childrens clothing had been left in the rain; and the task of ransacking boxes for dry ones, and drying the bed clothes though it gave us some profitable experience, was not at all an enviable one. But all hands set to work, and we got through alright with the exceptions of burning one good woolen quilt. After eating a late breakfast we started on, and we began to find riding as well as walking, a little uncomfortable, as there was seven grown persons and fifteen children to ride in three loaded wagons. The eldest child a boy of the thirteen years rode horse back to drive the stock. After all we had pretty good luck that day, and camped at night on the Sevier river opposite Pettersons place. Next morning we got an early start, and we met my brother Norman who had the tongue of his wagon broken by he and Isaac Alens running their wagons together. That day our travel was along the Sevier a beautiful river which tried to make itself as interesting as possible but the barren hills on either side unlike the lovely scenery of dear old Long Valey was very monotonous. The day wore slowly away and we camped reluctantly on account of the short distance traveled at the Panguitch bridge. We had a pleasant evening a good nights rest and an early start next morning. Just as we were starting William S. Butler came along bringing the unwelcome news of his fathers arest for unlawfull cohabitation. We went into the little town of Panguitch, which is well filled with pretty houses and ugly streets and fences, and did some trading. It took us longer than the others, and our team got so far behind that we did not "catch up" till noon. That night we camped in circleville canyon at Keslers place. Supper over we women did a little washing and all retired for the night. But about midnight it began to rain and rained just enough to scare us out of our cozy resting places and quit untill we comenced to get breakfast then it continued to rain nearly all day; but not heeding the rain we had prayer ate breakfast packed away the things and started. Our host and the men had not been able to agree on the price of pasturage, so it was not paid before we started. But we had not been going long when they concluded to pay the bill and have a conscience void of offence. So H. A. Fowler rode back through the rain and paid two dollars and ten cents for turning ten head of horses and seven head of horned stock in a field where the hay had been cut and hauled and the fence was down. We had a disagreable day and camped early in the Circleville school house. It was Sunday and after prayers and supper were over, the children were called together and each of the men talked to them awhile, as we were not disturbed at all that night, we thought there must be a quiet set of boy[s?] in Circleville. Next morning after having prayer and a good warm breakfast we started on again. This was a very cold day. We nooned with some old friends by the name of Barnson. Then we traveld till long after dark and camp south of Merry Ville at bro. Hows place. He and his family were very kind to us, furnishing us shelter fuel and the use of their only stove free of charge. Next day we came through Monroe and camped outside of town. It snowed on us during the night. Next morning the men concluded to go over the Glenwood hill thereby leaving the only chance we would have of meeting my father and mother whom I would dearly loved to have seen before moving so far away from them. That night we camped about a mile from Glenwood at Frank Walls whose wife Mary is a step sister to H. F. and Harriet. The time with them was spent pleasantly listening to some choice songs accompanied by the Organ. Also music from the fiddle and Organ. Then men and children also went to a childrens dance, which was in a school house close by. When they came home and after a heart felt prayer we retired for the night, and next day we went to Salina bought some salt, Harriet wrote a card home, and then we went on and camped outside of town. Next day we came as far as may field where we learned we could not go through north bend canyon on account of deep snow. So we camped south of town, and next morning Ammon and Albert each saddled a horse and rode over to Manti. Isaac and family went the day before, and with the help of the children Harriet Eliza and my self did some washing patching and drying the bed clothes that had been wet several days. We were quite comfortable all day but when night came and no men in camp, some of us felt a little nervous. After all had retired but my self one of the horses came up and as they did not usually come to camp at that hour I went to see what was the matter. The nose sack had been left on which I took off and then called Willie and found that two more were in the same condition. We lit the lantern and after a long search we found the others one had got his nose sack off and Willie took off the other one which by the way was a tin bucket worked in to a nose sack through the ingenuity of his father. We then retired without making farther search for the missing sack. Next morning was as lovely a sabbath as ever I beheld and the day was agreeably spent taking care of the things around camp reading writing and talking of those we had left at home and those we were to meet at the end of our journey. About three oclock Albert and Ammon came from Manti and in the evening Isaac came bringing with him his two daughters whom he had left in Manti on his trip south. And we prepared to retrace our steps a ways and go through Salina canyon. When monday morning came we got a good start, and had fair skies with beautiful scenery on all sides. But we soon came to mud, and oh such mud! We could almost imagine that we had got in to natures glue pot. However we got through this about the middle of the afternoon alright excepting that every body in camp especialy the teams were awfully tired. Then some of us immaginary creatures supposed we would have better road but we were soon brought to sense the facts, for we had only had a breathing spell when we came to the twist, and I donot care to ever take part in such twisting again. There were many curious things to be seen on that short but never to be forgotten road, but realy we did not have time to look at them, for with turning so many short corners going over large rocks and down and up such steep pitches we had no time for any thing but to hang on. However time will wear away and so did the distance, and night found us camped on the Salina river, where we would have been quite comfortable had it not been for a sharp wind blowing. We prepared to make an early start next morning but during the night some of the animals strayed off and after quite a search were found at a mans hay stack for which Isaac paid 25 cts and Ammon 30. When they were returning to camp Ammon was kicked by one of his horses on the knee which made it nearly impossible for him to get around. At noon he had some wild sage leaves bruised and moistened with tincture of lobelia, and a poultice of it put on his knee & that together with the blessings of Heaven, helped him so much that next day a limp was hardely perceptible. Of course we did not get the early start we had anticipated but we hitched up and started. We had not been going long when we came to the rattlesnake hill and some of us wished it had kept ahead of us, for we thought it a terrible hill; But we found it only a small sample of the road we had to travel that day. That night it was a tired set that camped at what is called the hanging rock. Our campfire and most of the beds were made under it. We had plenty of wood and water close by and a pleasant atmosphere. In the night we were aroused and some of us frightened half to death by the most hideous howling I ever heard. None of us could exactly account for it but next morning we were on the move in good time and the problem of the howling was solved by a pup coming from its hiding place among the ledges, and H.A.F. persuaded it to come along with us. That morning we commenced crossing the Salina creek (fording it) and it occured so often and was so disagreable on account of the banks being frosen and slipery making it often necessary to double teams and then hovering [?] the wagons slip back in the creek occasionally that it was very discouraging to some of us. So much so that the remark was made by one that it would take millions of dollars to make a road through that canyon. To which the encouraging reply was made that a thousand would make it pretty good. Then the first speaker replied I don't believe the wealth of the whole world could do it. The cenery all the way through the canyon was beautiful; this seemed to partely atone for the rough roads. We left the creek in the afternoon then the roads were much better and we camped on wet ground that night; But there was plenty of brush close by to put under the beds so the ground was not as disagreable as it might have been. The gultch differed widely from what my ideas were of a gultch. I expected to see a country cut up by washes and floods but this was only a piece of my ignorance; for it was a nice grassy country much more open than long valley with not a wash to be seen. By some sort of a miscalculation our flour was now nearly gone with no chance of getting more. But there was some shorts in camp and we found warm shortcake to be very palitable to sharp appetites. We were quite comfortable that night excepting that the whole camp was aroused by the men running after their horses. Next day we came over the divide and as far as the mouth of red creek canyon where we had a comfortable camping place. But as soon as H.A.F. unhitched his hourses they went off; not even waiting to get their grain. As that was something unusual the men were afraid they had taken the road for the muddy and H.A.F. went eight or nine miles in that direction while those at the camp looked up the creek on the hills and in the side canyons but it was all to no purpose for the horses were not found that night. Next morning as soon as it was light Ammon and Albert started out again and Isaac after satisfing himself that the horses were not close by hitched up his team and went on leaving word that if he found the horses he would either bring or send them back. But he did not have this trouble as they were brought to camp about ten oclock having been found about two miles away and we were soon on the move. But we had a stormy day before us and we were all glad when evening came and we were under shelter in the muddy school house. But Albert had taken cold and was sick with the cramp all night. As another family was camped there the house was pretty well filled leaveing merely a path from the door to the fireplace when the beds were all made down. It was now November 15th. We had another cloudy stormy day so that we could see nothing by the slippery hills and sticey mud over which we traveled. We did not see the sun atal that day. We made no camp at noon but came to Ferron where we were kindly welcomed by Fred and Marrion Core and their families; and where we were entertained more as invited guests than mere campers. In the evning all came together and the time was spent with songs speeches recitations and music. Next day was sunday and as it was still storming we spent the day with our kind friends who strongly urged it. That day and evening passed very pleasantly. And the next morning as soon as the horses could be found breakfast eaten and things packed away we started on the last days travel of that trip. It was a lovely day and we had a good road. We nooned at the Castledale bridge. In the afternoon brother Simeon Allen came with his team to meet us and we arived at Huntington about six oclock. All well and feeling that it was good to come to the end of so tedious a trip.

It is clear that Mary Fowler, like many other women of the period, read and reread her diary, and in this case used it to fashion a lengthier, fuller account of this momentous journey.[42] On the other hand, her husband, Henry Ammon's account of the journey in his later autobiography is confined to one terse paragraph:

We left Orderville in November and made our journey through fair weather until we got to Ferron, a town twenty miles south of Huntington. At Ferron, it rained practically all night so we had a hard time getting on to Huntington. We had to camp out every night of our trip.

Although the journey was certainly an important one for Mr. Fowler, Mary Fowler's account reveals just how intensely this move affected her life. As we have seen in the preceding chapters, the concept of interconnection was paramount for Mary Fowler, and any separation from loved ones became the context for an expression of pain and longing through writing. In this lengthy prose piece, Mary comes to terms with such separation in reconstructing a new self, and she deals as effectively as possible with leaving the old self behind: "Ere we left the dear place I picked up a little peble which though tiny and simple, is to be placed among my keepsakes." The

Harriet Fowler Allen and Florence Fowler Adair, Mary Susannah
Fowler's sisters-in-law, who traveled with Mary and Henry Ammon
Fowler from Orderville to Huntington. Photo courtesy of Virginia
Fowler Rogers.

diary, like the "peble," stands as a metanym for the dramatic change in her
own life.

The fact that diaries are constantly in process, constantly chronicling
change suggests that they also avoid closure. Carolyn Heilbrun notes that
"because the diary form avoids closure in the traditional sense, writing and
critiquing diaries may enable women to envision their narratives and their
lives differently."[43] It is the very form of the diary, allowing for interrup-
tion and discontinuity at the same time it signals process and continuous
development, that makes it so discursively significant for Mary Fowler, and
I suspect for many, many other women like her. Because the diary moves
in separate units of experience, always in present tense, the perspective of
the diarist is one of immersion, not of distance. A diary is completed when
there are no more pages left on which to record one's daily activities, not
necessarily when one's life has reached its denouement.[44]

Given the emphasis on the discontinuous, immersed, processual nature
of women's diary keeping, one might assume that our interest in such texts

might be merely to examine voyeuristically the detritus of a woman's daily life by delving into the pages of her diary, what Mary Fowler's contemporary, Virginia Woolf called "that capacious hold-all in which one flings a mass of odds & ends."[45] On closer examination, however, that capacious hold-all which seems initially so chaotic and haphazard often reveals a rhythmic pattern that the reader comes to recognize.[46] Often those rhythms are located in strategies of repetition as well as in silences and gaps. The interpretive reader is then charged with paying particular attention to the dynamics of repetition and silence in the daily writing of women. As Margo Culley suggests: "Because diaries are periodic in creation and structure, incremental repetition is an important aspect of the structure of most journals, and the dynamic of reading the periodic life-record involves attending to what is repeated."[47] In addition, though, the silences that fill these pages also demand critical attention, for the self-presentation in women's diaries often reveals the truth by leaving out as much as leaving in. Just as the absence of a thematic focus on specific Mormon virtues in Mary's poetry is suggestive of her own particularly intense attention instead to the primary metaphor of interconnectedness, so, too, the silences in her diary need to be understood in relation to the details provided. For example, while Mary does not discuss her relationship with Eliza, her sister-wife, with any degree of specificity in the diary, she nonetheless does briefly recount several occasions on which she provided Eliza and her children with both medical attention and financial support. Like those Mormon virtues that are absent from the poetry, so the description of the nature of her relationship with Eliza is something so basic to her sense of self that apparently Mary Fowler does not need to elaborate upon it in writing.

It is through the careful reading of both repetition and silence that we can come to understand what James Olney has called "metaphors of self." Only when we begin to see the rhythm, the pattern in the play of repetition and silence, is the prosaic, straightforward style of the diary allowed to reveal its real power. Because Mary Fowler's diary and many other diaries of nineteenth-century women contain almost no metaphors and very few adjectives, it is the accumulation of factual details that provides the real rhetorical force that might in other genres accrue to metaphor.[48] The repetitive rhythm of details and silences in Mary Fowler's diary, then, assumes a profound metaphoric power.

Such metaphoric self-representation has been described by some diary scholars in thematic terms. Suzanne Bunkers, for example has suggested that there are four primary themes that emerge in the midwestern women's diaries she has studied: (1) the woman's need to view the use of her time and energies as worthwhile; (2) the need for connection with other human beings; (3) the need for an outlet for emotions such as intense grief or anger which her culture did not deem appropriate for public expression by a woman; and (4) the writer's need for a forum for commentary on such subjects as marriage, religion, politics, and world events.[49] Bunkers seems to suggest that while not all midwestern women's diaries evidenced all of these themes, most exhibited at least some of them. As we examine the repetitions and silences of Mary Susannah Sumner Fackrell Fowler's diary, we begin to understand the ways in which her own self-representation includes some of these same themes. Yet these themes are in some way complementary to her own construction of self, not models for it. In other words, the metaphors of self employed by Mary Fowler in her diary, as well as her poetry and essays, symbolically create an identity that is responsive in some ways to the themes Bunkers identifies. For Mary Susannah, metaphors of self revolve around the recognition that she is a woman committed to her community, especially the community of her family, her female acquaintances, and her church; that she is a healer, standing between a healthy life and death; that she is a woman of words, who is gifted with the ability to express through poetic language the values she represents within her own community. It is these personal themes that emerge in the diary and that both complement and expand upon Bunkers's more general thematic concerns.

HENRY AMMON FOWLER'S DIARY

While much of the preceding discussion is relevant to an analysis of the diary Henry Fowler kept on his mission to Oklahoma and Indian Territory from 1900 to 1902, there are also some major differences. As suggested above, men's diaries were often less elliptical, more fully developed narratives of their participation in significant (or what they deemed to be significant) historical events than the daily recordings of women's journals. This is generally the case with Henry Ammon's diary, although from a particular perspective. As a missionary for the Church of Jesus Christ of Latter-day Saints, Henry Fowler considered the recording of his daily activities to be at least in major part an account of the active furthering of the Kingdom of God. The very title of his diary suggests this: "Journal of the Travels of Henry A. Fowler of the Church of Jesus Christ of Latterday Saints While in the South Western States Mission Oklahoma and Indian Teritory Chickasaw Nation." LDS historian Davis Bitton in the introduction to his massive bibliography *Guide to Mormon Diaries and Autobiographies* has suggested that "perhaps the largest single category of Mormon diaries is made up of those kept by missionaries."[50] Bitton goes on to point out that while in some cases the recording of mission experiences was simply part of a longer diary kept over many years, many diaries were kept by individuals only while they were serving mission assignments. The missionary diary is what Bitton calls "a very good example of a standardized account."[51] In almost all Mormon missionary diaries the following themes and topics are set forth in greater or lesser detail: mission call, preparation, and farewells; trip; companions; proselyting; members; contact with home; sightseeing; release; return trip.[52] While Davis Bitton is careful to point out that such standardization does not imply that these diaries are "insincere, inaccurate, or lacking in significance to their authors," there is obviously a tendency for structural repetition.[53] Such is certainly the case in Henry Ammon Fowler's journal.

Fowler gives the specifics of his mission call to Oklahoma, then details his journey from Huntington to Salt Lake City with members of his family and his leave-taking from them. He also records his subsequent railroad journey to Oklahoma, the trials of the trip, and meeting his companion:

> I left my Home in Huntington Emery Co Utah Oct 5th 1900 and arrived in Salt Lake City 6 at 12:45 PM was in time [to] attend the last meetings of Conference spent the time visiting with friends 2 PM 10th went to the Temple and in the annex was set apart for a mission to the southwestern States by elder Jos W McMurrin. Left City 8:20 PM Oct 11th on D&R.G.RR arrd in Grand Junction on 12th our company of 18 Elders parted here 9 of us going on CSL Midland & 2 on D&RG crossed a very high range of mountains in the afternoon & through a Tunnel 2 miles took 5 min to go through. passed by Leadville on the left a short distance could see it through the mountains the cenery is grand, but the road is very crooked arrd in Col Springs at 7 AM we here found Elders Siddoway & Gee of the Col Mission they were very much pleased to meet us & they staid with us till we boarded the Train again at 11:45 PM While here we strolled down the town our accomodations the first night from Salt Lake City was anything but good. So many people on the Train but from Col Springs we had a chair car and I soon fell asleep to wake about daylight to find we had left the mountains far behind. . . . Oct 17th . . . When we left Newkirk next morning we left our grips in the room & went in search of our future companions. They came in from the country for their mail about 10 AM so we found them Elder H.D. Hold my companion & Elder Orlin Cox with Elder Ruby walked a mile together then we all kneeled down & thanked the Lord for his blessings sang a Hymn then parted Elders Cox & Ruby South of town & we to go North our labors soon began we stay all night with a Mr. Henrie they treeted us well I enjoy the sweet potatoes here & everybody raises them.

As the above diary entry suggests, Henry Ammon includes the names of the members he visits and stays with, and he also lists the names and locations of those he converts. His diary is explicit in noting the number of miles traveled each day in proselyting: "Elder Holt went to bed early but

I set up til 10:30 talking on the Gospel & our people had a good bed walked 8 miles. . . . The stove was warm & a joney cake in the oven so we ate some of it & syrup thanked the Lord for his blessings then slept in his bed walked 14 miles" (November 2, 1900); and in describing the various sights he sees: "After writing our Journals this morning we took a walk with Mr Baxter to what is called Lost City it is on the Bluff South of the Arkansas River. The City so called is nothing but a long series of narrow passages among the Rocks the Rocks have been heaved apart in narrow lanes 6 to 12 ft apart and the rocks are 10 to 15 ft high and Trees of different kinds all among them and flowers and ferns. It is quite a pretty place" (July 3, 1902).

One of the most frequent entries in his journal, interspersed with his own activities, is an account of the letters he receives from home and often the content of those letters. For our purposes here this is most fortunate, since Henry Ammon often describes events in Huntington in much greater detail than Mary Susannah's own diary. For example, on September 13, 1901, he wrote:

> I got a letter from Mary saying Arno had come Home and the cow had been bloted & stuck and JW Washburn had come Home from his mission and she had the janitor work again for the School House. also a letter from Eliza. Carl had given her money so she had bought 25 bu. of wheat. Said Mary's cow had died it made me feel nearly sick I also got a letter from Rey he said he wanted to take music lessons this next winter but he bought Ma a cow and she needed it so bad and the cow was a good one so he did nt care but he will feel different when he hears she is dead.

It is also clear that Henry Ammon intends for his journal to be read and kept by his family; in fact, on February 8, 1901, he writes: "I have begun writing in another book and will send this Home for the folks to read and criticise." This acknowledgment of his audience also suggests the reasons that Henry Ammon might spend far more time citing details of his life than he might otherwise have done. Apart from the larger issues concerning gender and genre, it is also clear that this particular familial audience had certain expectations of his diary keeping, and that in addition to his own purposes, Henry also tried to write what his family would most want to read.

When I first began researching Mary Susannah's life, I initially discounted the importance of reading Henry's missionary journals—at least in part because I expected them to be the standardized repetition of houses visited and converts baptized. However, I later discovered that the juxtaposition of Henry's diary with Mary Susannah's record for the portion of this period where the two journals overlap is particularly fascinating. From the interplay of these two private writings, the reader can get a much fuller picture of life in Huntington for Mary and her family. Often Henry's account cites letters from Mary in which she discloses her illnesses that are sometimes glossed over in her own diary: "E is improving but M has a pain moving thro her limbs and makes her hand cramp so her letter was very short" (May 7, 1901).

Henry's diary interestingly provides a context for photographic documentation as well. On March 15, 1901, he writes:

> Bro Hendrics went to the P.O. and brought me letters from Home conveying the news that Mary & family had their pictures taken and Eliza was some worse again and a short note from O Gynon saiing he and Ellen were thinking of getting married and desiring to know "if I were for or against it" Mary said she was having another spell of toothache and Apostles J H Smith and A H Lund were in town and held meeting.

And on May 11, 1901, he adds, "We went to the P.O. for our mail the long looked for Picture of Mary and family came with a letter also she is better Arno and Eben are at Price shearing sheep." Henry's journal for April 12, 1901, also notes the arrival of a picture of Mary with "the Club," her women's literary group: "I got letters from Home also one from Bro E Fane at Gowen and the long looked for Picture of the Club and also of the Martial Band myself being one of them."

Through the immediacy of Henry Ammon's recounting of Mary's letters the reader can also begin to see the ways in which the same themes and metaphors of self that emerge in her own diary are articulated in another discursive form. By far the most prominent theme mentioned in Henry's accounts of Mary's letters to him is the health and well-being of their children, and also of Eliza and her children. Since Mary's own writing reveals and elaborates upon both the theme of interconnection, especially familial interdependence, and the theme of the healer as nurturer, Henry's reports of her letters to him situate this understanding in a broader context. This brief example demonstrates Mary's concerns: "February 21, 1901 two letters from Home Arno is better & Fred has been sick and is better Harry fell on the water Pail and cut his nose. Eliza is better My letters were encouraging it had been 10 days since hearing from home." The importance of Mary's family, whether the health of her children or the welfare of her distant husband, is a constant and abiding theme in the letters to her husband. The extent to which Henry Ammon obviously relies on letters, especially letters from Mary, to keep his spirits up cannot be overstated; for Mary, maintaining the interconnective bonds is of paramount concern, and it is clear that letters sent and received are a sustaining force for them both.

Just as the rhythm of detail and silence in Mary Fowler's diary provide the reader with an understanding of the relative significance of particular concerns, it is especially interesting to examine the silences in Henry's own diary. Although Mary's memory notes of items to mention in her letters suggest that she did occasionally write about her activities with other women in the community, Henry's own diary entries never mention these relationships. Clearly her activities and her relationships with other women were far more important to Mary Susannah than they were to her husband.

Although Henry Ammon does not frequently write about the ministering of his wife to other Huntington women in his diary, he does note the significance of her care for his plural wife Eliza and her children. On January 26, 1901, he writes: "I got two letters from Home saiing E is still unable to leave Home & Sister Rowley is Dead." Other entries indicate that it is Mary who lovingly cares for the ill Eliza and also for Eliza's son Leo. In fact, Mary also cares for Henry himself, even though he is so distant; on July 1, 1902, Henry writes that "I went to the P. O. and received a small Box of medicine sent from Home (Herbes)." And after one particularly severe illness, Henry wrote, "I missed the nursing of a tender wife in such spells and I hope I shall not have any more sickness till I go where I can get it."[54]

Mary's influence on Henry in terms of healing can also be evidenced in the list of remedies that appears in his diary. One such remedy is entitled "recipe for week women" and reads:

Blood Root 1/2 oz	nutmeg 1 oz
Cinamon 1 oz	cloves "
Senica Snake Root 1 oz	Blue cohush 1 oz
Black snake Root 1 "	Wahoo bark 1 "
Camomile 1 "	Yellow dock 1 "
Qaking asp Bark 1 oz	
Cotton Wood Bark 1 "	
Camomile Flour 1 "	
Put in 1/2 pt of alcohol and	
cork tight in a qt Bottle for	
24 hours then fill with water	
Dose Tea Spoon full 3 times a day	

Not only do Henry's journals reveal that Mary suggested remedies for her husband when he suffered from numerous complaints during his mission, but she also supplied him with a number of traditional cures for use with other individuals. The theme of healing and of Mary as healer for the community is reaffirmed through her husband's diary as he labored for two years in Oklahoma.

Similarly, another "metaphor of self" found in Mary's own diary and in her collected writings is represented in Henry's journal—the theme of Mary Susannah as a woman of words. On December 7, 1900, only a month after his mission had begun, Henry notes, "I got a letter from Mary with verses written for my birthday"; and in an accompanying notebook he records one of these poems in his own handwriting. Henry's appreciation for his wife's poetic gifts and his recognition of her writing abilities recur throughout the diaries. For example, after discussing a meal he shared with a Mormon family, Henry writes: "After supper I sang a song with Sister Harless to learn her the Tune the Song is one Mary composed at Orderville when on a visit in 1890."[55] Mary's verses are both treasured personal remembrances for Henry and meaningful thoughts worth sharing with others as well.

What is clear from Henry Ammon's diary entries concerning his wife Mary is that the way in which she is constructed through his discourse draws on several of the same themes that she herself articulates in her own writing. While Mary's concern with the larger community, especially the community of women, is not specifically focused on in Henry's journal writing, the importance of family, her work as a healer, and her talents as a poet are central to the construction of Mary Fowler that emerges in her husband's diaries.

PERSONAL LIFE HISTORIES, AUTOBIOGRAPHIES, AND PERSONAL ORAL NARRATIVES

In some ways diaries are the opposite of autobiographies or memoirs, which "invariably gloss over or eliminate most of life's irregularities."[56] Autobiographies, like reminiscences and oral narratives of personal experience, are situated and articulated through time and memory. As K. J. Gergen has suggested, "We may view personal remembrance not as an intimate portrayal of one's uniquely configured interior, but as a deployment of a public resource. The discursive traditions of one's culture supply a wide variety of memorial devices" such as autobiography, memoir, and personal reminiscence.[57] In fact, we might think of formal autobiography, reminiscence or memoir, oral personal experience narrative, and diary as existing along a kind of continuum of self-revelation, of time and memory. Each of these forms holds very particular generic possibilities for the tellers of life stories, and each differs from the others in terms of the discourse's reliance on memory, the relationship of writer or teller to audience, and the kind of self-reflexivity allowed by particular generic constraints.

While the diaries of Mary Susannah and Henry Ammon Fowler, written for themselves or for their immediate families, are grounded in the immediacy of daily writing that reveals particularly significant thematic nuances, the autobiographical writings of Henry Ammon also provide a perspective influenced by the passage of time, the sometimes ephemeral nature of memories that are used to construct an alternative yet complementary "self" for Mary Fowler. Both the seventeen-page "diary"—actually a memoir written after his seventy-fifth birthday that includes occasional diary-like entries from that point until his death in 1941—and the shorter "A Condensed Sketch of the Life of Henry Ammon Fowler—Taken from His Diary" add the dimension of Mary's work in the community to the thematic constructions that have already appeared in his missionary journals.

During the late nineteenth and early twentieth centuries, Mormon faithful had several models for writing personal life histories. Of course, the formal, carefully crafted autobiography was a genre familiar to all literate Mormons, and it was one particularly significant to those early church leaders who desired to record the history of the church through their own personal experiences, both of spirituality and of organizational progress. While such published autobiographical volumes were considered important discursive models by faithful Mormons, they more frequently adopted a somewhat abbreviated version of the formal autobiography, a form they referred to as "personal history." These personal histories usually consisted of a kind of life synopsis that noted significant events, charting relevant family history and important personal accomplishments. According to Mormon theology,

> Adam kept a written account of his faithful descendants in which he recorded their faith and works, their righteousness and devotion, their revelations and visions, and their adherence to the revealed plan of salvation. To signify the importance of honoring our worthy ancestors and of hearkening to the great truths revealed to them, Adam called his record a *book of remembrance*. . . . Similar records have been kept by the saints in all ages.[58]

By the turn of the twentieth century, the church officially encouraged the writing of these personal histories as part of family books of remembrance; there was clearly a direct connection between this practice and the growing importance of genealogy work in the church. Around the beginning of the twentieth century, after Joseph F. Smith had a revelation about the importance of genealogy, not only did he encourage individual Mormon faithful to pursue their own genealogies, but he also encouraged the growth of the Family History Library and the Church's Archives, where many personal histories were deposited.[59] As we have seen earlier, Mary Fowler was among the leaders of the genealogical endeavors in Huntington, instructing the women in both the Relief Society and the Young Ladies Mutual Improvement Association in the strategies of genealogical research and writing, including the compiling of personal histories.

The writing of personal histories was also encouraged by the Daughters of Utah Pioneers. Founded in 1901, at least partially as the Mormons' response to the founding of the Daughters of the American Revolution, the DUP strongly advised individual "camps" or DUP sections to encourage the writing and publishing of personal histories. Many of these personal histories are stored in the archives of both the individual DUP camps and the main DUP library/museum in Salt Lake City. Not only were these histories deposited in various church archives, but they were also the main components of individual families' "books of remembrance," where the family genealogy was fleshed out by compiling as many personal histories of family members as possible. Writing on November 19, 1947, Mary Susannah's daughter Fanny Harriet Fowler Harper suggests that the practice of writing such personal histories continued to grow during the first half of the twentieth century: "My daughter has asked me to write a sketch of my life that she can use in her book of remembrance, that is one of the requirements for her Mutual group. . . ."[60]

It was early in this period of active encouragement of the writing of personal histories that the form expanded to include not only one's own history, but that of relatives, especially relatives who had been significant contributors to the westward journey of the Mormon pioneers. If someone in the family had not left a personal life history, then a child or sibling or spouse would write one so that the family history itself would be more complete and so that the significance of the life of the individual would not be forgotten. In fact, Mary Fowler was the first to contribute to her own family history by reconstructing the personal histories of several ancestors from the stories she had heard from her parents. These fragmentary narratives were written carefully in a foolscap notebook reserved solely for this purpose.

The personal histories that contribute to the discursive construction of Mary Fowler herself fall into three categories—those written by an individual connected in some way to Mary (her husband, or sister, or child) about that individual's own life with some reference to Mary Fowler; those written by others about a close relative of Mary Fowler; and those written by others specifically about Mary Susannah Sumner Fackrell Fowler. Each of these types of life story provide additional insight into her life and the construction and reconstruction of her "self."

Henry Ammon Fowler's own autobiographical writings, for example, amplify the constructed Mary of his earlier missionary diaries, as I have suggested above. Not only does the longer autobiography indicate the extensive medical practice of Mary Susannah and her extraordinary closeness to her children and husband, but in several places Henry also acknowledges the significance of Mary's contributions to the community. In describing his return from the mission field, Henry notes that "Mary was much in demand among the sick of the town and was secretary of the Relief Society which was building a large hall so that when I came home from my mission she was nearly worn out."[61] In describing Mary Susannah Fowler's funeral, he writes, "A very large funeral was held, in spite of the rain and muddy weather, and many nice things were said of Mary's various works in public ways and her nursing the sick. . . . In appreciation of the many labors of Mary in the Relief Society, that organization gave me $40 to help pay expenses."[62]

While it is clear that Henry Ammon's personal history is focused on his own achievements, trials, travels, et cetera, it is also the case that in the brief references to his wife Mary, a picture consistent in many ways with both that presented in her diary and that of his own diary begins to emerge, albeit somewhat peripherally. Of the thirty-three references to Mary in Henry's personal history, thirteen concern her relationship with her children, eight involve the way in which Mary's nursing saved his life in a number of different dangerous situations, six describe journeys either to visit Mary's family or to move her from one place to another, and three involve Mary's work in the larger community. There is one reference to their marriage and another to a blessing they received together at the temple in Salt Lake City. The significant point here is that even when Henry Ammon is mentioning Mary somewhat peripherally, he nonetheless focuses on several of the metaphors of self already articulated in her own writing.

The same is true of the personal life histories written by Mary's daughters Laura Fowler Roper and Fanny Harriet Fowler Harper about their own lives. Each of these women describes her early life in her mother Mary's care as particularly significant; when Fanny muses

> I wonder how Mother put up with so much confusion. She taught us to make paper flowers and many other homely tasks. . . . Our clothes were all home-made, from our wraps to our factory and outing-flannel underwear. Mother corded, spun, and dyed the wool to make our stockings, mittens and fascinators.[63]

She is reminded of how amazing her mother must have been to accomplish all these household tasks at the same time she was engaged in caring for and educating her children. Laura Fowler Roper, on the other hand, focuses not only on Mary's abilities as a seamstress and homemaker, but also on her place within the larger Mormon community:

> Mother made a lasting impression on me by most always going to Sunday School and other church gatherings with us, taking all "us children." Our home life was happy though we were poor. Other children enjoyed coming to our place to play. Mother spent many hours after we went to bed

preparing clothes suitable for us to wear to school and church gatherings, and Christmas brought many happy surprises for us; though not more than a few cents were spent for each. There were eight children for Santa Claus to visit.[64]

In the case of the personal histories written specifically about Mary by her children, the discursive focus is even clearer. Unlike the autobiographical writings of her husband and daughters, the life histories of Mary Susannah Fowler written by her daughter Laura Fowler Roper and her son Fred Fowler are discursively evaluative and laudatory. The rhetorical thrust of both these life histories is no doubt determined by the purpose and audience for which they were intended: to recall with affection and admiration the life of their mother to be included in family books of remembrance or similar genealogical and historical publications. For example, Laura Fowler Roper writes of her mother:

> It was a trial to Mother to leave her folks and a comfortable home, and it was many years before things grew any where near as luxurious as they were in Orderville. However Mother was patient and cheerful and faithful, prayer being her mainstay. The people were all poor together and had to be resourceful. Mother was a real homemaker. She made Father's and the boy's suits and hats. She carded and spun wool, making all our stockings, mittens, and other things. . . . Mother was very efficient as a practical nurse. . . . But despite her training, Mother attributed her success as a nurse in sickness to the faith she exercised. Many give her credit for saving their own or their children's lives.[65]

In many ways, this brief passage crystallizes and melds together the salient thematic metaphors of Mary Fowler's life.

The introductory paragraph of her son's forty-eight-page typewritten life history of Mary Susannah Fowler, written twenty-five years after her death, sets the discursive tone for the rest of his manuscript:

> Mary Susannah Sumner Fackrell Fowler came into the world endowed with unusual intelligence. A keen sensitivity, manifest from earliest childhood throughout her life, gave her a quick awareness of the feelings of others. With these two outstanding capacities she developed an unrelenting passion for spiritual, ethical, and aesthetic values. This great drive for the good, the true, and the beautiful permitted her to find satisfactions beyond the limitations of constant and continued poverty. She sought and found these values in the ordinary and everyday things of life. But even more she developed the ability to extend her horizons and spiritualize deprivations and crushing trials.[66]

Fred Fowler's biographical tribute to his mother is not merely a factual recounting of the events that comprised her life, but rather a reconstruction of the woman she had come to be for him twenty-five years after

her death. This is not to say that what Fred writes is incorrect or misguid-
ed, rather it is to suggest that the evaluative process of selecting events to
record and the manner in which those historical moments are realized discursively produces a distinct, though strangely familiar, self for Mary Fowler.
The very fact that Fred reproduces within the lines of this introductory
paragraph Mary's own sense of the necessity of enduring earthly trials in
order to be spiritually reunited with one's family in heaven is a testament to
the rhetorical force of his mother's own writing, and to the way in which
she lived her life. In these biographical life histories produced by her children, then, and in the tributes sent to the family by friends and community members after Mary Fowler's death, a particular public persona is created
and re-created. Significantly, many of the characteristics of that persona are
in accord with Mary's own self-representation in diaries, essays, and poetry,
and yet it is through the family lens, adjusted carefully through time and
memory, that Mary Fowler's life comes into a particular focus for us.

A similar process occurs in the relating of oral personal experience
narratives. In fact, many of the personal histories involved in this study
actually evolve from, or are written versions of, oral narrative. Take the
"Autobiographical Sketch of the Life of Laura Fackrell Chamberlain," for
example. Laura, Mary Sumner Fackrell Fowler's sister, begins her personal
history with, "I remember what our mother told us, of what her mother
had told her, of their history,"[67] clearly grounding her written account in
oral history. What is especially interesting about this particular history is
that some of the significant "facts" reproduced are simply erroneous.

When I gave Mrs. Virginia Rogers, Mary Fowler's granddaughter, a
draft of the first chapter of this book to read and critique, she called me the
next day to report that I had gotten one fact wrong: Mary Fowler's maternal grandmother had not married her second husband in St. Louis, but in
Lancashire, England. I told Mrs. Rogers that I knew I had taken that information from several family histories, but she insisted, until I brought her the
primary source I had used—Laura Fackrell Chamberlain's "Autobiographical
Sketch." Laura Chamberlain had written: "She [Sarah Bromley] came to St.
Louis, Mo. There she met a man by the name of John Parker who had lost
his wife. He had three little girls. He and my grandmother were married."[68]
Yet when Mrs. Rogers countered by showing me the ship roster that indicated that John Parker and Sarah Bromley were already married when they
came to America, I had to admit that the family history was simply wrong.
Together we laughed about the mistake, and Mrs. Rogers said, "Sometimes
the facts aren't really the only important part of the story."

And she is right. Whether the factual error occurred in one of the
many oral tellings or just in Laura Chamberlain's written version isn't really significant; what *is* important in all of these forms of oral or written

reminiscence is that they are frequently marked by a reflective glance back through time that often presents an individual's life not chronologically, but in terms of important themes that organize and reformulate life experiences. The theme of the journey that recurs frequently in not only these personal histories, but in Mary's own writings as well as in other examples of Mormon reminiscence, achieves a particularly significant metaphorical effect when individual life journeys are fit within the journey of the Mormons as a people of God. In Mary Fowler's case, her own understanding of the personal trials to be endured on earth in order to reach eternal interconnectedness mirrors her belief in the Mormons' own cultural and spiritual journey towards God.

In *Listening to Old Voices*, Patrick B. Mullen has suggested that in the reminiscences of elderly people

> the past is viewed from the perspective of the present: when an old person tells a story about the past, it is not necessarily an absolutely factual account of the ways things were; rather, the story is filtered through the imagination of the teller and influenced by what has happened in the intervening years and by the current situation of the storyteller.[69]

Even though the oral personal experience stories involved in this work are usually not first-person accounts, but rather family stories that have been passed along, they have taken on many of the characteristics of first-person narration in combination with oral history. Here, the story is filtered through the imagination of the teller in particular ways and for particular rhetorical purposes:

> When talking about their lives, people lie sometimes, forget a lot, exaggerate, become confused, and get things wrong. Yet they are revealing truths. These truths don't reveal the past as it actually was, aspiring to a standard of objectivity. They give us instead the truths of our experiences. . . . Unlike the reassuring Truth of the scientific ideal, the truths of personal narrative are neither open to proof nor self-evident. We come to understand them only through interpretation, paying careful attention to the contexts that shape their creation and to the worldviews that inform them.[70]

When the story you are telling is not your own, but that of a cherished grandparent now deceased, the kinds of narrative strategies you employ to tell the story are intended to evoke a particularly positive response in the audience. The truths of the experiences are not only those of the subject of the narrative, but those of the teller as well. In the case of Mary Susannah Fackrell Fowler, usually the oral narratives of her grandchildren are grounded in a remarkably similar worldview.

In this respect, too, these personal narratives become part of what William A. Wilson has termed "the family novel."[71] In arguing the literary merits of his own mother's stories, Wilson points out that individual stories are "always related to other stories and other background events and can be understood only as they are associated with these."[72] He goes on to suggest:

> It is through this intertextuality that characters in the family oral novel emerge into full-blown, three dimensional individuals, just as well-developed characters emerge gradually from the pages of a written novel—no character is ever fully defined on the first page of a novel. It is also through this intertextuality that events in a number of the stories interlink into coherent meaningful wholes, just as events in a novel unfold and interlink as we push our way through page after page.[73]

With oral personal experience or reminiscence, then, one of the teller's goals is to draw the hearer into a process of meaning-making that is somehow negotiated during the very act of narration. Central to that process is the recognition and elaboration of particular themes. Sharon Kaufman, writing about the reminiscences of the elderly says:

> In the description of their lives, people create themes—cognitive areas of meaning with symbolic force—which explain, unify, and give substance to their perceptions of who they are and how they see themselves participating in social life. As each life is unique, so too are the themes. But all themes have their sources in the historical, geographical, and social circumstances in which people live, the flow of ordinary daily life, the values of American society, and cultural expectations of how a life should be lived.[74]

Life stories that continue to be told through the family and those narratives about family members that are constructed through time also participate in this kind of meaning-making. In fact, I would suggest that the constant renegotiation of the "self" of parents and grandparents and great-grandparents is very much involved with the creation or elaboration of themes that often have emerged in the narratives, written and oral, of the individual who is the focus of such storytelling. In our case, Mary Fowler's diary, poetry, and essays provide a kind of point of origin for particular themes that "unify the various strands of the story, relating the images, metaphors, and symbols together around the central meaning."[75]

William A. Wilson elaborates on the process of coming to terms with the articulation of thematic structures in personal narratives when he suggests:

> My attempt in studying my mother's stories . . . has been to discover how the individual narratives through which she explains herself to others are systematically related—that is, linked together into an artistic whole—by clustering around certain themes and individuals important to her. The unity in her family novel lies not in a linear plot leading from event to event toward any logical conclusion, but rather . . . in the clustering of motifs around given themes.[76]

Although they are brief, the oral narratives of Mary Fowler's grand-children, Virginia Rogers, Milton Roper, Eudora Clements, Rae Spellman, Marice Wilcox, Elmabeth Nielsen, and Eileen Freckleton, do just that. Most of these descendants were born after Mary Fowler died in 1920, and the others were young children who have only vague memories of actual-ly being with their grandmother. None of these individuals could actually relate incidents in Mary Fowler's life that they had witnessed themselves. However, each of these narrators spoke enthusiastically about Mary's love of learning, about the importance of words, about her healing abilities and care for others in the community, and foremost about her faith and spiri-tuality. More importantly, perhaps, they connected this grandmother they never knew with their own inherited abilities and with their own Mormon values. In this way, stories about their grandmother serve to rein-force their own belief system, while providing evidence of the virtues of this remarkable ancestor. The metaphors and themes so central to earlier versions of Mary Fowler's life reemerge in these oral narratives, not as records of the past, but as dynamic links to their own lives.

Virginia Rogers, the family genealogist and record keeper, was help-ing me sort through the hundreds of pages of documents she had accu-mulated, when she stopped and said,

> Now here is a copy of the Fowler family Bible—in Mary's handwriting! And I tried to get track of that. Lily Fowler McAfee said that she had seen it on the floor and the kids penning in it. And apparently it had been destroyed and discarded long ago, but Mary had gone in and did this very precise copying. I'll tell you Mary was no slouch. She was something![77]

By connecting the perseverance and dedication to genealogy of her grandmother with her own efforts, Virginia Rogers takes Mary Fowler's life story into a new discursive space. She is no longer a part of the past, but a liv-ing encouragement for Mrs. Rogers's own endeavors. Likewise, Marice Wilcox finds in Mary Fowler the source of her own delight in words. After discussing Mary's lack of a formal education and her prolific poetic work, Mrs. Wilcox said, "I use words naturally that I think . . . well, what else could you use, you know. It's the word that is just there in your mouth. And I know in my writing they are the ones that come up. And I know when I read what I've written it's usually well-constructed."[78] Although she knows few stories about her grandmother, Mrs. Wilcox still delights in connecting her own ver-bal abilities with those of Mary Fowler. In this way, her grandchildren recon-struct a particular version of the woman they never really knew and bring her to life in their own undertakings. Interestingly, these narratives in histor-ically reconnecting grandmother and granddaughters create a certain kind of recapitulation of the past that highlights the relationship between women across generations. In so doing, the themes of nurturance and women's community, so important in Mary Fowler's own self-representations, are once more brought to the fore. As William Wilson has pointed out, this process is "similar to what one finds in epic traditions where unity is derived from the accretion of narratives around cultural heroes and heroines and around dominant cultural values."[79]

The process is also one that draws me as a woman scholar into the cross-generational web of retellings. As I construct my own version of Mary Fowler, I am necessarily influenced by the personal relevance of those same thematic concerns. My own relationship with Virginia Rogers, developed over the last three years, no doubt affects the ways in which I represent her grandmother. One of the hardest parts of the kind of reciprocal ethnography espoused by folklorists like Elaine Lawless is coming to understand that the very reciprocity we seek complicates any ethnographic "reading" we might subsequently offer. At times it might even become difficult to determine precisely whose perspective is being represented. Here, while I honestly believe that there is very little I have not "told" in my rendering of Mary Fowler's life, I know there may have been issues I have interpreted in a particular way because of the closeness of my relationship with Virginia Rogers, for example.

Perhaps even more telling in this regard, though, is a misreading that almost caused me to confront these very issues head on. Early in my attempts to collect all of the extant diary entries and personal writings of Mary Fowler, I discovered in a small notebook where she jotted a miscellany of household expenditures, notes of conference lectures, addresses, and a poem or two, lines that seem to indicate that Mary herself might have been interested in a man other than Henry Ammon. Immediately preceding a notation concerning the date of a priesthood meeting in Orangeville, Mary had penned, "I'm trying so hard to forget you" and "Meet me tonight in dreamland." I was shocked, intrigued, and most of all extremely concerned about how—or even whether—I should include this evidence in her life story. As I grew to know Mary better, I became even more incredulous about these lines, but only when I went back to read them in the context of other entries inserted between the two I had found so disturbing did I come to realize that these were not Mary's romantic musings concerning an absent lover, but rather the titles or first lines of songs she wanted to remember! This experience both alerted me to the danger of taking any piece of writing out of its immediate and extended contexts and reminded me how powerful the voice of the ethnographer can be in any retelling. While I am relieved that I did not have to confront the decision of whether or not to include that information in this book, I know that subtler decisions may have been made throughout of which I am not nearly as conscious.

Certainly, for example, my desire to represent Mormonism in a fair and measured light shades the reading that I offer here. As a non-Mormon, I want to portray this cultural context as accurately as possible. It may be that in an attempt to do so, I err by withholding judgment about issues that in other situations I would be more willing to critique. The story of Mary Fowler that you read in these pages is one I have constructed as a woman, a folklorist, a non-Mormon, an academic, a family friend; it becomes yet another discourse added to those others described in the preceding chapters.

For, it is in the interaction of each of the discourses discussed here that the negotiation and construction of the identity of Mary Susannah Fowler takes place. In the discursive intersection of oral narrative and diary, of personal life history and church record, the salience of particular themes emerges and the symbolic force of these metaphors of self, identified first in Mary Fowler's own journal, becomes increasingly powerful. Alone, any one of these discourses would provide an interesting, perhaps provocative, glance at a woman who lived a century ago; together, as these multiple discourses reflect each on the other, readers are allowed to engage in a kind of collaborative, ongoing reconstruction of Mary Susannah Sumner Fackrell Fowler. And in the process, we each begin to experience for ourselves the interconnectedness Mary Fowler so prized.

Notes

INTRODUCTION

1. Susan Miller, *Assuming the Positions: Cultural Pedagogy and the Politics of Commonplace Writing* (Pittsburgh: University of Pittsburgh Press, 1998), 2.

2. Susan Stanford Friedman, "Women's Autobiographical Selves: Theory and Practice," in *The Private Self*, ed. Shari Benstock (Chapel Hill: University of North Carolina Press, 1988), 42.

3. See, for example, Patrick B. Mullen, *Listening to Old Voices: Folklore, Life Stories and the Elderly* (Urbana and Chicago: University of Illinois Press, 1992); Kirin Narayan, *Mondays on the Dark Night of the Moon: Himalayan Foothill Folktales* (New York: Oxford University Press, 1997); and William A. Wilson, "Personal Narratives: The Family Novel," *Western Folklore* 50 (1991): 127–49, and "In Praise of Ourselves: Stories to Tell," *Brigham Young University Studies* 30 (1990): 5–24. For an insightful critique of the changing relationship between researcher and subject, see Beverly J. Stoeltje, Christie L. Fox, and Stephen Olbrys, "The Self in Fieldwork," *Journal of American Folklore* 112 (1999): 158–82.

4. Elaine J. Lawless, *Holy Women, Wholly Women: Sharing Ministries through Life Stories and Reciprocal Ethnography* (Philadelphia: University of Pennsylvania Press, 1993), 5.

5. James Olney, "Autobiography and the Cultural Moment: A Thematic, Historical and Bibliographical Introduction," in *Autobiography: Essays Theoretical and Critical*, ed. James Olney (Princeton: Princeton University Press, 1980), 19.

6. Patracinio Schweickart, "Reading Ourselves: Toward a Feminist Theory of Reading," in *Contemporary Literary Criticism: Literary and Cultural Studies*, ed. Robert Con Davis and Ronald Schleifer (New York and London: Longman, 1989), 133.

7. Barbara Myerhoff and Jay Ruby, "Introduction," in *A Crack in the Mirror*, ed. Barbara Myerhoff and Jay Ruby (Philadelphia: University of Pennsylvania Press, 1982), 4.

8. Francoise Lionnet, *Autobiographical Voices: Race, Gender, Self-Portraiture* (Ithaca and London: Cornell University Press, 1989), 28.
9. Maureen Ursenbach Beecher, ed., *The Personal Writings of Eliza Roxcy Snow* (Salt Lake City: University of Utah Press, 1995; rpt., Logan: Utah State University Press, 2000), ix.
10. Laurel Thatcher Ulrich, *A Midwife's Tale: The Life of Martha Ballard, Based on Her Diary, 1785–1812* (New York: Vintage, 1991), 35.

CHAPTER 1

1. Fred Fowler, "Mary Fowler," Utah State Historical Society Archives, Salt Lake City, Utah, MSS A 312, 1–6.
2. Olive Fackrell Norwood, "Mother's History," photocopied manuscript in author's possession, courtesy of Lois Worlton, 42.
3. Laura Fackrell Chamberlain, "Autobiographical Sketch of the Life of Laura Fackrell Chamberlain," manuscript, Daughters of Utah Pioneers Archives (hereafter DUP Archives), Salt Lake City, Utah.
4. Henry Ammon Fowler, "Autobiography," Utah State Historical Society, MSS A 599.
5. F. Fowler, "Mary Fowler," 13.
6. Ibid., 14.
7. Kate B. Carter, "Living the United Order in Orderville," in *Heart Throbs of the West*, ed. Kate B. Carter, vol. 1 (Salt Lake City: Daughters of Utah Pioneers, 1938), 12–13.
8. H. Fowler, "Autobiography," 6.
9. Carter, "Living the United Order," 13–14.
10. See chapter 2 for a more complete discussion of the dissolution of the order.
11. H. Fowler, "Autobiography," 7.
12. Fanny Harriet Fowler Harper, "Life History," photocopied manuscript in the author's possession, courtesy of Lois Worlton.
13. Laura Ellen Fowler Roper, "Mary Susannah Sumner Fackrell," photocopied manuscript in the author's possession, courtesy of Virginia Fowler Rogers and Lois Worlton.
14. Harper, "Life History," 2–3.
15. F. Fowler, "Mary Fowler," 33–34.
16. H. Fowler, "Autobiography," 9.
17. Stella McElprang, *Castle Valley: A History of Emery County* (Castle Dale, Utah: Emery County Daughters of Utah Pioneers, 1949), 209.
18. H. Fowler, "Autobiography," 9.
19. Ibid., 8.
20. Laura Ellen Fowler Roper, "A Brief History of My Life," photocopied manuscript in the author's possession, courtesy of Lois Worlton and Virginia Fowler Rogers.
21. Mary Susannah Sumner Fackrell Fowler, manuscript diary, November 1899–July 1900, Marriott Library, University of Utah, Salt Lake City, Utah, original in the possession of Virginia Fowler Rogers.

22. H. Fowler, "Autobiography," 15.

23. Ibid., 13.

24. Ibid., 15.

25. Ibid., 14.

26. Jessie Manwaring Fowler, "Life History of Jessie Manwaring Fowler," photocopied manuscript, courtesy of Dianne K. Still.

27. H. Fowler, "Autobiography," 18.

28. Ibid., 16.

CHAPTER 2

1. Dean May, "The Making of Saints: The Mormon Town as a Setting for the Study of Cultural Change," *Utah Historical Quarterly* 45 (1977): 86.

2. Dorothy Noyes, "Folk Group," *Journal of American Folklore* 108 (1995): 472.

3. Ibid., passim.

4. May, "The Making of Saints," 86.

5. Dean May, *Three Frontiers: Family, Land, and Society in the American West, 1850–1900* (Cambridge: Cambridge University Press, 1994), 63.

6. "General Epistle from the Council of Twelve Apostles to the Church of Jesus Christ of Latter-day Saints Abroad, Dispersed throughout the Earth," *Millennial Star* 10 (March 15, 1848): 81–88.

7. May, *Three Frontiers*, 68.

8. Ibid., 230.

9. Leonard Arrington, et al., *Building the City of God: Community and Cooperation among the Mormons* (Urbana: University of Illinois Press, 1992), 265.

10. Ibid., 266.

11. Quoted in WPA, *Utah: A Guide to the State* (New York: Hastings House, 1941), 81.

12. Ibid.

13. Arrington, et al., *Building the City of God*, 146.

14. Quoted in Arrington, et al., *Building the City of God*, 268.

15. C. Gregory Crampton, *Mormon Colonization in Southern Utah and in Adjacent Parts of Arizona and Nevada, 1851–1900* (Salt Lake City: n.p., 1965), 152.

16. "Orderville Articles of Confederation," in Orderville Historical Record, 1873–1911, Archives of the Church of Jesus Christ of Latter-day Saints, Salt Lake City, Utah (hereafter cited as LDS Archives).

17. Mark A. Pendleton Papers, Marriott Library, University of Utah.

18. Phil Robinson, *Sinners and Saints* (London: n.p., 1883), 231–32.

19. Arrington, et al., *Building the City of God*, 271. Dean May has pointed out to me that this is a carefully chosen and symbolic date, since July 24 marked the anniversary of the Saints' arrival in the Salt Lake Valley.

20. Pendleton Papers, n.d.

21. *Orderville: Heart of the United Order* (Hurricane, Utah: Homestead Publishers, 1985), 13.

22. David B. Fackrell, *Deseret News*, July 28, 1875, 410.

23. Laura Fackrell Chamberlain, "Life History of David B. Fackrell," DUP Archives.

24. Quoted in Adonis F. Robinson, ed., *History of Kane County* (Salt Lake City: Utah Printing Co., 1970), 328.

25. Orderville Ward Record, February 14, 1880, LDS Archives.

26. *Orderville: Heart of the United Order*, 15.

27. Martha Jane Carling Webb Porter, "Life History of Porters in Orderville," DUP Archives.

28. Quoted in Arlen M. Clement, *Families of Destiny: A History of Fackrell and Sorensen Families and Their Posterity, 1690–1990* (n.p., 1991), 42.

29. A. Robinson, *History of Kane County*, 329.

30. Charlotte Cox Heaton, "A Pioneer Heritage and Early Years in Polygamy and the United Order in Southern Utah," (n.p., 1969), 7.

31. Emma Carroll Seegmiller, "Personal Memories of the United Order of Orderville," *Utah Historical Quarterly* 7 (1939): 186.

32. Ibid.

33. *Orderville: Heart of the United Order*, 15.

34. Quoted in Clement, *Families of Destiny*, 41.

35. A testament to that understanding lies in the fact that Mary Susannah Fowler compiled a list of names of over two hundred women who lived in the United Order in Orderville. See A. Robinson, *History of Kane County*, 556.

36. Norwood, "Mother's History."

37. Heaton, "A Pioneer Heritage." A chart like the one described by Heaton is preserved in the Daughters of Utah Pioneers museum in Orderville.

38. Norwood, "Mother's History," 45.

39. *Orderville: Heart of the United Order*, 20.

40. Heaton, "A Pioneer Heritage," 20.

41. Seegmiller, "Personal Memories of the United Order," 188–89.

42. Quoted in A. Robinson, *History of Kane County*, 342.

43. M. Porter, "Life History of the Porters," 589.

44. Seegmiller, "Personal Memories of the United Order," 176.

45. Heaton, "A Pioneer Heritage," 5–6.

46. Clement, *Families of Destiny*, 46G.

47. Heaton, " A Pioneer Heritage," 6.

48. This flag is now housed in the Daughters of Utah Pioneers museum in Orderville, Utah.

49. Phoebe M. Carling Porter, "Life in Orderville," manuscript, DUP Archives.

50. F. Fowler, "Mary Fowler," 11.

51. Seegmiller, "Personal Memories of the United Order," 178.

52. Henrietta P. Fackrell, "Mary Susannah Fackrell," manuscript, DUP Archives.

53. See chapter 1.

54. L. Roper, "Susannah Sumner Fackrell," manuscript, DUP Archives.

55. Henrietta P. Fackrell, "Life History of David B. Fackrell," DUP Archives, 11.

56. Lois Worlton, interview by author, Salt Lake City, Utah, September 12, 1996.

57. Ibid.

58. See, for example, Jessie Embry, *Mormon Polygamous Families: Life in the Principle* (Salt Lake City: University of Utah Press, 1987), and Richard Van Wagoner, *Mormon Polygamy: A History* (Salt Lake City: Signature Books, 1992).

59. Virginia Fowler Rogers, interview by author, Salt Lake City, Utah, July 23, 1996.

60. Mary Susannah Sumner Fackrell Fowler, "Mary Fowler's 2nd Book of Origanal and Selected Pieces," holograph in the possession of Virginia Fowler Rogers.

61. The following quotations are taken from the Huntington Relief Society Minutes in the LDS Archives.

62. See the next chapter for additional descriptions of Mary's ministering to Eliza and her children.

63. Lois Worlton, interview by author, Salt Lake City, Utah, July 13, 1996.

64. Chastie V. Stolworthy Esplin, "Memories of My Early Life," in *Esplin Pioneers of Utah*, ed. Arthur D. Coleman (Provo, Utah: J. Grant Stevenson, 1968), 170.

65. Anne Firor Scott, *Making the Invisible Woman Visible* (Urbana: University of Illinois Press, 1984), 274.

66. Ibid. See also Anne Firor Scott, *Invisible Allies* (Urbana: University of Illinois Press), 1991; Theodora Penny Martin, *The Sound of Their Own Voices: Women's Study Clubs, 1860–1910* (Boston: Beacon, 1987).

67. Scott, *Invisible Allies*, 111.

68. See Scott, *Making the Invisible Woman Visible*.

69. F. Fowler, "Mary Fowler," 12.

70. Jill Mulvey Derr, Janath Russell Cannon, and Maureen Ursenbach Beecher, *Women of Covenant: The Story of the Relief Society* (Salt Lake City: Deseret Book, 1992), 112–18.

71. Bearing one's testimony is a significant part of LDS religious expression that involves attesting to one's personal knowledge of the truth of the gospel.

72. For example, see chapter 1 for an account of Mary Susannah meeting Henry Ammon in the shoe shop where he worked.

73. Eliza Roxcy Snow, "Simplicity," *Woman's Exponent* 32 (September, 1903): 25.

74. These publications will be discussed in more depth in chapter 5.

75. Norwood, "Mother's History," 45.

76. A. Robinson, *History of Kane County*, 363.

77. See Anne Ruggles Gere, *Intimate Practices* (Urbana and Chicago: University of Illinois Press, 1997) for a discussion of missionary efforts among Indian tribes by Mormon women in particular.

78. See Huntington Relief Society Minutes, May 5, 1892; June 2, 1892; July 7, 1892, for example.

79. For a contemporary example of such collaborative work by women in a religious context, see Elaine J. Lawless, *Women Preaching Revolution* (Philadelphia: University of Pennsylvania Press, 1997).

80. H. Fowler, "Autobiography," 11.

81. Derr, et al., *Women of Covenant*, 155.
82. Huntington Relief Society Minutes, May 3, 1898.
83. Rae Spellman, interview by author, Salt Lake City, Utah, July 30, 1996.
84. Ibid.
85. L. Roper, "Mary Susannah Sumner Fackrell."
86. Derr, et al., *Women of Covenant*, 157.
87. Snow, "Simplicity."
88. Derr, et al., *Women of Covenant*, 158–59.
89. F. Fowler, "Mary Fowler," 20–21.
90. Ibid., 21–22.
91. Ibid., 25–26.
92. Huntington Relief Society Minutes, January 20, 1910.
93. *Woman's Exponent* 40 (April, 1912).
94. Quoted in Derr, et al., *Women of Covenant*, 161.
95. Ibid.
96. Huntington Relief Society Minutes, November 6, 1913.
97. Derr, et al., *Women of Covenant*, 193.
98. See chapter 5 for a more detailed account of the nature of this writing.
99. Derr, et al., *Women of Covenant*, 193.
100. Huntington Relief Society Minutes, May 17, 1917; July 13, 1919.
101. Ibid., January 20, 1920.
102. F. Fowler, "Mary Fowler," 45.
103. Baptism for the dead is explained: "Vicarious baptism for the dead was prac-
     ticed by the early Christians. These baptisms for the dead were performed
     so that the dead, not having heard the gospel on earth, but accepting it in
     the spirit world, might, by their acceptance of the vicarious baptism in their
     behalf, conform to the law of salvation" (John A. Widtsoe, *An Understandable
     Religion*, quoted in Melvin R. Brooks, *LDS Reference Encyclopedia* [Salt Lake
     City: Bookcraft, 1960], 40).
104. F. Fowler, "Mary Fowler," 26–27.

CHAPTER 3

1. The concept of "folk healer" has been used in a number of different ways.
   Here, when I use the term, I am referring to an individual whose health
   care practices originate within her community; she has gained medical
   knowledge traditionally from members of that community, most often from
   other women. Scholars have alternately used the terms "domestic healers"
   or "lay healers" to distinguish such practitioners from professional physicians
   (see, for example, Lamar Riley Murphy's *Enter the Physician: The
   Transformation of Domestic Medicine, 1760–1860* [Tuscaloosa: University of
   Alabama Press, 1991]). In Mary Fowler's case, her domestic healing traditions
   came both from traditional practices passed down through her family and
   from the popular medical philosophies of Samuel Thomson discussed later
   in this chapter.
2. F. Fowler, "Mary Fowler," 43.

3. Marilyn Ferris Motz, *True Sisterhood: Michigan Women and Their Kin, 1820–1920* (Albany: SUNY Press, 1983), 98.

4. See, for example, the life story of Texan Jewell Babb, whose narrative articulates this same theme of interconnectedness: Jewell Babb, *Border Healing Woman* (Austin: University of Texas Press, 1981).

5. Sharon R. Kaufman, *The Ageless Self: Sources of Meaning in Late Life* (Madison: University of Wisconsin Press, 1986), 149–50.

6. For a fuller discussion of thematic considerations in folk narratives of life history, see Mullen, *Listening to Old Voices.*

7. James Olney, *Metaphors of Self: The Meaning of Autobiography* (Princeton: Princeton University Press, 1981).

8. Karen Baldwin, "Aesthetic Agency in the Folk Medical Practices and Remembrances of North Carolinians," in *Herbal and Magical Medicine: Traditional Healing Today,* ed. James Kirkland (Durham: Duke University Press, 1992).

9. Carol McClain, *Women as Healers: Cross-Cultural Perspectives* (New Brunswick, New Jersey: Rutgers University Press, 1989).

10. Barbara Ehrenreich and Deidre English, *For Her Own Good: 150 Years of the Experts' Advice to Women* (New York: Doubleday, 1978), 30.

11. Mary Brasher, "Letter," photocopy in the author's possession, courtesy of Virginia Fowler Rogers.

12. Catharine E. Beecher and Harriet Beecher Stowe, *The American Woman's Home* (Hartford: Stowe-Day Foundation, 1972 [1869]), 342–43.

13. Motz, *True Sisterhood,* 99.

14. Ehrenreich and English, *For Her Own Good,* 36.

15. Murphy, *Enter the Physician,* 5–6.

16. Ibid., 33.

17. The fact that the terms "Brother" and "Sister" are used to refer to adult members of the Mormon community is indicative of just this kind of extension of the family outward into the larger social group.

18. F. Fowler, "Mary Fowler," 43.

19. See Murphy, *Enter the Physician,* 73.

20. Motz, *True Sisterhood,* 100.

21. Ibid., 101.

22. Murphy, *Enter the Physician,* 39.

23. Ibid.

24. See Motz, *True Sisterhood,* 103.

25. Quoted in Murphy, *Enter the Physician,* 64.

26. Catharine Beecher, *Miss Beecher's Housekeeper and Healthkeeper* (New York: Harper & Brothers, 1873), 485.

27. Virginia Fowler Rogers, interview by author, Salt Lake City, Utah, July 27, 1996.

28. Ehrenreich and England, *For Her Own Good,* 43.

29. Murphy, *Enter the Physician,* 71.

30. Ibid., 46–47.

31. Ibid., 71.

32. Lucy [Mack] Smith, *Biographical Sketches of Joseph Smith the Prophet and His Progenitors for Many Generations* (Lamoni, Iowa: Reorganized Church of Jesus Christ of Latter Day Saints, 1912), 61–65.

33. John Heinerman, *Joseph Smith and Herbal Medicine* (Manti, Utah: Mountain Valley Publishers, n.d.), 4.

34. The Book of Mormon, Alma 46:40.

35. Priddy Meeks, manuscript journal, Marriott Library.

36. According to Bruce R. McConkie, *Mormon Doctrine* (Salt Lake City: Bookcraft, 1966), 845: The Word of Wisdom refers to "a revelation given to Joseph Smith, February 27, 1833, containing a *part* of the revealed counsel in the field of health, because it begins, 'A Word of Wisdom, for the benefit of . . . the church' (Doctrine and Covenants 89:1), and is now commonly known as the Word of Wisdom. As a revealed law of health, dealing particularly with dietary matters, it contains both positive and negative instructions. Its affirmative position gives directions for the use of meat and grain by both man and animals; its prohibitions direct man to refrain from the use of certain specified harmful things (Doctrine and Covenants 89). . . . Accordingly, the negative side of the Word of Wisdom is a command to abstain from *tea, coffee, tobacco,* and *liquor.*"

37. Meeks, manuscript journal.

38. Heinerman, *Joseph Smith and Herbal Medicine,* 30.

39. Claire Noall, *Guardians of the Hearth: Utah's Pioneer Midwives and Women Doctors* (Bountiful, Utah: Horizon Publishers, 1974), 103.

40. Meeks, manuscript journal, 177–78.

41. Quoted in Noall, *Guardians of the Hearth,* 16.

42. Ehrenreich and English, *For Her Own Good,* 48.

43. H. Fowler, "Autobiography," 10.

44. Ibid., 11.

45. Ibid., 12–13.

46. Ibid., 14.

47. Milton Roper, interview by author, Huntington, Utah, August 22, 1996.

48. Eudora Clements, interview by author, August 30, 1996.

49. Spellman, interview.

50. Emma R. Olsen, ed., *Pioneer Health Care* (Salt Lake City, Utah: Daughters of Utah Pioneers, 1994), 2.

51. Quoted in Sherilyn Cox Bennion, "The Salt Lake Sanitarian: Medical Advisor to the Saints," *Utah Historical Quarterly,* vol. 57, no. 2 (1989): 125.

52. Austin Fife and Alta Fife, *Saints of Sage and Saddle* (Bloomington: Indiana University Press, 1957), 101–2.

53. Quoted in Bennion, "The Salt Lake Sanitarian," 125.

54. Joseph Smith, *History of the Church of Jesus Christ of Latter-day Saints,* ed B. H. Roberts, 7 vols. (Salt Lake City: Deseret News, 1949), 4:603.

55. Brasher, "Letter."

56. Norwood, "Mother's History," 10.

57. Kathryn Sklar, *Catharine Beecher: A Study in Domesticity* (New Haven, Connecticut: Yale University Press, 1973), 214.

58. Quoted in F. Fowler, "Mary Fowler," 42.
59. J. Fowler, "Life History of Jessie Manwaring Fowler."
60. Samuel Thomson, *New Guide to Health; Or Botanic Family Physician* (Montpelier, Vermont: n.p., 1851), 43.
61. Ibid., 44.
62. Spellman, interview. Priddy Meeks includes a description of this method of steaming in the manuscript journal on page 344.
63. Clements, interview.
64. Eula Fackrell Carlson, interview by author, August 13, 1996.
65. *Emery County Progress*, November 30, 1901, 3.
66. F. Fowler, "Mary Fowler," 47.
67. Ibid.
68. McConkie, *Mormon Doctrine*, 57.
69. Ibid., 165.
70. Henry A. Fowler, "Journal of the Travels of Henry A. Fowler of the Church of Jesus Christ of Latterday Saints While in the South Western States Mission Oklahoma and Indian Teritory Chickasaw Nation," LDS Archives.
71. Elizabeth Brockbank, "Tribute to Mary Fowler," photocopy in the author's possession.

CHAPTER 4

1. Miller, *Assuming the Positions*, 5.
2. Chamberlain, "Life History of David B. Fackrell."
3. F. Fowler, "Mary Fowler," 8–9.
4. Lois Worlton, interview by author, Salt Lake City, Utah, July 31, 1996.
5. H. Fackrell, "Mary Susannah Fackrell."
6. Worlton, interview, July 31, 1996.
7. F. Fowler, "Mary Fowler," 10.
8. See the following chapter for a fuller description of this incident.
9. F. Fowler, "Mary Fowler," 8.
10. Laura Fackrell Chamberlain, "Biographical Sketch," LDS Archives.
11. See Miller, *Assuming the Positions,* passim.
12. *Woman's Exponent* 6 (December 25, 1877): 108.
13. *Orderville: Heart of the United Order*, 16.
14. A. Robinson, *History of Kane County*, 329.
15. Seegmiller, "Personal Memories of the United Order," 183.
16. Ibid.
17. Emma Carroll Seegmiller, "Voices From Within: The Story of the United Order," Brigham Young University Archives, Provo, Utah, MSS 522.
18. Emily B. Spencer, "A Visit to Orderville," *Woman's Exponent* 6 (February 15, 1878): 139.
19. "Woman against Woman," *Woman's Exponent* 7 (May 1, 1879): 234.
20. A. Robinson, *History of Kane County*, 353. Here the newspaper Robinson is referring to is the *Deseret News*.

21. Ibid., 363.
22. Hattie Blackburn, "Living the United Order in Orderville," in *Heart Throbs of the West*, ed. Kate B. Carter, vol. 4 (Salt Lake City: Daughters of Utah Pioneers, 1949), 36.
23. Gere, *Intimate Practices*, 102.
24. Ibid., 198.
25. *Woman's Exponent* 22 (June 15, 1894): 149.
26. Gere, *Intimate Practices*, 198.
27. *Young Woman's Journal* 5 (1894): 159–60.
28. Ibid., 161.
29. *Young Woman's Journal* 7 (1895–96): 31.
30. Ibid., 31–32.
31. "Women in Literature," *Woman's Exponent* 5 (November 15, 1876): 91.
32. Ibid.
33. Ibid.
34. An article in the *Young Woman's Journal* 3 (1892), for example, focused on the process of "invention."
35. Ibid., 68.
36. Mary Susannah Sumner Fackrell Fowler, "Originality of Character," in "Mary Fowler's 2nd Book of Origanal and Selected Pieces."
37. This legitimization of women's knowledge and experience as a kind of authority is also noted by Maureen Beecher in her discussion of the life of another, more famous, Mormon woman in *The Personal Writings of Eliza Roxcy Snow* (Salt Lake City: University of Utah Press, 1995; rpt., Logan: Utah State University Press, 2000), xvii.
38. *Young Woman's Journal* 8 (1896): 229.
39. "For Young Writers," *Juvenile Instructor* 22 (1887).
40. *Young Woman's Journal* 8 (1896): 233
41. "For Young Writers."
42. *Young Woman's Journal* 4 (1893): 528.
43. *Young Woman's Journal* 2 (1891): 221.
44. *Young Woman's Journal* 2 (1891): 461; *Young Woman's Journal* 8 (1896): 57, 226; *Woman's Exponent* 1 (June 1, 1872).
45. Karen J. Blair quotes Catharine Beecher in pointing out that in the nineteenth century, novels and romances, at least, "produce mischievous effects" and corrupt the mind. (Karen J. Blair, *The Torchbearers* [Bloomington: Indiana University Press, 1994], 17).
46. Ibid.
47. *Young Woman's Journal* 5 (1894): 196.
48. Ibid., 197.
49. *Young Woman's Journal* 2 (1891): 462.
50. Mary Susannah Fowler, diary, March 24, 1900.
51. Quoted in Martin, *The Sound of Their Own Voices*, 118.
52. Susa Young Gates, "With the Editor," *Young Woman's Journal* 5 (1894):196.
53. See chapter 2.

CHAPTER 5

1. See especially Roger Renwick's *English Folk Poetry* (Philadelphia: University of Pennsylvania Press, 1980) and Pauline Greenhill's *True Poetry: Traditional and Popular Verse in Ontario* (Montreal and Kingston: McGill-Queen's University Press, 1989) for additional consideration of the definition of "folk poetry."

2. Pat Mullen has pointed out that even my characterization of Mary's use of "strikingly original" contractions above suggests that I may be aligning myself with a "folk" aesthetic here.

3. In the discussion that followed my paper presentation on Fowler's poetry at the 1999 American Folklore Society meetings, Frank deCaro asked me why I thought it was so much easier for folklorists and the public in general to value folk art than it is to truly appreciate folk poetry. I don't have *the* answer, but I suspect it has something to do with our willingness to alter our own aesthetic judgments, to suspend belief in particular artistic values just as one might suspend disbelief in listening to a legend, in order to appreciate the particular community aesthetic in which the painting or poem is produced. One factor contributing to the suspension or transformation of aesthetic judgments obviously has to do with how far apart those judgments are to begin with.

4. Renwick, *English Folk Poetry*, 3.

5. Pauline Greenhill, "Shakespoke: Selves, Others and Folk Poetry," *Canadian Folklore- Folklore Canadien* 19 (1993): 5.

6. Ibid., 10.

7. Renwick, *English Folk Poetry*, 3.

8. Because most of Mary Fowler's poetry that still exists is from the period between 1888 and 1893, a time of intense political ferment over the issue of polygamy and statehood, many of her verses included references to the trials endured by polygamist families.

9. See chapter 2.

CHAPTER 6

1. Marlene Kadar, "Coming to Terms with Life Writing—From Genre to Critical Practice," in *Essays on Life Writing from Genre to Critical Practice*, ed. Marlene Kadar (Toronto and London: University of Toronto Press, 1992), 2–3.

2. Ibid.

3. Ibid., 4.

4. Ibid., 12.

5. Ibid.

6. Laura Ellen Fowler Roper, "Susannah Sumner Fackrell," DUP Archives.

7. Laura Fackrell Chamberlain, "Biographical Sketch," LDS Archives.

8. Suzanne L. Bunkers and Cynthia A. Huff, eds., *Inscribing the Daily: Critical Essays on Women's Diaries* (Amherst: University of Massachusetts Press, 1996), 3.

9. Felicity Nusbaum, "Eighteenth-Century Women's Autobiographical Commonplaces," in *The Private Self: Theory and Practice of Women's Autobiographical Writings*, ed. Shari Benstock (Chapel Hill: University of North Carolina Press, 1988), 128.

10. Ibid., 129.

11. Ibid.

12. Lionnet, *Autobiographical Voices*, 8.

13. Kadar, *Essays on Life Writing*, 11, 82.

14. Jane Marcus, "Invincible Mediocrity: The Private Selves of Public Women," in *The Private Self*, 137.

15. Margo Culley, *A Day at a Time* (New York: Feminist Press, 1985), 21.

16. Harriet Blodgett, *Centuries of Female Days* (New Brunswick, New Jersey: Rutgers University Press, 1988), 8.

17. See Lynn Z. Bloom, "'I Write for Myself and Strangers': Private Diaries as Public Documents," in *Inscribing the Daily*, 27.

18. Culley, *A Day at a Time*, 21.

19. Ibid., 4.

20. Nancy F. Cott, *The Bonds of Womanhood* (New Haven, Connecticut: Yale University Press, 1977), 15.

21. Blodgett, *Centuries of Female Days*, 31.

22. Joseph Smith, "Journals," LDS Archives, December 11, 1841.

23. Bruce R. McConkie, ed., *Doctrines of Salvation: Sermons and Writings of Joseph Fielding Smith* (Salt Lake City: Bookcraft, 1998), 2:200–201.

24. Dean May, personal communication with author, October 1998.

25. Henrietta Embree, manuscript diary, Barker Texas History Collection, University of Texas, Austin.

26. Susan Newcomb, manuscript diary, Barker Texas History Collection, University of Texas, Austin.

27. Ibid.

28. Blodgett, *Centuries of Female Days*, 40.

29. Catherine Hobbs, ed., *Nineteenth-Century Women Learn to Write* (Charlottesville: University of North Carolina Press, 1995), 200.

30. Estelle Jelinek, *The Tradition of Women's Autobiography* (Boston: G. K. Hall, 1986), 104.

31. Cinthia Gannet, *Gender and the Journal: Diaries and Academic Discourse* (Albany: SUNY Press, 1992), 223.

32. Suzanne Juhasz, "Towards a Theory of Form in Feminist Autobiography," in *Women's Autobiography*, 221–24.

33. Culley, *A Day at a Time*, 14.

34. Elizabeth R. Baer, "Ambivalence, Anger, and Silence: The Civil War Diary of Lucy Buck," in *Inscribing the Daily*, 212.

35. Juhasz, "Towards a Theory of Form," 224.

36. Culley, *A Day at a Time*, 8.

37. See Blodgett, *Centuries of Female Days*, 32; Jelinek, *Women's Autobiography*, passim.

38. Blodgett, *Centuries of Female Days*, 42.

39. Elizabeth Hampsten, *Read This Only to Yourself*, 234.

40. See Penelope Franklin, *Private Pages, Diaries of American Women, 1830s–1970s* (New York: Ballantine, 1986), xxi.

41. Culley, *A Day at a Time*, 8.

42. Ibid., 13.

43. Carolyn G. Heilbrun, *Writing a Woman's Life* (New York: Norton, 1988), 30.

44. See Jelinek, *Women's Autobiography*, 224.

45. Virginia Woolf, *The Diary of Virginia Woolf*, ed. Anne Olivier Bell (New York: Harcourt, 1977–84), April 20, 1919.

46. See Baer, "Ambivalence, Anger, and Silence," in *Inscribing the Daily*, 211.

47. Culley, *A Day at a Time*, 19.

48. See Hampsten, *Read This Only to Yourself*, 21.

49. Suzanne Bunkers, "Midwestern Diaries and Journals: What Women Were (Not) Saying in the Late 1800s," in *Studies in Autobiography*, ed. James Olney (Oxford: Oxford University Press, 1988), 190–210.

50. Davis Bitton, *Guide to Mormon Diaries and Autobiographies* (Provo, Utah: Brigham Young University Press, 1977), vii.

51. Ibid., viii.

52. Ibid., vii–ix.

53. Ibid.

54. H. Fowler, "Journal of the Travels," March 12, 1902.

55. Ibid., August 17, 1901.

56. Franklin, *Private Pages*, xxvi.

57. Kenneth Gergen, *Realities and Relationships: Soundings in Social Construction* (Cambridge: Harvard University Press, 1994), 95.

58. Bruce R. McConkie, *Mormon Doctrine*, 100.

59. May, personal communication.

60. Harper, "Life History."

61. H. Fowler, "Autobiography," 11.

62. Ibid., 16–17.

63. Harper, "Life History."

64. Laura Ellen Fowler Roper, "Laura Fowler—Her Own Life," Photocopied manuscript in the author's possession, courtesy of Virginia Fowler Rogers, 2.

65. Ibid.

66. F. Fowler, "Mary Fowler," 1.

67. Chamberlain, "Autobiographical Sketch."

68. Ibid.

69. Mullen, *Listening to Old Voices*, 3.

70. Personal Narratives Group, *Interpreting Women's Lives: Feminist Theory and Personal Narratives* (Bloomington: Indiana University Press, 1989), 4.

71. Wilson, "Personal Narratives," 137.

72. Ibid.

73. Ibid.

74. Kaufman, *The Ageless Self*.

75. Mullen, *Listening to Old Voices*, 15.
76. Wilson, "Personal Narratives," 141–42.
77. Rogers, interview, July 23, 1996.
78. Mrs. Marice Wilcox, interview by author, Salt Lake City, Utah, August 8, 1996.
79. Wilson, "Personal Narratives," 142.

Bibliography

Manuscript Sources

Brasher, Mary. "Letter." Photocopy in the author's possession, courtesy of Virginia Fowler Rogers.

Brockbank, Elizabeth. "Tribute to Mary Fowler." Photocopy in the author's possession.

Chamberlain, Laura Fackrell. "Autobiographical Sketch of the Life of Laura Fackrell Chamberlain." Daughters of Utah Pioneers Archives, Salt Lake City, Utah (hereafter cited as DUP Archives).

————. "Biographical Sketch." Archives of the Church of Jesus Christ of Jesus Christ of Latter-day Saints, Salt Lake City, Utah (hereafter cited as LDS Archives).

————. "Life History of David B. Fackrell." DUP Archives.

Embree, Henrietta. Manuscript diary. Barker Texas History Collection, University of Texas, Austin.

Fackrell, Henrietta P. "Life History of David B. Fackrell." DUP Archives.

————. "Mary Susannah Fackrell." DUP Archives.

Fowler, Fred. "Mary Fowler." Utah State Historical Society Archives, Salt Lake City, Utah, MSS A 312.

Fowler, Henry Ammon. "Autobiography." Utah State Historical Society. Salt Lake City, Utah, MSS A 599.

————. "Journal of the Travels of Henry A. Fowler of the Church of Jesus Christ of Latterday Saints While in the South Western States Mission Oklahoma and Indian Territory Chickasaw Nation." LDS Archives.

Fowler, Mary Susannah Sumner Fackrell. Manuscript diary, November 1899–July 1900. Marriott Library, University of Utah. Salt Lake City, Utah. Original in the possession of Virginia Fowler Rogers.

————. Manuscript diary, September–December 1900. Original in the possession of Mrs. Marice Wilcox.

————. "Mary Fowler's 2nd Book of Origanal and Selected Pieces." Holograph in the possession of Virginia Fowler Rogers.

Harper, Fanny Harriet Fowler. "Life History." Photocopied manuscript in the author's possession, courtesy of Lois Worlton.

Huntington Relief Society Minutes. LDS Archives.

Meeks, Priddy. Manuscript journal. Marriott Library, University of Utah, Salt Lake City, Utah.

Newcomb, Susan. Manuscript diary. Barker Texas History Collection, University of Texas, Austin.

Norwood, Olive Fackrell. "Mother's History." Photocopied manuscript in author's possession, courtesy of Lois Worlton.

"Orderville Articles of Confederation." Orderville Historical Record, 1873–1911, LDS Archives.

Orderville Ward Record, February 14, 1880, LDS Archives.

Porter, Martha Jane Carling Webb. "Life History of Porters in Orderville." DUP Archives.

Porter, Phoebe M. Carling. "Life in Orderville." Manuscript. DUP Archives.

Roper, Laura Ellen Fowler. "A Brief History of My Life." Photocopied manuscript in the author's possession, courtesy of Lois Worlton and Virginia Fowler Rogers.

———. "Laura Fowler—Her Own Life." Photocopied manuscript in the author's possession, courtesy of Virginia Fowler Rogers.

———. "Mary Susannah Sumner Fackrell." Photocopied manuscript in the author's possession, courtesy of Virginia Fowler Rogers and Lois Worlton.

———. "Susannah Sumner Fackrell." DUP Archives.

Seegmiller, Emma Carroll. "Voices from Within: The Story of the United Order." Brigham Young University Archives, Provo, Utah, MSS 522.

Smith, Joseph. "Journals." LDS Archives.

———. *History of the Church of Jesus Christ of Latter-day Saints*, ed B. H. Roberts, 7 vols. (Salt Lake City: Deseret News, 1949), 4:603.

INTERVIEWS

Carlson, Eula Fackrell. Interview by author. August 13, 1996.

Clements, Eudora. Interview by author. August 30, 1996.

May, Dean. Personal communication with author. October 1998.

Rogers, Virginia Fowler. Interview by author. Salt Lake City, Utah. July 23, 1996.

———. Interview by author. Salt Lake City, Utah. July 27, 1996.

Roper, Milton. Interview by author. Huntington, Utah. August 22, 1996.

Spellman, Rae. Interview by author. Salt Lake City, Utah. July 30, 1996.

Wilcox, Marice. Interview by author. Salt Lake City, Utah. August 8, 1996.

Worlton, Lois. Interview by author. Salt Lake City, Utah. July 13, 1996.

———. Interview by author. Salt Lake City, Utah. July 31, 1996.

———. Interview by author. Salt Lake City, Utah. September 12, 1996.

SECONDARY SOURCES

Arrington, Leonard, et al. *Building the City of God: Community and Cooperation among the Mormons*. Urbana: University of Illinois Press, 1992.

Babb, Jewell. *Border Healing Woman*. Austin: University of Texas Press, 1981.

Baer, Elizabeth R. "Ambivalence, Anger, and Silence: The Civil War Diary of Lucy Buck." In *Inscribing the Daily: Critical Essays on Women's Diaries*. Ed. Suzanne L. Bunkers and Cynthia A. Huff. Amherst: University of Massachusetts Press, 1996.

Baldwin, Karen. "Aesthetic Agency in the Folk Medical Practices and Remembrances of North Carolinians." In *Herbal and Magical Medicine: Traditional Healing Today*. Ed. James Kirkland. Durham: Duke University Press, 1992.

Beecher, Catharine E., and Harriet Beecher Stowe. *The American Woman's Home.* Hartford: Stowe-Day Foundation, 1972 [1869].

Beecher, Catharine. *Miss Beecher's Housekeeper and Healthkeeper.* New York: Harper & Brothers, 1873.

Beecher, Maureen Ursenbach, ed. *The Personal Writings of Eliza Roxcy Snow.* Salt Lake City: University of Utah Press, 1995. Reprint, Logan: Utah State University Press, 2000.

Bennion, Sherilyn Cox. "The Salt Lake Sanitarian: Medical Advisor to the Saints." *Utah Historical Quarterly*, vol. 57, no. 2 (1989).

Bitton, Davis. *Guide to Mormon Diaries and Autobiographies.* Provo, Utah: Brigham Young University Press, 1977.

Blackburn, Hattie. "Living the United Order in Orderville." In *Heart Throbs of the West*. Ed. Kate B. Carter. Vol. 4. Salt Lake City: Daughters of Utah Pioneers, 1949.

Blair, Karen. *The Torchbearers.* Bloomington: Indiana University Press, 1994.

Blodgett, Harriet. *Centuries of Female Days.* New Brunswick, New Jersey: Rutgers University Press, 1988.

Bloom, Lynn Z. "'I Write for Myself and Strangers': Private Diaries as Public Documents." In *Inscribing the Daily: Critical Essays on Women's Diaries*. Ed. Suzanne L. Bunkers and Cynthia A. Huff. Amherst: University of Massachusetts Press, 1996.

Brooks, Melvin R. *LDS Reference Encyclopedia.* Salt Lake City: Bookcraft, 1960.

Bunkers, Suzanne L., and Cynthia A. Huff, eds. *Inscribing the Daily: Critical Essays on Women's Diaries.* Amherst: University of Massachusetts Press, 1996.

Bunkers, Suzanne. "Midwestern Diaries and Journals: What Women Were (Not) Saying in the Late 1800s." In *Studies in Autobiography*. Ed. James Olney. Oxford: Oxford University Press, 1988.

Carter, Kate B. "Living the United Order in Orderville." In *Heart Throbs of the West*. Ed. Kate B. Carter. Vol. 1. Salt Lake City: Daughters of Utah Pioneers, 1938.

Child, Lydia Maria. *The American Frugal Housewife*, 16th ed. Boston: Carter, Hendee and Co., 1835.

Clement, Arlen M. *Families of Destiny: A History of Fackrell and Sorensen Families and Their Posterity, 1690–1990.* N.p., 1991.

Cott, Nancy F. *The Bonds of Womanhood.* New Haven, Connecticut: Yale University Press, 1977.

Crampton, C. Gregory. *Mormon Colonization in Southern Utah and in Adjacent Parts of Arizona and Nevada, 1851–1900.* Salt Lake City: n.p, 1965.

Derr, Jill Mulvey, Janath Russell Cannon, and Maureen Ursenbach Beecher. *Women of Covenant: The Story of the Relief Society.* Salt Lake City: Deseret Book, 1992.

Ehrenreich, Barbara, and Deidre English. *For Her Own Good: 150 Years of the Experts' Advice to Women*. New York: Doubleday, 1978.

Embry, Jessie. *Mormon Polygamous Families: Life in the Principle*. Salt Lake City: University of Utah Press, 1987.

Esplin, Chastie V. Stolworthy. "Memories of My Early Life." In *Esplin Pioneers of Utah*. Ed. Arthur D. Coleman. Provo, Utah: J. Grant Stevenson, 1968.

Fife, Austin, and Alta Fife. *Saints of Sage and Saddle*. Bloomington: Indiana University Press, 1957.

"For Young Writers." *Juvenile Instructor* 22 (1887).

Franklin, Penelope. *Private Pages, Diaries of American Women, 1830s–1970s*. New York: Ballantine, 1986.

Friedman, Susan Stanford. "Women's Autobiographical Selves: Theory and Practice." In *The Private Self*. Ed. Shari Benstock. Chapel Hill: University of North Carolina Press, 1988.

Gannet, Cinthia. *Gender and the Journal: Diaries and Academic Discourse*. Albany: SUNY Press, 1992.

Gates, Susa Young. "With the Editor." *Young Woman's Journal* 5 (1894):196.

"General Epistle from the Council of Twelve Apostles to the Church of Jesus Christ of Latter-day Saints Abroad, Dispersed throughout the Earth." *Millennial Star* 10 (March 15, 1848).

Gere, Anne Ruggles. *Intimate Practices*. Urbana and Chicago: University of Illinois Press, 1997.

Gergen, Kenneth. *Realities and Relationships: Soundings in Social Construction*. Cambridge: Harvard University Press, 1994.

Greenhill, Pauline. "Shakespoke: Selves, Others and Folk Poetry." *Canadian Folklore-Folklore Canadien* 19 (1993).

———. *True Poetry: Traditional and Popular Verse in Ontario*. Montreal and Kingston: McGill-Queen's University Press, 1989.

Heaton, Charlotte Cox. "A Pioneer Heritage and Early Years in Polygamy and the United Order in Southern Utah." N.p., 1969.

Heilbrun, Carolyn G. *Writing a Woman's Life*. New York: Norton, 1988.

Heinerman, John. *Joseph Smith and Herbal Medicine*. Manti, Utah: Mountain Valley Publishers, n.d.

Hobbs, Catherine, ed. *Nineteenth-Century Women Learn to Write*. Charlottesville: University of North Carolina Press, 1995.

Jelinek, Estelle. *The Tradition of Women's Autobiography*. Boston: G. K. Hall, 1986.

Juhasz, Suzanne. "Towards a Theory of Form in Feminist Autobiography." In *Women's Autobiography*. Ed. Estelle Jelinek. Boston: G. K. Hall, 1986.

Kadar, Marlene. "Coming to Terms with Life Writing—From Genre to Critical Practice." In *Essays on Life Writing from Genre to Critical Practice*. Ed. Marlene Kadar. Toronto and London: University of Toronto Press, 1992.

Lawless, Elaine J. *Holy Women, Wholly Women: Sharing Ministries through Life Stories and Reciprocal Ethnography*. Philadelphia: University of Pennsylvania Press, 1993.

———. *Women Preaching Revolution*. Philadelphia: University of Pennsylvania Press, 1997.

Lionnet, Francoise. *Autobiographical Voices: Race, Gender, Self-Portraiture.* Ithaca and London: Cornell University Press, 1989.

Marcus, Jane. "Invincible Mediocrity: The Private Selves of Public Women." In *The Private Self: Theory and Practice of Women's Autobiographical Writings.* Ed. Shari Benstock. Chapel Hill: University of North Carolina Press, 1988.

Mark A. Pendleton Papers. Marriott Library, University of Utah, Salt Lake City, Utah.

Martin, Theodora Penny. *The Sound of Their Own Voices: Women's Study Clubs, 1860–1910.* Boston: Beacon, 1987.

May, Dean. "The Making of Saints: The Mormon Town as a Setting for the Study of Cultural Change." *Utah Historical Quarterly* 45 (1977).

———. *Three Frontiers: Family, Land, and Society in the American West, 1850–1900.* Cambridge: Cambridge University Press, 1994.

McClain, Carol. *Women as Healers: Cross-Cultural Perspectives.* New Brunswick, New Jersey: Rutgers University Press, 1989.

McConkie, Bruce R. *Mormon Doctrine.* Salt Lake City: Bookcraft, 1966.

McElprang, Stella. *Castle Valley: A History of Emery County.* Castle Dale, Utah: Emery County Daughters of Utah Pioneers, 1949.

Miller, Susan. *Assuming the Positions: Cultural Pedagogy and the Politics of Commonplace Writing.* Pittsburgh: University of Pittsburg Press, 1998.

Motz, Marilyn Ferris. *True Sisterhood: Michigan Women and Their Kin, 1820–1920.* Albany: SUNY Press, 1983.

Mullen, Patrick B. *Listening to Old Voices: Folklore, Life Stories, and the Elderly.* Urbana and Chicago: University of Illinois Press, 1992.

Murphy, Lamar Riley. *Enter the Physician: The Transformation of Domestic Medicine, 1760–1860.* Tuscaloosa: University of Alabama Press, 1991.

Myerhoff, Barbara, and Jay Ruby. "Introduction." In *A Crack in the Mirror.* Ed. Barbara Myerhoff and Jay Ruby. Philadelphia: University of Pennsylvania Press, 1982.

Narayan, Kirin. *Mondays on the Dark Night of the Moon: Himalayan Foothill Folktales.* New York: Oxford University Press, 1997.

Noall, Claire. *Guardians of the Hearth: Utah's Pioneer Midwives and Women Doctors.* Bountiful, Utah: Horizon Publishers, 1974.

Noyes, Dorothy. "Folk Group." *Journal of American Folklore* 108 (1995).

Nusbaum, Felicity. "Eighteenth-Century Women's Autobiographical Commonplaces." In *The Private Self: Theory and Practice of Women's Autobiographical Writings.* Ed. Shari Benstock. Chapel Hill: University of North Carolina Press, 1988.

O'Connor, Bonnie Blair. *Healing Traditions: Alternative Medicine and the Health Professions.* Philadelphia: University of Pennsylvania Press, 1995.

Olney, James. "Autobiography and the Cultural Moment: A Thematic, Historical and Bibliographical Introduction." In *Autobiography: Essays Theoretical and Critical.* Ed. James Olney. Princeton: Princeton University Press.

———. *Metaphors of Self: The Meaning of Autobiography.* Princeton: University of Princeton Press, 1981.

Olsen, Emma R., ed. *Pioneer Health Care.* Salt Lake City: Daughters of Utah Pioneers, 1994.

Orderville: Heart of the United Order. Hurricane, Utah: Homestead Publishers, 1985.

Personal Narratives Group. *Interpreting Women's Lives: Feminist Theory and Personal Narratives.* Bloomington: Indiana University Press, 1989.

Renwick, Roger. *English Folk Poetry.* Philadelphia: University of Pennsylvania Press, 1980.

Robinson, Adonis F., ed. *History of Kane County.* Salt Lake City: Utah Printing Co., 1970.

Robinson, Phil. *Sinners and Saints.* London: n.p., 1883.

Schweickart, Patracinio. "Reading Ourselves: Toward a Feminist Theory of Reading." In *Contemporary Literary Criticism: Literary and Cultural Studies.* Ed. Robert Con Davis and Ronald Schleifer. New York and London: Longman, 1989.

Scott, Anne Firor. *Invisible Allies.* Urbana: University of Illinois Press, 1991.

———. *Making the Invisible Woman Visible.* Urbana: University of Illinois Press, 1984.

Seegmiller, Emma Carroll. "Personal Memories of the United Order of Orderville." *Utah Historical Quarterly* 7 (1939).

Sklar, Kathryn. *Catharine Beecher: A Study in Domesticity.* New Haven, Connecticut: Yale University Press, 1973.

Smith, Lucy [Mack]. *Biographical Sketches of Joseph Smith the Prophet and His Progenitors for Many Generations.* Lamoni, Iowa: Reorganized Church of Jesus Christ of Latter Day Saints, 1912.

Snow, Eliza Roxcy. *Woman's Exponent* (1903).

Spencer, Emily B. "Women." *Woman's Exponent* 6 (1878).

Thomson, Samuel. *New Guide to Health; Or Botanic Family Physician.* Montpelier, Vermont: n.p., 1851.

Ulrich, Laurel Thatcher. *A Midwife's Tale: The Life of Martha Ballard, Based on Her Diary, 1785–1812.* New York: Vintage, 1991.

Van Wagoner, Richard. *Mormon Polygamy: A History.* Salt Lake City: Signature Books, 1992.

Wilson, William A. "Personal Narratives: The Family Novel." *Western Folklore* 50 (1991).

———. "In Praise of Ourselves: Stories to Tell." *Brigham Young University Studies* 30 (1990).

Woolf, Virginia. *The Diary of Virginia Woolf.* Ed. Anne Olivier Bell. New York: Harcourt, 1977–84.

WPA. *Utah: A Guide to the State.* New York: Hastings House, 1941.

NEWSPAPERS AND PERIODICALS

Emery County Progress, November 30, 1901.
Deseret News (1875–1920).
Woman's Exponent (1872–1915).
Young Woman's Journal (1890–1896).

Index